W9-AAT-894

Wild and Rare

Wild and Rare

Tracking Endangered Species in the Upper Midwest

Adam Regn Arvidson

MINNESOTA
HISTORICAL
SOCIETY PRESS

The publication of this book was supported, in part, by a gift from an anonymous donor.

Unless otherwise indicated, all photographs are by the author.

The shiner chapter appeared in similar form in *Briar Cliff Review* (2012). The prairie bush clover chapter appeared in similar form in *Michigan Quarterly Review* (spring 2012).

www.mnhspress.org

The Minnesota Historical Society Press is a member of the Association of University Presses.

Manufactured in Canada

10 9 8 7 6 5 4 3 2 1

♾ The paper used in this publication meets the minimum requirements of the American National Standard for Information Sciences—Permanence for Printed Library Materials, ANSI Z39.48–1984.

International Standard Book Number
ISBN: 978-1-68134-087-6 (paper)
ISBN: 978-1-68134-099-9 (e-book)

Library of Congress Cataloging-in-Publication Data
Names: Arvidson, Adam Regn, author.
Title: Wild and rare : tracking endangered species in the upper Midwest / Adam Regn Arvidson.
Description: St. Paul, MN : Minnesota Historical Society Press, [2018] | Includes bibliographical references and index.
Identifiers: LCCN 2017044449 | ISBN 9781681340876 (pbk. : alk. paper) | ISBN 9781681340999 (ebook)
Subjects: LCSH: Endangered species—Middle West. | Wildlife conservation—Middle West.
Classification: LCC QH76.5.M53 A78 2018 | DDC 591.680977—dc23
LC record available at https://lccn.loc.gov/2017044449

This and other Minnesota Historical Society Press books are available from popular e-book vendors.

To

my MOM
and
my DAD

for taking me outside
and seeding my curiosity

Contents

Introduction   3

1.   Lily   11

2.   Mussels   37

3.   Plover   67

4.   Roseroot   97

5.   Bush Clover   125

6.   Butterflies   159

7.   Lynx   177

8.   Orchid   205

9.   Shiner   229

10.   Wolf   257

Epilogue: *Bat*   281

Narrative Bibliography   293

Acknowledgments   303

Wild and Rare

Introduction

A howling wolf is never merely an animal making a sound. It is the call of wilderness itself, the mournful beckon of freedom. Or it is the dark and ominous coming of night, with all its terrors. It ignites the desire to conquer nature—or to conserve and nurture all living things. It is the story of all human history: our evolution, our domestication of other animals, our civilization of the land, our tortured relationship with the earth and its nonhuman denizens. A wolf howl is the only sound in nature with all this baggage. A howling wolf is never simple.

I am safely behind plate glass at the International Wolf Center in Ely, Minnesota, listening to a scruffy-bearded twenty-something teach a group of mostly teens and toddlers about wolf ecology. Throughout the talk, the five members of the resident pack have been gradually sauntering down from the woods to the clearing near the windows. Then Grizzer, the largest male, climbs up on a rock outcrop, puts his nose to the sky, and begins to moan—begins to wail.

His mouth becomes a dark O in his gray-black face. He senses from nostril to tail, a strong line of energy channeled up from the earth into the spring air. His voice seems conjured from the stones, from the groaning of continents moving across the hot core of the planet. The others join him, dissonant and harmonic at once, each standing stock-still, rooted to the soil, the rock, the grass, and the last dregs of snow. Their eyes squint, their tails are poised but relaxed, their coats a-frizz with the soulful song. Their howls seem to come not from them but from somewhere farther away than the actual animal standing before me. It is an old, old melody, at once exuberant and aching.

It takes me a moment to realize that they have become the only sound. The kids, the parents, the teacher—all have fallen silent. We all watch the pack. We are stirred somehow. My skin tingles. It is a sad song that at times breaks into playful yips and yawns and gargles. There are moments that sound almost human, as one voice drops low and grumbles, like a scolding grandfather.

And that's through the PA system, in the scrubbed air of the building, in my human world. As I leave the center, they begin again, and I stand frozen in the parking lot to listen. The air permeates my light sweater as the bones of leafless birches shine in the afternoon light. I can still see them, in my head, their bodies channeling the very sounds of the earth.

As quickly as they started, they fall silent once more. The world falls silent with them. But they are still there. I know they are. That's how the north woods feels: the wolves are always there, somewhere. You can feel them all the time, whether they're singing or not.

Today there are around twenty-five hundred wolves in the woods of Minnesota, but that wasn't always the case. There used to be a lot more, and they used to roam every state in the union. Wolves are incredibly adaptable and can survive wherever there is food—wherever there are deer, moose, elk, rabbits, buffalo, skunks, squirrels, or just about any other four-legged animal. And that includes cows, sheep, and goats. Throughout the 1800s and 1900s, when European settlers flooded across the landscape of North America, the government, with paid sharpshooters and bounties for dead wolves, began to systematically exterminate this king of the forests and prairies and mountains. *Systematically* is the right word. The slogan "the only good wolf is a dead wolf" was a rallying cry for hunting parties, and areas were considered "cleared" and safe for habitation once there were no wolves left.

In 1973, when the Endangered Species Act was passed—and the gray wolf, controversially, became one of the initial protected species—there were fewer than three hundred wolves in the entire lower forty-eight. There were packs in far northeastern Minnesota (the so-called Arrowhead), where they could feed on moose and benefit from the relative safety of Canada and the inaccessible reaches of what is now the Boundary Waters Canoe Area Wilderness And there were isolated groups on Isle Royale, a rocky island in Lake Superior. The act ended bounties and forbade killing of wolves by the public, but that was only the beginning of the controversy over protection.

I was born in 1974, so the Endangered Species Act is, in a way, a chart of my life. The list of plants, animals, insects, fish, and invertebrates grows and shrinks, changes, and exhibits colossal failures, tremendous successes, and unresolved conflicts. The bald eagle, symbol of America, is off the list, thanks, yes, to the outlawing of DDT, but also to the act's habitat protection requirements. So, too, the alligator and the manatee: recovered from the brink of extinction. And wolf numbers have rebounded beyond expectations. The act has even changed perceptions of some of these endangered animals. A 1914 picture shows children grinning under a clothesline strung with more than a dozen wolf skins. In 2010 I overheard a child say, "I want a pet wolf."

About a week before my trip to Ely, I sit down with Rich Baker, endangered species coordinator for the Minnesota Department of Natural Resources. He is responsible for managing the state's own endangered species list and also coordinating with the US Fish and Wildlife Service, which oversees the federal list. "The wolf is such an anomaly," he tells me, between bites of Vietnamese rice vermicelli salad. "It has engendered such love and hate in equal measures. That's because of the polarizing nature of the beast: it looks like a dog, and people love dogs, but then it goes and kills livestock."

I love lists, and the endangered species list is about as big, complex, diverse, and rife with controversy as they come. The Endangered Species Act as we know it today was signed by Richard Nixon in 1973. An earlier 1966 law called the Endangered Species Preservation Act identified species in danger of extinction, but it had no teeth. The 1973 act does. It generally forbids any taking of listed plants and animals for any purpose on federal lands or on projects with federal funding. There are exceptions, of course, but the general idea is that the best way to conserve a species is to take the pressure off. The act sets forth a process for listing, requires development of a recovery plan and periodic updates of species status (five-year reviews), and envisions delisting species when the goals in the recovery plans are met. It also calls for the designation of critical habitat, essentially a recognition that certain geography is critically important for species conservation.

A species can come onto the list as either *endangered* or *threatened*. The former means the species is in danger of extinction. This is the strictest category with the most stringent rules on taking, harassment, and capture. A threatened species is one that could become endangered without proactive protection. Rules on the taking of threatened species can be more flexible, but these species still benefit from the same mandate to study, monitor, and report. And all that reporting happens in the public eye, with open comment periods before any decision and the publication of everything in the Federal Register, the official notice service of the US government. Think of the register as an ever-evolving set of rules that apply to the entire nation.

The endangered species list itself, too, is an ever-growing tome of wild and rare plants and animals. Some species have come off the list, but many more have been added in the ESA's more than four decades. At the core of decision-making is science. The act is specific about the use of scientific fact to list and delist species, which requires an army of experts across America to study and document its nonhuman residents.

That first time I had lunch with Rich, there were twelve federally listed species in Minnesota, and I wanted to see every one of them. Today, there are nineteen, and that number may change by the time you read these words. The wolf has been delisted and relisted several times during my explorations for this book. Following the endangered species list in Minnesota has taken me to the north woods to follow a canine and a feline, to the shores of the northernmost lake in the United States and to the southern Gulf Coast to spot a pair of bird species, to the western prairies to see a minnow and an ancient species of prairie legume, to the northwestern plains to search for an orchid and two butterflies, to the rivers of the Twin Cities metro area to haul aboard five unusually named freshwater mussels, into deciduous forests to net a bat, and to rugged bluff country to examine a rock-clinging ice-age succulent, an iridescent blue butterfly, and a tiny spring woodland wildflower that is found only in Minnesota. (The nineteenth species, a bumble bee, came onto the list so recently that I never sought one for this book—though it seems my Minneapolis backyard might be one of the best places to see it.)

I have also gotten to know those who study these plants and animals. From wading hip-deep in prairie creeks with a fisheries professor who can identify every type of minnow under the muddy surface, to scaling cliffs with a biologist seeking to genetically reclassify an ice-age leftover, to speeding across Texas bayous with a bird expert, I have met extraordinary people and seen beautiful landscapes across the Upper Midwest and beyond. Those people are as much a part of this story as the wild and rare beings they study and love. Those landscapes are at the core of these species' existence, a vast web that nourishes and shelters them. And these people and places are just as different from each other as the wolf is from the dwarf trout lily.

Therein lies a major aspect of my fascination. On one end of the spectrum of this list is a moving, snarling predator—inspiration for fairy tales, instigator of centuries of government policy, killer of sheep and backyard pets, in some cultures a revered brother, a family animal whose social structure is hauntingly like ours, a wide-ranging omnivore capable of existing just about anywhere. On the other is a fleeting flower, a poor reproducer, sequestered on fewer than six hundred acres in southern Minnesota. Yet both inspire protection, extensive research, passion, and a fair degree of coddling.

Above all, the Minnesota (for now) nineteen are a cross section of the human relationship with nature. They cover many bases. Species type: mammal, insect, crustacean, bird, fish, plant. Habitat: woods, rivers, creeks, prairies, lakeshores. Threat: deliberate extirpation, general rareness, conversion of prairie to farmland, draining of wetlands, recreational lakeshore development, industrial and agricultural water pollution, increased rain runoff from urban development, habitat loss due to global climate change. Human perspective: utter adoration, vile hatred, complete indifference.

What can this list of federally endangered species tell us about our part of the world? What can it tell us about us? Let's find out, species by endangered species.

Minnesota dwarf trout lily

1

Lily

The fleeting upper midwestern spring is a five-week romance—cool, fresh, bright, and unfurling. Soon it will settle into the swelter and deep shade of June. The deciduous forest of south-central Minnesota transforms quickly and often from April through May. Plants and animals remember themselves in succession, remember that they are green beings after all, and that they can flower; or remember that they can sing, chortle, croak, cheep, chitter, hoot, and gobble. The woods are still open to traveling sounds, and the sun still comes all the way down to the duff. Now is the time to hurry, if you're a woodland wildflower—bloodroot or hepatica or jack-in-the-pulpit: the leafen umbrella will open soon.

In the valley of Prairie Creek in April 2012, white trout lily carpets the hillsides. Yellow marsh marigold traces the seeping freshets, its glossy greenness like polished houseplants strewn on the browning leaves. Cutleaf toothwort, of the rhythmic percussive name, lives up to its moniker with jagged greenery and contrasts it with delicate white bullhorns. Virginia waterleaf looks shade-dappled even in full sun. (A friend with whom I saw this plant told me her mother always called it Virginia Waterford, as if a stately British dame were reclining in the spring woods.) Ferns, sedges, and wild ginger are cliquish, sticking to their own kind in pockets of some soil or other, some level of moisture or other, some ray of sunlight or other. And the ramps look like baby coconut palms, somehow too tropical in appearance for these bare woods.

Collectively, these are spring ephemerals. They run their yearly course before the maples, oaks, hickories, and lindens can leaf out. They drink the spring sun, pack it all down into their roots, and by late June at the latest (with a few exceptions, like the ginger and the waterleaf) give up their aboveground existence. The forest floor in summer is shady and mostly brown. Spring is ephemeral. These woods are a manifestation of that. Go ahead and load up spring with symbolic meaning, call it newness, call it a fleeting romance (as I did a few paragraphs ago), call it a resurrection. I see spring actually slipping away with every moment. Those deciduous leaves are coming on quickly.

I walk down from the picnic area at Nerstrand Big Woods State Park onto the boardwalk that winds between trees, stepping always downward to Hidden Falls. The boardwalk is here to protect these delicate flowers—one in particular.

The Minnesota dwarf trout lily (*Erythronium propullans*) is the most ephemeral of spring ephemerals. It is small, about two or three inches high, and simple: its visible parts are limited to a single greenish-silvery-brown leaf in years it decides not to bloom, and two of those leaves and a whitish-pink flower in years it decides to. Its bloom time is shorter than most all of its forest-floor kin, and its flower is barely the size of a grain of rice. The flower can have anywhere between three and six tiny petals perched atop an impossibly delicate grayish stem, which rises directly from the ground between the leaves. In the morning the flower is shy, closed and pointing downward. As the sun warms, the petals open and curl back on themselves. Small bees, flies, and butterflies may feed on its nectar and pollinate it in the process.

The way to tell the dwarf trout lily and the white trout lily (*Erythronium albidum*) apart is by the flower: though the cousins' leaves are the same size, the dwarf's tiny bloom gives it away. Nerstrand Big Woods is one of just a few places the dwarf grows in the world. Endemic to Minnesota, the dwarf trout lily grows in only three counties. That's it.

The walkway has signs that say "Sensitive Area, Please Stay on Boardwalk." At the bottom is a sign explaining this little plant's significance and its similarity to the white trout lily, which appears in abundance here and throughout the eastern forests, from Maine to Ontario to Tennessee. The sign says the dwarf is here, but the actual colonies and individuals are not marked. That's okay: I like a search. I've been here before, but I don't remember exactly where they are. And that might not matter, because a particular trout lily (this is true of white, yellow and dwarf) might not flower in a given year, and might not even put up leaves. Without the flower, it's impossible to tell the difference between dwarf and white. Their speckled leaves (like a trout's side, so it's said, but I don't see it) are identical in general size, color, and shape. Hunting dwarf trout lilies is like finding the smallest needle in a haystack made of needles.

A Minnesota dwarf trout lily in bloom

But there's one, growing up from between the exposed roots of a small maple. Ranunculus vine climbs the tree. A trio of bloodroot leaves, like strangely shaped satellite dishes, rises nearby. The lily is two feet from the boardwalk. And here's another, two inches in front of the toe of my boot. And one more, down the slope to the creek behind the tree that cradles the first. The flowers aren't fully open yet. They offer just a hint of the downward-facing star with the yellowish throat that will soon present itself to spring woods pollinators.

The dwarf trout lily was first found by a European American in 1870, by Mary B. Hedges, a botany instructor at St. Mary's School in Faribault, on the school grounds. Of course it is likely the local indigenous people knew of the plant, though any uses they may have had for it are unknown. It was sent to Harvard University's herbarium (where a pressed specimen can still be found), where botanist Asa Gray wrote a paper on it (in which he noted how "peculiar" the plant was), thereby officially recognizing it as a species. Two additional sites were found in the late 1800s. No dwarves have ever been found outside the 275-square-mile triangle traced by these first sites. That triangle is generally centered on Faribault, Minnesota, and includes portions of Rice, Steele, and Goodhue Counties.

Between the 1960s and 1980s, plant expert, author, and University of Minnesota professor Thomas Morley set off to find every dwarf population, and he added many sites to the list of known occurrences. He also kept meticulous records of places he thought he might find some but did not. About fifteen more sites were found by the Minnesota Department of Natural Resources' County Biological Survey in the 1990s and 2000s, but none were outside those original three counties. This is the only plant endemic to Minnesota. Endemic and ephemeral.

In recognition of that long-known rarity, Minnesota botanists proposed the plant's inclusion on the endangered species list as early as 1975, just after the ESA's passage. It was finally listed as endangered in 1986, and a recovery plan was written in 1987. That plan already describes losses of colonies since the sixties: road construction and conversion to row crops at privately owned sites, motorbike activity at River Bend Nature Center, and illegal horticultural collecting within Nerstrand Big Woods State Park. The recovery plan says that delisting is possible when five hundred colonies on fifteen separate sites are fully protected and managed (the plan references nineteen target sites—there are now forty distinct recognized sites). It calls, quite logically, for careful protection and stewardship of "naturally occurring populations." It also recommends establishing a "grid system or other set of permanent markers on the ground" at each major trout lily site, for the purpose of better understanding change in populations over time as well as soil sampling at each site, to better understand correlations between the plant and the substrate.

Unlike some other listed species, which see almost yearly notices, lawsuits, plan amendments, critical habitat designation modifications, and other federal paperwork, the dwarf trout lily has—legally speaking—been pretty quiet. The only other item worth a Federal Register notice is the 2011 five-year review. (Five-year reviews, incidentally, are supposed to be prepared, as the name suggests, every five years, but funding and staff time is rarely available to do so—for any species. A 1991 review included all species listed before that time and did not substantially alter the status of the lily. So the lily's five-year review is only fifteen years late.)

The big takeaway from that 2011 review is that none of the criteria for delisting have been met. Furthermore, the species was classified as having a high degree of threat and a low potential of recovery, and it may be in conflict with economic development. Not a good outlook.

The review also identifies additional threats to the species not covered in 1987, most notably storm water runoff from urban areas that exacerbates flooding. A large percentage of known lily populations lie in the valleys of the Cannon and Straight Rivers, which are the receiving waters for runoff from the streets of Owatonna, Faribault, and Northfield. The review document even goes so far as to recommend a surface-water management plan be prepared for Faribault as a way of protecting this endangered plant. This recommendation comes directly from Minnesota

Department of Natural Resources botanist Nancy Sather, who watched with dismay as the spring floods of 1998 destroyed portions of most major populations, including those at Nerstrand.

Today, when perusing the literature on the dwarf trout lily—and, in reality, any rare Minnesota plant—it is hard to escape the name of Nancy Sather. I first encountered Nancy at River Bend Nature Center in Faribault. I had volunteered for a survey of dwarf trout lilies to be led by Nancy and fellow DNR botanist Derek Anderson. We were going to walk "the grid," one of the oldest permanent monitoring areas for the species. I say "encountered" Nancy because we weren't formally introduced that day, and it would be years before I was able to meet her face-to-face. Derek started the day and Nancy came later, when the dozen or so volunteers were already in the woods, walking in a long line looking for lilies. That day in 2011 was the first time I ever saw a dwarf trout lily. As we walked the grid, I could hear Nancy's high voice piercing the forest, the tone a mix of instruction and excitement: "Do you see any lilies? You should be into the lilies right about now." I remember her surprise that we weren't seeing many lilies. I remember her disappointment.

Nancy worked at the Minnesota DNR beginning in 1979; she is recently retired. She has been a key part of the Minnesota Biological Survey, an effort begun more than thirty years ago to catalog plant and animal species, county by county, across the state (the survey has completed eighty-three of eighty-seven counties as of 2017). She has made an important career of studying and conserving rare species. Her passion for plants is infectious.

I first sit down with Nancy in a rather stale, gray office in the DNR headquarters in St. Paul. She wears her gray-white hair in a loose ponytail. Her face has the bright vibrancy of a life lived outdoors. She wears glasses and dresses simply and practically, with sensible shoes, seemingly ready to go into the field on a moment's notice. She is comfortable and confident in her knowledge, and on several occasions she has unabashedly commandeered my notebook to make sketches or draw maps to explain her points. Maps of Minnesota and its plant species seem to float just behind her eyes, to be called forth verbally or with an ink pen whenever necessary.

Nancy started working with dwarf trout lilies in the late 1980s. She had the idea to set up the grid at River Bend. This was in the days before GPS, so the grid is old-school: staking and measuring and surveying techniques. In the 1990s she started looking for more trout lily sites. Morley had had the last say in the seventies but Nancy was eager to find more. She searched forests around the edges of the known areas, forests that seemed to be the right places, but didn't find any more. As she moved eastward, she noticed the soil became more sandy, and this seemed to correlate to the edge of the known populations. The soils on which the dwarves grow are highly silty; Nancy calls this the "old gray till," and it comes from the Decorah shale.

The 2011 five-year review (on which Nancy was extensively consulted) suggests an association between dwarf trout lilies and Decorah shale, and it includes a map showing the areas underlain by that stone, as a guide to where further searches might turn up lilies. The mud that became the Decorah shale was deposited in a shallow sea that covered the Midwest about 450 million years ago. The Decorah is a gray stone full of fossils—its outcrops are known as the best places in Minnesota to find trilobites, horn corals, and gastropods. Above the Decorah is the light tan sandstoney Cummingsville Formation. Below it is the famous Platteville limestone, an erodible gray stone that forms Minnehaha Falls and St. Anthony Falls in Minneapolis and is featured in innumerable building foundations, facades, and bridges. The Platteville is also the rock over which Hidden Falls plunges in Nerstrand. Glaciers smashed and finely ground the Decorah shale, turning it into the old gray till. This defines the dwarf trout lily triangle: mounds of gray silt created by glaciers from the Decorah, cut through by twisting rivers, and sitting on a flat, mostly buried expanse of Platteville limestone.

Weathered Decorah shale seems to be the best thing for dwarf trout lilies (unlike their white relatives, which don't seem to care much about their bedrock). But it is possible to have too much of a good thing. In 2011, the summer after I walked the River Bend grid, a midyear flood deposited six to eight inches of old gray till on the dwarf trout lilies there. The flood was unexpected, but these unexpected floods seem to be arriving more frequently. The lily population there has collapsed. Some lilies were buried; some were washed away by the river as it cut new channels through the silt.

The population has also crashed at a private Nature Conservancy preserve. There used to be hundreds of plants at the volunteers' preferred lunch spot, but in the past two or three years, says Nancy, there have been just ten or so. She has noticed the landscape there has also changed: more glacially delivered rocks seem to be sitting on the surface of the land. Whether this indicates a depositional event like a flood or an erosional event that has taken away the silt and exposed the rock is unknown, but in either case the substrate has been affected and the lilies are nearly gone.

The fear presented by both these locations is that they were protected, well studied, stewarded carefully by volunteers, nonprofits, and the DNR. The dwarf trout lily recovery plans focus primarily on the protection of habitat sites, to ensure populations will not be plowed under, dug up, or collected. But what to do if even the fully protected sites are crashing? And why else might they be crashing?

In order to understand that, so much more needs to be learned about the dwarf trout lily. Nancy says it is an odd little plant, and that most of the original description of it—and even the life history cataloged in the 1987 federal recovery plan—should be taken with a degree of skepticism. Truth be told, we are still learning how this plant works. But it is very hard to study a briefly blooming perennial in the wild, especially one with so few numbers and such a limited range. Nancy can't very well go digging up plants to see if they are putting out runners or small bulblets, which is another way the lilies can reproduce. She can't transplant them elsewhere and do trial studies of their ability to reestablish. Such activities could threaten the entire species.

Thankfully, the dwarf trout lily has been successfully transplanted to two places outside its original southern Minnesota range. One population lives in a park in Minneapolis, having been brought there by an early-nineteenth-century botanist, Eloise Butler long before the Endangered Species Act. Those lilies live a wild life amidst other woodland ephemerals and trees also brought there by Butler. The other population can be found at the Minnesota Landscape Arboretum. They were moved to the botanical garden exactly for the purpose of study.

Much has been learned about the species in the arboretum garden plots, where conditions are controlled and individual plants are tracked as best they can be. Studies here have debunked much of the description of the plant included in the 1987 recovery plan. That document asserted that trout lilies reproduced rather poorly. They could be pollinated by a small bee and a few other insects, but they never seemed to set seed unless in the presence of white trout lilies. It was believed they mostly reproduced by means of a small shoot growing off the side of the subterranean part of the stem, and that a bulb could be produced only by a plant while in flower. By creating a dwarf-only planting (and not being afraid to uproot plants at will), the arboretum was able to show that dwarf trout lilies are better at making babies than was thought. Non-flowering plants do set new bulbs, and plants can make more than one bulb. Arboretum botanists have also been able to calculate a more accurate percentage of the number of plants flowering in a given year—around 15 percent. In all, it seems the pessimistic reproductive analysis in the 1987 report wasn't exactly correct. Though admittedly it's still no milkweed: the dwarf trout lily produces few if any seeds, and its bulbs don't get far from their parents.

But the biggest mystery is the anomalies. Nancy tells me about anomalies during our conversation in the DNR conference room. She draws them, in fact, on a scrap piece of paper: odd mutations from the normal structure of the lily, as many as nine different aberrations. Some plants might open with just one or two petals, rather than the normal four to six. Some develop a hook-like green structure, or an extra leaf-like appendage with a different texture or in an odd location on the stem. Some have no outer flower parts at all—just stamens. These stamens are truly weird, sometimes seemingly having no relationship with the architecture of the rest of the plant. They seem alien—wrong, somehow.

Nancy is the first person to have formally documented these anomalies. She initially thought that some agricultural chemical might be causing them, but they have since also cropped up in both transplanted populations at the Eloise Butler garden and at the Minnesota Landscape Arboretum, places well shielded from agricultural runoff. They are still a mystery.

Nancy has thought about them a lot, devising theorems impossible to test. As we talk, she exhibits a strange mix of emotions. She is concerned for these plants, for the implications of this strangeness. But she also seems a little excited at the prospect of another investigative door opening up. These unassuming little plants have thrown her a curveball, and she loves them for it.

Her most interesting theory reveals a nuanced, more long-term perspective on the issue. Maybe the anomalies really aren't. "We the botanists walk in on plants at a point in time, in the nineteenth or twentieth or twenty-first century," she says, hearkening back to Mary Hedges in 1870, "and what we see is what we think is real. But of course nature just keeps marching on." Maybe, she suggests, how the plant was described in the late 1800s is not the whole story, just like the depictions of the now arid West during the early 1900s were likely describing a far wetter than average time. "Are we looking at [the lily's] genetic experiments? Is the plant experimenting with ways to be a lily? Or are we looking at an interaction between some environmental thing and the forces that trigger plant anatomical development?"

All she knows is that she has seen the result. "Over and over," she says, "the anomalies go up and up in a population, and then the population crashes."

In 2013 I camp at Nerstrand State Park with my two boys and my mother. My wife, Kerri, is out of town on an extended trip and my mom has come to help with childcare. We have planned on two nights—Friday and Saturday—but it pours on Friday, so we watch the weather forecast and wait. On Saturday morning I pack the car in the rain. The radar shows the Twin Cities in dark blue downpour, but the storm edge is just to the south, meaning clear skies merely an hour away. My mom thinks I am crazy, taking us camping in this spring gully washer. But I persevere. The precipitation peters out near the County Highway 1 exit from Interstate 35, then clears entirely as we drive through Dundas. By noon we are setting up camp under sunny skies and getting ready to hike down to Hidden Falls. Ethan, four and a half tests himself on the limestone scarp beside the waterfall. He falls near the bottom but brushes it off. Then he goes all the way up and stands on the top edge beside the cascade's precipice, beaming with pride. Mason, just two, stays near the plunge pool, venturing nearer and nearer the water, testing his limits. Then he trips and soaks his clothes. I do not have backups, but he doesn't mind, and he struts a little in a toddler's brag about his brush with danger.

Hidden Falls is unexpected in this landscape. A buried lens of limestone stretches like a dam across the gentle valley of Prairie Creek. It's only about twenty feet high, and wider than that. A scraggly ash tree holds a peninsula together at the base of the falls. Above, the water gives no signal of its coming drop. Below, it carries on as if not noticing the

At Hidden Falls with Ethan and Mason, 2013

momentary excitement of rock. All around, the hills are soft, rounded, glacial, eroded to gullies with meanders at their bottoms. And then this hard edge amidst the forest, jutting from the duff, its name both trite and perfect.

We four walk from the falls up the boardwalk. We look for dwarf trout lilies and find them: two, close to the boardwalk, near but not exactly where I have seen them before. I share them with the boys and my mom, and then walk on. The landscape is freckled with trout lily leaves.

At camp I grill burgers and cook beans in the can in the coals. After s'mores, I put the boys to bed in the tent, flop in a camp chair, and gaze up at the deep black sky speckled with stars. My mom and I drink whiskey and reminisce about camping together. About the time at White Pines Forest in Illinois when we unpacked all our food and decided to take a little walk around camp—allowing just enough time for every jay and squirrel and raccoon to avail itself of our stockpile. About the times in Kohler-Andrae State Park on the Lake Michigan shore when my brother and I would find unusually shaped cedars and perch in their swoopy limbs. About our three days in the Boundary Waters to celebrate her sixtieth birthday—this excursion a constant inspiration to me: to be able and willing to backcountry camp with Ethan and Mason on my own sixtieth birthday.

After a time I look up at the stars and find the whole cosmos has rotated. Hours have passed. We sip our last and turn in.

My interest in the spring ephemerals starts with my mom during my childhood in Illinois. Though of course I never saw a dwarf trout lily before moving to Minnesota in 1998, our half-acre suburban yard was rich with white and yellow trout lilies that hugged the trunks of grand white and bur oaks rising from the manicured lawn. In the mid-eighties, when I began to be tasked with mowing that vast (when compared to surrounding lots) greensward, I was under strict instructions from my mother to stay back from the trees in spring. She loved those trout lilies, the way they circled the bases of the trees like atolls in an otherwise uniform ocean.

The trout lilies in the yard were mini-monocultures—landscapes of uniform green-and-liver spikes, not unlike how they occur at Nerstrand, or anywhere else I have seen them. Unlike most other spring ephemerals, they colonize entire hillsides and glades. They are the background upon which the bursts of other species rest.

The understory landscape was populated with trout lilies, too, in Muncie, Indiana, within the cool shade of Christy Woods. In this patch of preserved deciduous forest on the campus of Ball State University, I learned about plants—studied plants for the first time. It was an introductory ecology course, somewhat geared toward students in related majors for whom this would likely be their only ecology class. It was a required part of the landscape architecture curriculum. We studied the woods empirically, designing experiments meant not to demonstrate some new scientific finding but rather our ability to think like scientists. I set up meter-square plots at varying distances from a trail edge and counted species, working to determine if trails had an impact on diversity. The trout lilies seemed unaffected by the trail. They grew right up to the edge and formed their spiky colonies deep into the woods, under the redbuds and spicebushes and dogwoods.

I did not take another ecology course, but I signed on as a volunteer docent at Christy Woods. I learned the plants—tree, shrub, and perennial—and led school groups and senior walking clubs along the dim trails. I pointed out the ginger and the Dutchman's breeches and the bluebells and the jack-in-the-pulpit.

Spring in central Indiana always seemed about to break and then never seemed to break. It wasn't unusual for the weather to take on that cool, drizzly, fresh character starting in early February and then stick with it through April. The school-year window for spring ephemerals was short. By the time I was talking with third graders about trout lilies, I was also into finals, and then home to Illinois for the summer. It was the curse of the college romance: after a winter of hibernation, once everyone got in the mood to fall in love, it was time to scatter.

I, landscape architecture degree in hand, scattered eventually to Minnesota, for no reason other than a job offer. I have now seen more than eighteen springs here. Wild ginger, bloodroot, and jack-in-the-pulpit grow in my yard. No trout lilies though, of any kind. I'm not sure why exactly, now that I think about it. They are not the kind of plant typically for sale by the purveyors of natives. And I have focused on species that hold at least some green through the year—with the exception of bloodroot, my personal favorite, which I enjoy for just a week or so every April.

My dwarf trout lily sightings were always just one here, another there until the day in 2016 when I walk into the woods with Jerry and Karen Ibberson. We meet early on a Wednesday morning at Clinton Falls Dwarf Trout Lily Scientific and Natural Area on the banks of the Straight River just north of Owatonna—a name derived from the Dakota word for "straight." The state purchased this site in 2011, and the Ibbersons became its stewards the following year. They remove invasive plants, tear out barbed wire, and count plants—all on their own time. They are in their late sixties and seem like they have been married for decades. But no, their romance is recent: a match.com connection and marriage just nine years ago. Though they share no children, they have fourteen grandchildren between them. They live nearby and seek the wonder of nature near and far, once spending four months camping in Alaska, and also once visiting Nerstrand to search for dwarf trout lilies. They met Nancy Sather that day—she happened to be in the park preparing to count plants by herself—and she recruited them into her network of working plant lovers.

We chitchat in the little grass parking lot sandwiched between the river and County Highway 45, then gear up and head into the woods. This SNA has an odd geography caused by the convulsions of the nearby watercourse. Unexpectedly, in light of its name, the Straight River swings around in a great S-curve, creating two peninsulas, both cut off from adjacent public lands by the river and private property. This isolation can be partly thanked for the profusion of lilies I am about to see.

Jerry slings a backpack over his shoulder and straps on a homemade holster (PVC pipe closed at one end and with a strap on the other) filled

with bright orange flags. He pulls gaiters over his khaki-colored hiking
pants and nestles a baseball hat on his head. Karen hefts her own backpack and a bright-red cooler—the Ibbersons will be out here all day. She
wears a bright blue windbreaker, a flash of color compared to Jerry's
near camouflage. Both carry hiking poles. Karen has been having trou-
ble with her knee.

After an easy ten minutes through the open woods, we arrive at the
bright yellow "state land" sign, with a little glacial boulder beside it. This
rock is home base. Jerry and Karen set down their gear. The plan is for
me to walk for a little while with them, before the arrival of another
volunteer and Derek Anderson from the DNR. Then we will commence
with the real work—setting out long-term monitoring grids. As soon
as we reach the rock, the phone calls start. The volunteer is n the parking lot and doesn't know where to go. Derek isn't there yet to guide
her in. So Karen heads back to the cars, even though Jerry is quite sure
Derek will arrive the minute Karen clears the woods (which of course,
is exactly what happens).

In the meantime, Jerry shows me the land. It's flat, a plateau above
the curve of the Straight, with thin young trees, an overhead canopy just
beginning to leaf out. A not-too-distant shooting range means our
walk is punctuated with echoing blasts. But that's the only sound—that
and Jerry naming plants. False rue anemone is out in force. Waterleaf is
fully leafed and just beginning to bud. Bluebells ginger, and something
yellow—a buttercup, perhaps—gather in small conclaves. My spirits are
lifted even before I see any lilies. A walk in the spring woods is my tonic.

Then Jerry casually points out "a few" lilies. A few, here, means a
dozen, two dozen. I stop in my tracks, afraid of crushing the tiny flowers, but suddenly they are everywhere—not "suddenly" like they just
suddenly started blooming, but "suddenly" like my eyes became attuned
and I began to notice them everywhere. Ten, forty, sixty, a hundred.
They are impossible to count. I am incredulous. I have been visiting
Nerstrand for years for the thrill of finding a half dozen, and have failed
many years at even that. But here they thrive. Pure colonies of dwarves
stretch for yards in every direction—every blooming trout lily a dwarf.

I crouch low and gently lift a flower for a closer look. I would never do this at Nerstrand, but here it seems appropriate, to make that brief physical contact, an affectionate touch. I rise and continue on. I tiptoe through the woods—it's the only way to avoid these lilies.

Jerry and I circle back around and return toward the rock. Derek is arriving with Karen and the other volunteer, Marcia Richards. Marcia has been walking the woods counting lilies since 1987, when she read an article by (who else?) Nancy Sather and called her up to volunteer. She's a spry seventy-ish, with a gleam in her eye. As we five walk together to begin the survey, I ask why she comes out here. "To be able to go out into the woods in this season of the year is just magical," she says without hesitation. "I love the woods with the trees just barely green." Ah, yes, I agree.

The work begins. The task today is to set up fifty permanent tracking plots, each a meter square. Back at his office, Derek laid a one-meter grid across the entire SNA on his computer, then randomly selected fifty of those squares. Permanent plots are one of the techniques Nancy has recommended for counting lilies when they're in abundance at sites like these (it's called for in the recovery plan, remember?). The old idea of "colonies" as described in the early recovery plan for the species (and a condition of the plant's delisting) is not truly effective in the field. How to define a colony? Where does one colony end and another begin? But it would also be impossible to count every plant here. "With these numbers," explains Derek, "you'd spend a week with ten people to count them all." So the plots are representative. They allow Derek and Nancy to estimate the total population and also return to the same squares to track change over time.

Jerry runs the GPS and starts flagging coordinates. Marcia carries a clipboard with a numerical list of the squares. Derek has two squares made out of white PVC and a bag of short green stakes. I arrive at site #33. Derek hands me a white square, which I place on the ground so the flag Jerry labeled with #33 is in the northwest corner of the square. Derek knows the site well enough to find the cardinal directions by gut, but I need my phone's compass to get it right. When it's set, we put small green stakes at two corners and remove the orange flag. The green stakes will stay there (that's the "permanent" part of the permanent grid). The rules of an SNA say that no apparent human-made elements can exist there, thus these unobtrusive interventions that Derek and others can nevertheless locate again with GPS.

With the grid in place, Derek and I start counting lilies. Marcia and Karen are counting another square somewhere nearby. We place an orange flag beside each dwarf lily flower we see. Some are growing under the leaves of larger plants, like waterleaf, so we gently pet the vegetation to reveal any flowering dwarves. Every time I think I have found them all, I look again and see two more. Gradually, this little square sprouts a forest of orange flags.

Once we are sure we have flagged all the lilies in the square (some are right on the edge, so we count only those rooted within—the scientific purity of the randomized sample!), I pull and count the flags.

Derek Anderson, Jerry Ibberson, and Marcia Richards counting lilies, 2016

Twenty-three lilies. I lift the white square and walk over to a new numbered flag. On the way I tell Marcia what I found: twenty-three lilies in
square #33. That is more dwarf trout lilies than I have seen in my entire
previous life.

Not all grids are as fecund. #19: 0, #34: 4, #4 and #16: 0. Then a big
one: forty-three lilies in #15. But even this figure isn't all that impressive
to Derek. He recounts squares here and at other sites with up to 150 lilies
in a single meter. I imagine the color: a mass of orange hovering above
a single meter of land in this vast green forest. A rare, retiring species
highlighted and ostentatious.

I reluctantly leave the group before lunch. We have completed perhaps a dozen of the fifty squares. It seems simple, this laying down of
squares, counting of plants, and moving on. The data are elementary:
numbers in a spreadsheet that, even at high quantities like here, still
reinforce the scarcity of this plant everywhere else. Since lilies have been
counted at many other sites—Nerstrand, River Bend, others—the numbers have gone down. Here: who knows? Volunteers and scientists will
come out each year to count the same grids. Thus the data will grow—
whether or not the lily population does. These randomized permanent
grids are the most basic of basic science, but over time they can answer
big questions. Is this the place where lilies are most abundant? Are lilies
increasing or decreasing here? Can lilies in a certain area be expected to
flower more or less at similar rates each year? Are we anywhere near
achieving delisting?

Or should the dwarf trout lily ever be removed from the list? This
species has probably always been rare, a function of its range. Even if
every population on every site were permanently protected, it would
still be rare. Even under an optimal conservation scenario, this little
plant would still grow nowhere else in the world but three counties in
Minnesota. Would delisting be interpreted as a success story, or would
we instead forget about it—stop counting, stop removing buckthorn,
stop noticing, until it's gone?

Or what if, even with the goals met and all the appropriate land
protected, the numbers keep dropping? Maybe the dwarf is a genetic

anomaly that isn't built to last. An angiospermatic flirtation not a long-lasting love.

Or what if Mary Hedges never found that plant at St. Mary's School? What if no one noticed it? Wouldn't Nancy just study some other plant? My dwarf-less yard in Illinois and Christy Woods in Indiana weren't lacking for the absence of this one plant, just as my Minnesota woods don't lack for the absence of redbud or spicebush. But among my theoreticals this one is the least tenable. If not for Mary Hedges, some other botanist would have found and described it. That's what botanists (and all humans) do: we discover, describe, ascribe meaning, and, yes, give love to everything around us. This little plant, because it inherently once was on earth alongside us, was bound to be seen, known, cared for.

In fact, in 1910, long before the Endangered Species Act, and long before anyone ever thought to study this rare plant, and long before anyone realized it grew only in Minnesota, a botanist with a love of wild plants saw it, moved it to her new wild garden, and began caring for it. Eloise Butler was born in Maine in 1851, in an era of amateur and professional naturalists. She grew up in the wild and rural New England landscape at the very moment in history that Charles Darwin and Albert Russel Wallace were inspiring the world to rethink species. As a child she wandered forests and bogs with her sister, Cora, and even at that age seemed more drawn to plants than to people. In 1870 she graduated from high school and became a teacher in a one-room schoolhouse about four miles from where she grew up. But she had bigger goals. Unfortunately, most American colleges and universities were closed to women until the 1890s, so the remaining options were to continue to teach or to attend a normal (teacher-training) school. Eloise and Cora Butler both enrolled in the newly opened Eastern State Normal School, and Eloise graduated with high grades in 1873.

Almost immediately upon Eloise's graduation, the Butler family sold the farm in Maine and moved west to Indiana. She was unhappy there, likely out of sorts away from the wooded hills she knew so well. Within a year she had boarded a train north to Minneapolis, where she would spend the rest of her life and have a profound impact on at least one little corner of the city.

Today, the Eloise Butler Wildflower Garden sits within the largest green space in Minneapolis, the 750-acre Theodore Wirth Park. The prairie knolls are lovely in the fall, when the asters and coneflowers and goldenrod color the ground under monumental white oaks. The shady woods along the marshy creek are a joy in spring, as all the ephemeral wildflowers wake up in turn. Dwarf trout lilies live here, too. I saw them once, somewhat by accident, walking the cushiony wood chip trails with a friend and our two pairs of children. I knew they were there only because a naturalist was among them, counting. It was a Tuesday morning, and the naturalist had likely hoped no one would discover by her presence where these rare plants were living, but there I was, with a gaggle of preschoolers. She was visibly uncomfortable and did not speak to us. The sun was low and at my back, so I raised my hand in the air and used my shadow to point out the plants to my friend and the kids. That was a few years ago, and I have never found them again.

I can understand the naturalist's concern. This is an urban park, and people do love rare plants. Eloise Butler did, too. These lilies are here because Butler dug them up from somewhere else and planted them in her "Wild Garden," as she did with hundreds of prairie and woodland plants. She roamed other wild places in Minnesota and collected species. She brought back eastern plants when she visited Cora in New England. She rescued plants when woods were to be destroyed by, she said, "so-called improvements." She brought them all to the wild garden and installed them in places that seemed like their home habitats. She kept track of each in detailed journals and files like library cards—intending that the garden was both a place of solace and a place of science. The dwarf trout lily was just another plant to her. Her index card on the species says it was planted in the garden on May 17, 1909, and was collected from Cannon Falls. She noted that her specimens were "poor material, probably will not grow."

Some of her collected plants survived, some thrived, some struggled on for a little while and expired. The lilies have done well, despite her fears. All this collecting, transplanting, and cataloging—which Eloise called "botanizing"—has created a garden that is, yes, wild, but also curated. In this, the garden fits perfectly with the philosophy of landscape design that was prevalent at the time. Jens Jensen was crafting naturalized forests in Chicago in a careful balance of wild woods and deliberate interventions like stone council rings and pathways strategically placed to highlight particular views or landmark plants. Theodore Wirth, the superintendent of Minneapolis Parks during Butler's wild garden botanizing (and after whom the large park around the wild garden is named), expended monumental—for the time—energy and resources dredging lakes and sculpting hills in an effort to make the landscape at once natural looking but wholly constructed.

Butler, in her way, was in step with this prevailing thinking about the landscape. She felt that the natural landscape was restorative, healthful, and important for our very well-being. She also was not afraid to tinker with it.

When Butler arrived in Minneapolis in 1874, there were no parks at all. The park board was founded in 1883, while she was in the midst of a thirty-three-year high school teaching career. During that span, Butler continued to enrich her own scientific understanding by attending science summer schools, botanizing on her own time in the rural wilds just west of the city, traveling three times to Jamaica with Cora to pursue her complementary interest in marine algae, and spending a summer at the Marine Biological Laboratory in Woods Hole, Massachusetts (now the famed Woods Hole Oceanographic Institute). She also dragged her students out to her favorite haunts, including the tamarack bogs in what was to become Theodore Wirth Park and the wild garden.

Butler became interested in the idea of a wild garden around the turn of the century. In 1889 the park board had purchased the initial sixty-four acres of what would become Wirth Park. Butler visited the undeveloped park frequently beginning in 1891. She called upon her allies—other female botany teachers in the city—and drafted a petition to the park board to set aside space for a "natural botanic garden." In 1907 the board did just that, instructing superintendent Wirth to "select the proper place and make such minor improvements in the way of paths and fencing as may be necessary at an expense of not to exceed $200." The *Minneapolis Journal* headlined: "Shy Wild Flowers to be Given Hospice."

Though Butler was not officially appointed curator of the garden until four years after its founding, it was obvious she was in charge of it. Almost before the ink was dry on the park board authorization, Butler was out planting pitcher plants she had lovingly overwintered at her home. She became official at the behest of the Conservation Committee of the Minneapolis Woman's Club in 1911, when she retired from teaching high school. She stayed with the garden until her death in 1933, aged eighty-one. Others, almost all of them women, have continued her work at the garden.

Plenty of pictures of Eloise Butler exist today. Perhaps the most often seen (and the one that hangs on the wall of the current park board superintendent's office) is from 1921, when she was seventy. She wears a floppy, brimmed hat and a simple dress with a double row of buttons down the front and zigzag piping around the collar. She holds a sprig of some plant, maybe a goldenrod. Her face is soft and less wrinkled than you might expect for a seventy-year-old who spent her life in the wilds. The nose about which she was so self-conscious is a pleasant knob above lips set with confidence. Her eyes are downcast, studying the plant. She reminds more than a little of Nancy Sather.

There are two oddities in the image. On her right shoulder is a round clip from which hangs a pair of spectacles. I wonder if the cord is retractable, and whether she needed them for close looking or view gazing. She's not wearing them while studying this plant, but the photo could be posed. And on her left shoulder is a pin that can only be described as a sheriff's badge: a five-pointed metal star with little balls at each point. There are words on the star, but they're not legible.

Overall, this picture conveys an impression of success and satisfaction mixed with a little melancholy. Butler lived in a man's world—a world of science that was barely just beginning to allow women into the fold. Though the natural sciences were advancing rapidly at the time, opportunities for women were mainly restricted to teaching science and performing amateur botany. That's what Butler did, yet she still faced disdain for being unmarried, for unladylike yet happy tromping in the bogs in her free time, and for being too demanding. She wasn't alone. She collected like-minded women who advocated with her for the wild garden, for student greenhouses at local high schools, and for the opportunity to travel and study. Butler was a botanist—a scientist—though she had no advanced degree, no professorship, and no full-time job doing science. She created a legacy of knowledge and preservation, even though the gender roles of the day were stacked against her. And she paved the way for others. If Eloise Butler had been born a hundred years later, she would be Nancy Sather.

The Nerstrand boardwalk is full of people. This late April day in 2015—sunny, cool, refreshing—is begging Minnesotans to come into the woods. They bring sophisticated photography gear and binoculars, because the birds are also excited for this weather. Two ladies with thick Germanic accents are intrigued by the tiny flowers blooming through the brown leaf floor. I teach them a few common names: spring beauty, sharp-lobed hepatica, trillium. They repeat each with a strange roundedness—a way I have never heard these names in my head. A father walks down the steps with his three children. The middle one, a girl about six, carries a guidebook and a big backpack with a Yosemite Junior Ranger patch. It's clear whose idea this hike was. A couple walks with their daughter, maybe in her first years of college, wearing black stretch pants and a sparkly silver headband. Dad and daughter carry *Wildflowers of Minnesota* field guides. They are silent and peer down at the forest floor from the very edges of the boardwalk. They flow like creek currents from one side to the other. A volunteer naturalist, older and graying, greets passersby and dispenses identifications only if asked. I ask about the dwarf trout lily. "There's supposed to be thirteen in this area here," she says. "I've found about five."

A married pair, about sixty, in practical loose hiking clothing—him in a floppy hat and sporting a big gray beard, her hatless and with shoulder-length gray hair—ask me about the trout lily, mistaking me for a volunteer naturalist (I am walking very slowly and pretty much hanging around the area). I point out the two I have found. They smile widely. They are greatly pleased. "We've been coming here for twenty years, and this is the first time we've definitely seen one," he says, crouching, as people tend to do, to see the tiny flower more closely. "Now that you've actually seen them, they are definitely an order of magnitude smaller." They nod at each other, stand close together without touching, big smiles on their faces, and walk on.

I spend more than an hour on the boardwalk, looking for all thirteen trout lilies, seeing five or six, and deliberately trying to overhear people talking about nature. I wonder why people are here, why they visit Nerstrand, whether they know or care that a plant found only in this state is right here mere inches from their feet. Most don't understand the difference between the white trout lily and the dwarf. Most are enjoying the woods in total, more concerned with the pure beauty of the day: the barely leafed trees, the chickadees flitting through the branches, the murmur of the creek getting ready for its plunge, the golden unfiltered sunlight. To some the dwarf is a novelty, or a special find amidst an otherwise pleasant landscape.

Would the forest be less without it? The carpet of greenery and flowers that attracts people, including me, to this spring woods would be generally undiminished. Does the dwarf satisfy our need for biodiversity or our need for a puzzle, a scavenger hunt, a *Where's Waldo* of the woods?

I came to Nerstrand this time with my friends Dan and Amber, who are accomplished sketch artists and watercolorists and avowed nature lovers. As I eavesdropped, Amber drew a bloodroot. Dan tried to identify warblers whipping through. I expect they humored me in my obsession with the dwarf trout lily. It was only when I reminded them of its rarity, of the fact that this was the only plant found only in Minnesota, that they lit up. Are we attracted to the plant itself or its novelty?

Gradually, I followed them down to the falls. I called out marsh marigolds and cutleaf toothworts and early meadow rues and Dutchman's breeches. Below the limestone scarp we three sat on a wooden bench and produced drawings. My friends created watercolors that ranged across the folds of their journals and captured the April light cascading through the bare trees. I made a blocky ink sketch, trying to render the layers of rock that make up Hidden Falls.

I come here every year, sometimes alone, sometimes with family, sometimes with friends. Nerstrand Big Woods is a sacred place to me. It seems to me that in the European American tradition, places can be sacred to people but tend not to be universally sacred. They become sacred through some combination of one's own affinity for a landscape type, of one's own memories, of familiarity, and of a willingness to name it sacred. Sacredness is a human act, a bestowing of honor and respect. Once so honored, a place then begins to dwell inside oneself, to seem to have its own gravity and importance. Each visit compounds affinity, memory, and familiarity, and therefore the sacredness grows.

The first time I ever took each of my boys camping, it was at Nerstrand. I have come here every spring since moving to Minnesota, except for the one in 2011 when Mason was born, on an April day when the dwarf trout lilies were probably in bloom. That year I met Nancy at River Bend and saw my first dwarf trout lily.

My time has been measured by the eyeblinks of the spring ephemeral seasons, year after year, bloom after bloom. A plant grows up from the wet soil just rid of snow and raises its white flower to the fleeting sun.

Mussels, clockwise from left:
spectaclecase, sheepnose,
Higgins eye pearlymussel,
mapleleaf, snuffbox

2

Mussels

Mike Davis, moments after I enter his brightly lit, bubbling aquatics lab, reaches into a tank and hands me a mussel. The shiny brown animal rests between my fingers like a wave-washed stone, the perfect size for skipping, but fatter. It is roughly triangular and tinged greenish near the hinge end. A faint pattern—a slight interplay between brown and darker brown, like a fingerprint or snakeskin—seems somehow embedded in the shell, as if I were looking through layers of resin. It is satisfying to hold: hard, smooth, weighty for its size, substantial, and with a presence that proves somehow it is alive. It is, of course, alive—clamped tight against the threat of my hand and the air, but alive. Inside that shell are muscles, gills, siphons for taking in and pushing out water, teeth, a mouth, an entire digestive tract, and a complete reproductive system. A mussel is an efficient, self-contained little creature. It seems robust and impenetrable, indestructible even.

But Mike soon reminds me these are fragile animals. The mussel I am holding is a snuffbox (*Epioblasma triquetra*). It is federally endangered. Somewhat matter-of-factly, Mike says, "You're one of a dozen or so people in the world who have held one of those."

I let that sink in for a moment, then drop the snuffbox back in its tank. Around me in the warehouse the tanks bubble, fish swim lazily in blue water, and humans stroll about with casual purpose, opening valves, carrying trays, and repairing leaking pipes. This is the Minnesota

A snuffbox mussel in the Minnesota DNR's Lake City mussel laboratory, 2015

Department of Natural Resources' mussel laboratory, an unmarked faded yellow building on a dead-end road just north of Lake City. Mike Davis is the state's foremost mussel expert. He has been with the DNR since 1986, founded the mussel lab in 2015, and for the past five or six years has worked exclusively on studying, propagating, and reintroducing native Minnesota mussels to habitats across the state and region. Minnesota has forty-eight species of native mussels living in its creeks, rivers, and lakes. They are not all that hard to find. They tend to stay put. I see mussels regularly in the sandy bottom beneath the rickety dock up north, where I fish with my boys. The mussels get down in the muck and become camouflaged with algae, and my boys find some thrill in moving their hands close to them and watching them snap closed with a puff of water. Little mussels come up with handfuls of pretty rocks when I scoop southern Minnesota riverbanks just to hear that bright earthy clacking of stones.

Mike, who has snorkeled and scuba dived in the big rivers of the Twin Cities, describes mussel beds as freshwater coral reefs. He has seen communities of mussels with more than twenty species living together at densities of a hundred individuals per square yard. They lie half buried in the gravel, open to the river, eating the detritus carried toward them by powerful currents and filtering the water in the process. The average person might call some of these clams, but scientists like Mike call them all mussels, the main difference having to do with life cycle: true clams simply release larvae into the water, while mussels require the collaboration of another animal—but more on that later

Mike Davis grew up in Rochester, among the rolling hills and twisty rivers of southeastern Minnesota. He was always interested in the natural environment, farming, horses, and fishing He went to college to study environmental science, but found himself more suited to the land than to the classroom, so he took what he calls a "fifteen-year hiatus" from college. He did a little farming; he milked fifty cows every day for four years. He also was a commercial fisherman on the Mississippi River and a few lakes. In the early 1930s, the commercial price of freshwater mussels was going up. Mussel shells were being cut into beads and inserted into oysters in Japan to culture pearls. Mike switched to diving the mussel beds of Lake Pepin (mussels were a lot easier to catch), and he would sell them by the ton "I am personally responsible," he says with an ironic grin, "for the deaths of thousands of mussels."

Around that same time, his son suffered a head injury, which was not life threatening but which led doctors to discover a malformation in his blood vessels. Mike needed health insurance. So, at thirty-eight years old, he finished his final year of college and got a job with the DNR. By then, the price of mussels was up to twenty-five cents a pound—high at the time, but it would eventually climb to a dollar a pound—and the DNR was getting concerned about the effect on Lake Pepin populations (the Higgins eye pearlymussel [Lampsilis higginsii] was federally listed by then). Because Mike had a little experience catching and identifying mussels, he was tasked with a survey of the Cannon River in 1987. He was then named a biologist for the Mississippi River, and he set up monitoring sites in Lake Pepin. Gradually, through in-the-field experience, voracious reading, and participation on work teams for endangered species, he became a regional expert.

Mike still keeps horses and, of course, still loves to be around the water. He looks the part of the mariner, with a tousled swatch of gray hair, a lean, wiry body and limbs, and often a rough gray stubble about his cheeks and chin. He has an easy, somewhat crafty-looking smile to go with his flat and dry sense of humor. He has a spreadsheet brain that somehow can keep track of all those odd common names and the corresponding scientific names and state and federal statuses.

Mussels, perhaps more than any other group of plants and animals, have been hard hit by humans, especially in urban areas like the Twin Cities. Dams change water flows and prevent fish and mussel migration. Dredging for navigation alters the river bottom. Untreated municipal and industrial sewage used to be dumped into waterways. Referencing research into the historic occurrence and the more recent decline of mussels in the big rivers of central Minnesota, Mike says that "the arrival of Europeans seems to always be the culprit." Yes, there are still some reefs, but they are likely far less diverse, less extensive, and less wide-ranging than they once were. Five mussel species appear on the federal endangered species list: the snuffbox, the spectaclecase (*Cumberlandia monodonta*), the sheepnose (*Plethobasus cyphyus*), the winged mapleleaf (*Quadrula fragosa*), and the Higgins eye pearlymussel. Mike and his team have done work with each of these, and a few others like the mucket (*Lampsilis abrupta*), the plain pocketbook (*Lampsilis cardium*), the elktoe (*Alasmidonta marginata*), and the monkeyface (*Quadrula metanevra*).

As indicated by those above sentences, humans have granted this tribe the most fantastic lineup of names. Purple wartyback, threehorn wartyback, pimpleback. Elephantear, washboard, pistolgrip. Hickorynut, fawnsfoot. Ebonyshell, flutedshell, paper pondshell, fragile papershell, yellow sandshell. Creeper, flat floater, lilliput, spike.

The adult snuffbox Mike handed to me was in the last stage of a complex life cycle that has only fairly recently become understood. In the wild, male and female snuffboxes live near each other in rivers and creeks with swift current. The male releases sperm balls (spermatozygmata) into the water, essentially sowing his seed into the current and hoping for the best. A downstream female catches that spermball. As soon as she does, it explodes, releasing millions of spermatozoa, which she combines with her eggs, from which grow millions of first-stage larval mussels called glochidia. The microscopic glochidia don't look quite like adult mussels. They are more like seeds with sharp edges or pointed thorns. When the glochidia are ready, the female snuffbox plays a trick: she leaves her shell slightly agape but uses her rocklike appearance to blend in with the lake-bottom pebbles. A log perch—a small fish common in rivers—comes looking for food, turning over pebbles in search of aquatic insects. When the perch turns over the snuffbox, she catches the fish head with her shell teeth and immobilizes it with her vice grip. While holding the fish, the snuffbox mother pumps her glochidia into the fish's face and across its gills.

In moments, the fish is released, shakes itself off, and carries on with its river life. A few of the snuffbox's glochidia have snagged on the log perch's gills and are carried into the wide world with the peregrinations of their new host. It seems that with most mussel-fish relationships, the fish is not harmed by the growing mussel-lets in its gills. The fish goes on unperturbed while the mussel, now transforming from a larva into a juvenile that looks a little more like a tiny mussel, takes nourishment from the fish's blood and rides safely ensconced out of reach of waterway hazards. After a time, the baby snuffboxes drop off the fish and settle onto the river floor to begin filter feeding as mussels do.

At Mike's lab a larvae "harvest" is going on: grad students filter water from tanks and slide petri dishes under microscopes. I peer into the eyepieces, and it is like looking at outer space. A black background is studded with bright objects like stars and planets. The frame pulses hypnotically as odd beings wend their slow-motion way in this galactic landscape. A rotifer eats a midge larva; flatworms undulate aimlessly; larvae of mites and flies are as alien as anything I have ever seen. And amongst this flotsam of fishwater: mussels. Tiny, transparent, but fully mussels. I see the bivalve shell open slightly to allow the clear-white foot to stretch outward like putty. The foot stretches and then contracts the shell toward it. It makes decent pace, stretching and contracting, presumably seeking suitable substrate. The first dish contains a couple of plain pocketbooks, the second a few muckets. In the wild, these larvae would find themselves a spot with just the right kind of sand, gravel, or rocks, wedge in, and pretty much stay there for the rest of their lives. Which can be a long time. Mussels live for many decades in the wild. Mike and his team have found live spectaclecase mussels in the Upper St. Croix River that, based on their analysis of size and shell ridges, were nearly a hundred years old.

Two million people and three big rivers live in the Twin Cities metropolitan area. The Mississippi flows generally from the northwest to the southeast, with a big laying-down-S curve in the middle. The Minnesota comes in from the agricultural west between the cities: downstream of downtown Minneapolis and upstream of downtown St. Paul. The St. Croix flows down from the northern forests of Minnesota and Wisconsin and joins the Mississippi on the eastern edge of the metro, at Prescott, Wisconsin. After that confluence, the Mississippi soon becomes Lake Pepin, the only natural lake on that great river's entire journey to the Gulf of Mexico. Waterskiing was invented here, out of the marinas of Lake City, and this was also the hub of commercial mussel harvesting.

The geology through which these big rivers flow is pretty straightforward, but still creates a land unexpected in a midwestern city. The level layer cake of rock has three key components: the St. Peter sandstone on the bottom, the Platteville limestone on the top, and a thin layer of Glenwood shale between them. This is a good lineup for making waterfalls. The St. Peter is some of the softest sandstone in the world: visit the glade in Minnehaha Park and you can turn rock into sand with a gentle touch. Into the yellow-orange rock, people have carved caves that feel like being inside half a pumpkin. They have carved their names, lovers' names, and dates everywhere they can reach.

The Platteville is hard but has lots of cracks throughout. Water coming over the top of the limestone easily erodes the sandstone, creating an overhang. Then the limestone breaks apart and plunges downward, moving the waterfall upstream. St. Anthony Falls is the Mississippi River's version of this erosion event. Historically it was considered the fastest moving waterfall in the world, meaning it was advancing upstream more quickly than any other waterfall. The geological record indicates that twelve thousand years ago the falls was about where the Minnesota River is now, halfway between the two cities. The first European to record his visit to the falls was Father Louis Hennepin, a Belgian priest, who named it for his patron saint and claimed it for France—even though the local Dakota already had a few pretty good names for it (Owamni, meaning "falling water," or Owamniyomni, meaning "whirlpool") and claim to it.

With the advancement of the Mississippi up its valley and the resulting creation of a narrow gorge, other tributaries got stranded well above the river level. Minnehaha Creek has its own waterfall: a fifty-three-foot cascade at the head of a lovely box canyon in a park in Minneapolis. On the St. Paul side, a few small creeks have also cut canyons headward, most notably Hidden Creek. That cascade is no longer natural, though. The creek comes out of the cliff face in a sewer pipe and cascades through a series of stone pools constructed in the 1930s by the Works Progress Administration.

The Minnesota River has a different history entirely. It was one of the drainage outlets for massive Glacial Lake Agassiz in northwestern Minnesota. At its peak, that river was miles wide and hundreds of feet deep, a fact that can be understood today by looking at its wide valley stretching southwest through the suburbs toward Mankato.

The confluence of the Minnesota and Mississippi, known as Bdote, is sacred to the Dakota people, many of whom consider it the place where the Dakota first came to be. And on Pike Island, which sits at the sacred confluence, Dakota women, children, and elders were held by the US government in a concentration camp after the US–Dakota War of 1862. In the shadow of Fort Snelling during the winter of 1862–63 as many as three hundred Dakota people died, mostly from measles and other diseases, perhaps compounded by poor nutrition.

At the Minnesota River, the Mississippi turns northeast and its valley widens, having been carved by the same glacial power as the Minnesota's valley. Here the high ground pulls back from the river and low floodplains run all the way down through and past St. Paul. Like Minneapolis, St. Paul sits high above the river, but where the former overlooks a waterfall at the beginning of a gorge, the latter surveys a wide, lazy river beginning to feel more like the mighty Mississippi of midwestern lore. Here the river takes a hard right and heads southeasterly.

The St. Croix also has a glacial history, but a different geology. It flows across the gravelly glacial till of northern Minnesota and Wisconsin, then reaches a pinch point at Taylors Falls, where a massive plug of basalt betrays far older volcanic activity in the Upper Midwest. Because it also began life as a glacial meltwater river, it has managed to cut through the basalt and create a deep gorge known as the Dalles of the St. Croix. The basalt cliffs today rise hundreds of feet above the tannin-stained river. They are popular with rock climbers and pock-marked with potholes: smooth cauldrons in the rock that were carved by the abrasive action of sand and gravel during the torrential hundreds of years of glacial chaos. Some of these potholes are more than sixty feet deep, six feet across, and perched a hundred feet above the present river level. The St. Croix used to be two hundred feet deep.

After the Dalles, the St. Croix courses more calmly almost due south past several picturesque towns (Marine on St. Croix, Stillwater, Afton) and into the Mississippi. In many places it becomes almost lake-like and very popular for motor boating, especially near Hudson, Wisconsin, at the crossing of Interstate 94.

Of course, all these rivers were once free flowing, but the growth of cities and industry required changes. The rivers became the transportation lifeblood of the region, and Americans dreamed of the ability to reliably move goods and people on water from the Gulf of Mexico to the Twin Cities and back. The US Army Corps of Engineers was made responsible for river navigation. Beginning in the 1930s, the corps built a system of locks and dams to create a nine-foot-deep navigation channel, which barges still use today to haul grain, construction materials, and aggregate. Above St. Louis, Missouri, twenty-nine locks and dams create deep, flat pools, which are far easier to push barges through than the shallows and riffles that were there before.

The corps built four locks and dams in the Twin Cities metropolitan area: No. 2 at Hastings, just upstream of the St. Croix River, No. 1 just above the Minnesota (also known as the Ford Dam), and the Upper and Lower St. Anthony locks and dams in downtown Minneapolis. These latter two were significant upgrades of various attempts to control St. Anthony Falls since Minneapolis was founded in 1856. The falls are truly the origin of the city, powering grain mills on the waterfront. Millraces, chutes, embankments, and bridges have repeatedly been built, removed, and destroyed by the river. But in 1963 the corps completed the transformation of the falls into a concrete flume and finished construction of the extraordinary forty-nine-foot-high Upper St. Anthony lock to extend navigation out of the Mississippi gorge and onto the upper river. This opened development of industrial land in north and northeast Minneapolis.

Along with operating the locks and dams, the corps keeps the navigation channel open by regular dredging. The river wants to wander, and the new pools created behind the dams tend to silt up because the water is slower than it was. But nine feet means nine feet, so the corps digs the bottom down and puts the muck on large spoil piles scattered up and down the river.

These human-engineered changes are not good for mussels. More specifically, the slower current and the siltation are not good for mussels. The dams, which can block movement of fish, are not good for mussels. The barge traffic, according to Mike Davis, may not be good for mussels, because mussels will close up and stop feeding when things get too turbulent or loud. The more barges, the more sound and turbulence, the less the mussels eat. Not good for mussels.

However, despite what you might envision from the foregoing description as a fully industrial river, that is not actually the case. All three big rivers flow through corridors of protected green space and parkland

Several regional parks stack up end to end along the river: Harriet Island, Lilydale, Crosby Farm, Hidden Falls, Minnehaha, Mississippi Gorge, Central Mississippi. Trails above and below the bluffs offer an up-close experience with the Mississippi. Minnesota's only urban state park—Fort Snelling—occupies the confluence of the Minnesota and Mississippi. The Minnesota valley is a national wildlife refuge. And the entire seventy-two-mile Mississippi corridor through the Twin Cities metro area is a unique National Park Service unit called the Mississippi National River and Recreation Area. Within this area's boundary, the NPS collaborates with other agencies, like the City of St. Paul and the Minneapolis Park and Recreation Board, to provide people with interpretation and programming on the river. The St. Croix is protected as a National Scenic Riverway and features numerous state parks in both Wisconsin and Minnesota, including the stunning Interstate Park (in both states) at the Dalles.

On a couple of sunny and warm August days in 2015, I join nine people on three boats to help survey 270 Mississippi River sites in the heart of the metro. I arrive early at the Hidden Falls Regional Park boat landing in St. Paul. Six large Wilderness Inquiry canoes are staged on the shore, with stacks of paddles and life jackets nearby. On the far side of the river, in Minneapolis, dogs fetch sticks thrown into the water by owners sauntering on the sandy shoreline. Just to the side of the boat ramp, several anglers try their luck. I watch the Mississippi scoot quietly by. The surface is brown and smooth, seemingly stationary, but occasionally little bits of bark, foam, or bubbles betray the rapid current. One of the anglers, a portly African American man, reels in a fish. He gently removes the hook, then climbs the beach to the picnic shelter to show his catch to a man in a motorized wheelchair and two companions. They all nod and smile while the angler walks to the water's edge and drops the fish back in. Too small to keep.

Soon, Mike Davis arrives in a DNR pickup truck towing a boat on a trailer. With him is Zeb Secrist, one of Mike's assistants, whom I met when I visited the Lake City lab. Also here is Andrea Brandon from the

Nature Conservancy, aiming to get a feel for the river and various agencies' conservation efforts. Zeb and Mike ready the boat. Ropes are thrown and chains clank. On go our PFDs. Andrea, Mike, and I board the boat as Zeb backs us into the water. Then he parks the truck and joins us on board. Our boat is a flat-bottomed craft you might see in a southern bayou, but with an outboard and a few Zeb and Mike conversions. A large metal sorting table occupies the right side. A laptop on a moveable arm faces the table. As we launch, the second boat arrives: a pontoon full of other folks from a variety of federal and state agencies.

"They've got their bravest diver on board," says Mike.

"Who, Allie?" asks Zeb, standing up and looking over at the approaching boat. "The Allie-gator?"

Allie Holdhusen kneels on the pontoon's prow, outside the low white and silver walls that enclose the main part of the boat. She wears a full wetsuit with the top half pulled down around her waist to show a purple bikini top. Driving the boat is Byron Karrs, in a full National Park Service uniform, his gray goatee and thinning hair perfectly trimmed. Also aboard are Dan Kellner with the US Army Corps of Engineers and Tam Smith with US Fish and Wildlife. Dan is a big, jovial man in a football t-shirt and shorts. He strikes me immediately as a lovable coach character (and, it turns out, he has had a lot to do with coaching these agencies and his superiors to all work together toward mussel conservation). Tam is more retiring, in a long-sleeved shirt, long hiking pants, boots, sunglasses, and a wide-brimmed ranger-green hat.

"How's the water?" calls Mike, as the pontoon and its crew approaches. "Fast?"

"Fast," replies Byron.

"It went up about a foot since yesterday. Bad timing, always," says Mike. "You look cold, Allie!"

She grins. She looks ready to get in the water, and, seeing that, Zeb starts to suit up, too. While the group meets and greets, Zeb strips down to a swimsuit and pulls on his own wetsuit, then puts a pair of hiking boots over the wetsuit feet. Zeb is blond, young, and muscular. He loves to be on horses and underwater, claiming to have scuba dived in about

70 percent of the rivers in Minnesota. He reaches to grab a mooring line from the pontoon as it comes up quickly and bumps the DNR boat. "He really likes to abuse government property," Mike teases.

"Okay, where do you guys think you're gonna start?" calls Dan. Most of the group on the pontoon have pulled out sandwiches and snacks and are fueling up for the day.

"Well, you guys said you were going to start down by the Minnesota River and we were gonna start up here, but I see plans changed." Mike is ribbing them a little. He didn't expect to run into the federal boat here at Hidden Falls.

Soon, Mike and Byron start up the engines, and the little flotilla breaks up. The group decides to stick close together, so both boats motor upstream toward the Ford Dam. That's the upper end of about three river miles into which Higgins eye mussels were reintroduced beginning in 2000. The survey is specifically looking for how that particular species is doing, but it will also give managers an overall picture of the mussels in this reach. Mike has a map of the river with each of the 270 sites noted. They are also in a GPS receiver that Mike uses to get the boat to the right location. He and others have surveyed this set of sites before, and the accuracy of the ongoing study depends on returning to the same locations year after year. Just after noon, we arrive at site #9, which is below Lock No. 1 on the west side of a low island. We are in the wash of the Ford Dam, which stretches across the river like a horizon. Above it to the left are the massive stone and concrete walls that hold up the Minnesota Veterans Home. They dwarf the lock itself, which raises boats about thirty-eight feet to the level of the pool behind the dam and is tied for the second-tallest lock on the entire Mississippi River with Lock and Dam No. 19 in Keokuk, Iowa. (The tallest one, at forty-nine feet, is just upstream at Upper St. Anthony Falls, in downtown Minneapolis.) The lock's giant metal doors face us. The control tower looks a lot like the cockpit of one of those Star Wars AT-AT Walker vehicles.

Mike navigates the boat into position, coming in upstream of the GPS point. He and I drop anchors, which dig into the river bottom and hold the boat in the current. Mike is trying to judge the flow so that when the anchor lines are tight the boat will sit just about right on site #9. When the boat is stable, Zeb pulls his mask down over his face, puts his scuba regulator in his mouth, grabs a quadrat, and drops overboard. A quadrat—a metal square exactly one-half meter on each side—is a simple tool but a critical piece of equipment for underwater surveys. Attached to one edge of the square is a smaller metal rectangle that holds open a mesh bag. Underwater, Mike tells me, Zeb has placed the square on the bottom, digging in the toes of his hiking boots to keep stationary in the current, and is using his hands to scrape everything inside the square into the bag.

In about two minutes, Zeb comes up and heaves the full quadrat on board. Mike grabs the haul while Zeb re-enters the boat and lifts off his mask and regulator. Mike dumps out the entire contents of the bag on the metal table, spreads out the mess, and begins looking for mussels— dead or alive. Site #9 is a bust. Mike turns to the computer and enters that data (even absence of animals is data), including the type of river bottom (sand, gravel, boulders), which Zeb calls out from the front of the boat when asked. We haul anchor and move on to other sites.

It's not until we move around to the east side of the low island, at site #12, that we actually find some mussels. The quadrat comes up very heavy with rocks, gravel, and mussel shells. Andrea and I help sort, but we don't know the mussels, so we pull them aside for Mike. Several shells (dead mussels) stand out from the rocks: a pigtoe, a strange floater, a deertoe, and a fragment of a Higgins eye. We also find a live mapleleaf (not the endangered winged mapleleaf). Mike estimates its age and measures its length. With his help, I input the data into the computer.

At site #6, at 1:45, we find two large mussels: a twenty-two-year-old threeridge and an eighteen-year-old pigtoe. We skip site #10 because the current is too strong and the anchors won't hold the boat. At sites #17 and #20, Zeb drops into the water and comes immediately back out— we are right below the huge VA wall and the water is deep down to bedrock. At site #22 again the boat won't hold, and Mike decides to head farther downstream to get past the worst of the current coming over the dam. Mike checks in with the other boat (the Allie-gator is diving from

Sorting mussels on the Mississippi River below Lock and Dam No. 1, 2015

the pontoon just downstream of us), and we cruise down to the outlet of Hidden Creek, just above where we launched.

At site #45, we bring up a lot of rocks and a tiny baby mussel—a fragile papershell. I lay it in the palm of my hand and take a picture. Then Andrea wants to take a picture. We all say its name with some degree of awe. It is no bigger than my pinky fingernail, semi-translucent and yellow brown, with a dark blush near its hinge. A long string—the mussel's tether—stretches out to at least four times the length of its shell. Mike spells out its scientific name so Andrea can enter this little individual into the massive digital mussel database. Then I toss the tiny animal back into the churning, brown Mississippi.

We work through the afternoon in a rhythm. Though the processes of looking for endangered species—mussels, roseroots, trout lilies, lynx, Topeka shiners, plovers, and others—all have their own particulars, this basic science proceeds in a somewhat standard way. A scientist develops a list of sites. A team visits the sites one by one. A scientist catalogs the data in the field. Researchers analyze the data back at the office/lab/university and compare it with last year's data, and the data from the year before, and so on. During these surveys, the mood is most often jovial, filled with humor, and, in some ways, languid. Moving a boat from one GPS coordinate to another (each typically only fifty or so yards from each other) is a nice way to spend a day. Everybody is in a rhythm: park, anchor, dive, scrape, surface, dump, sort, enter data, haul anchor, move. On the Mississippi we listen to country music in the boat because that's what Zeb likes. We talk about topics ranging from mussels to horses to parks to music. We often don't talk at all. We eat our snacks and stay hydrated. We gaze pensively at the river.

At 3:30 the two boats regroup near the Hidden Falls landing. A third boat has arrived, brought by Bernard Sietman from Mike's lab. More greetings and ribbings and updates ensue. The three boats will continue on through the afternoon and evening, but I disembark for the day.

Perhaps it is appropriate at this time to have an endangered mussel roll call.

The three S's—spectaclecase, sheepnose, and snuffbox—were all listed together as endangered in 2012, the snuffbox in February and the other two in March. These listings are too recent for these species to have any recovery plans or five-year reviews. The snuffbox was discussed earlier—it's the one that lures in and holds onto a poor log perch and, as Mike says, "gets to have its way with that fish." The sheepnose is brown or yellow orange, up to four and a half inches, with a few barely raised knobs in a row on its shell. Mike and his team were involved with the sheepnose prior to its federal listing, including performing host fish studies. It was believed that walleyes carried the developing larvae, but Bernard was able to determine that in fact it's minnows that carry them. When the female sheepnose is ready to expel its glochidia it does so directly into the water in long, pinkish, mucusey strings (called conglutinates) that look a lot like little worms. Minnows eat these 'worms," breaking up the mess and flushing the babies over their own gills.

The spectaclecase is the one that's not like the others. It's much bigger, up to eight inches, and long and narrow, like, of course, a case for spectacles. Historically it was found in the Mississippi and St. Croix Rivers among boulders. "This is our enigma," says Mike. "We don't know how they reproduce." Though Mike and his team haven't done much with this species, they have found spectaclecases during general mussel surveys, and the locations and ages give some clue to its host fish. Reproduction has been documented for this species below the dam on the St. Croix at Taylors Falls—mussels of many ages can be found. Above the dam, only older individuals exist (many of them nearly a hundred years old). The Taylors Falls dam was built in 1907, making it just about as old as those mussels above it. Mike believes that the dam has prevented reproduction above it—all the individual mussels there now were there when the dam was built. That would suggest the host is a migratory animal than can no longer get above the dam. In addition, there is significant genetic similarity between Minnesota spectaclecases and those in Tennessee and Ohio, suggesting an extremely migratory host. Mike and Bernard think it might be eels, but they're still working on that puzzle.

The winged mapleleaf was listed as endangered in 1991. A recovery plan came in 1997 and a five-year review in 2015. The winged mapleleaf grows to about four inches and has prominent ridges near the outer edge of its oval body. Two rows of raised knobs radiate from the hinge area (scientists describe these knobs rather unfortunately as "pustules" or "tubercles"). This mussel tends to prefer faster-moving water and either sand or gravel bottoms. The winged mapleleaf's host fish is the channel catfish or blue catfish. Mike has found that small, young catfish don't host the mussels well, but once a cat reaches one or two years old, it does. Perhaps this is a distribution method for the mussel? Perhaps younger fish don't move around much, so the mussel is designed to wait for more mobile fish? No one knows for sure. The winged mapleleaf female moves her glochidia into a fleshy tower projected from her mantle and up into the river above her. She hopes a catfish will mistake this for food, and when the tower is disturbed she releases the larvae, hopefully to be inhaled by the catfish.

Mike and collaborators from the USFWS have worked with the winged mapleleaf since 2004, but, he admits, with less success than they have had with the Higgins eye. With the mapleleaf they used a cage technique, wherein they obtained host fish from Ohio and put them in wire cages in Lake Pepin and near Hudson, Wisconsin, in the St. Croix. After a while the fish were released but the cages were left in place to protect the mussels presumably (hopefully) growing in the substrate. Small winged mapleleafs are hard to count (or even see) because their bumpy shells blend in with the gravel. Mike and the others ended up abandoning both sites due to zebra mussel infestation and apparent lack of success. However, a more recent monitoring of mussel populations at the Hudson site turned up around six hundred winged mapleleafs. "Where we thought we had failed," says Mike, "we now have inadvertently reintroduced a population in Hudson."

The winged mapleleaf had an extensive range: large Mississippi River tributaries in eleven states, from Minnesota to Oklahoma. At the time of listing, however, and in the 1997 recovery plan, scientists lamented that it could be found only in the St. Croix River in Minnesota and Wisconsin, along a fifteen- to twenty-mile segment below the stunning Dalles at Taylors Falls. Delisting can occur when there are five sustaining populations in three different Mississippi River tributaries (along with additional study to ensure that's the right number of sites). The recent five-year review changes the picture entirely. Additional populations have been found in the Bourbeuse River in central Missouri, the Ouachita and Saline Rivers in Arkansas, and the Little River in Arkansas and Oklahoma. If a government technical document can sound surprised, this one does. To discover winged mapleleafs that far from what was considered the last remaining populations must have been thrilling and befuddling to scientists. If they had been found down by Prescott or Hastings, fine, but Oklahoma?

Nevertheless, the five-year review does not recommend delisting, for a few reasons having to do mostly with studies not yet completed. The recovery plan seems to say that the winged mapleleaf cannot be delisted because we have not completed the studies required by the listing to ensure we have the right delisting criteria. Within this seemingly circular logic, though, is a reference to a newer threat (which we'll get to in a moment), so perhaps the scientific caution is warranted.

The Higgins eye is a rather plain bivalve: oval and brownish black, sometimes with obvious rays fanning out from its hinge. It can grow up to six inches and prefers large rivers, where it can be found in just about any type of bottom. This animal is exciting because of its "minnow display." The female's mantle (the part that can extend beyond the shell to lure fish or to facilitate feeding) looks like it has a tail fin and eyespot. It conspicuously resembles a minnow. The Higgins eye's host fish are those that eat minnows, like sauger and bass—fish too big for it to capture. But one bite on that lure and the fish gets a powerful blast of glochidia. Despite this treatment, the fish don't seem to be often injured by mussels.

The Higgins eye is the mussel Mike has studied the longest, and also the species that has been in the federal mix the longest. The Higgins was historically found in the Minnesota, Mississippi, and St. Croix Rivers, and in other rivers in Wisconsin and Iowa, though it has likely been extirpated from the Minnesota River. It was listed as endangered in 1976. A recovery plan was written in 1983 and revised in 2004. In 2006 (thirty-plus years after listing) a five-year review was published.

A key piece of the recovery plan and five-year review for mussels (and, in fact, the main criteria for eventual delisting) is the establishment and monitoring of Essential Habitat Areas. Under the Endangered Species Act, the USFWS can designate critical habitat for species, and that critical habitat comes with special rules for federal projects. EHAs are a slightly different sort of vehicle, meant mainly for keeping track of a mussel's status but without any special regulations. These habitats are the places where Higgins eyes exist now. They are the core areas to protect, according to the plan. An initial seven EHAs were established in 1983 and another three were added in the 2004 revised recovery plan. In 2008 the USFWS, through an amendment, added another four. They occur in the Mississippi River in Iowa, Illinois, Wisconsin, and Minnesota; in the St. Croix River in Minnesota; and in the Wisconsin River in Wisconsin.

In order to be delisted, the original recovery plan requires sustaining, long-term populations of Higgins eyes exist at five EHAs, of which one must be on the St. Croix, one in Mississippi River pool fourteen (near Clinton, Iowa), and one in the Prairie du Chien, Wisconsin, EHA, which was considered the most viable, intact population of Higgins eyes anywhere.

However, the 2004 version considers revising that requirement. It states optimistically that studies since 1983 have extended the known range of the Higgins eye by 180 river miles. Unfortunately, it also advises removing the requirement that one of the sustaining populations be at Prairie du Chien, because that population has been profoundly affected by an invasive species of its own kin.

Though perhaps exactly the opposite of an endangered species, there is another mussel that must be included in this roll call: the invasive zebra mussel (*Dreissena polymorpha*). Zebra mussels, unlike the native mussels described in this chapter, don't need a fish host to reproduce. A female will produce between a hundred thousand and five hundred thousand eggs per year; these eggs turn into free-swimming larvae that form their own shells over the course of a few weeks and then settle to the bottom. Zebra mussels reproduce prodigiously and can quickly coat underwater structures, lake bottoms, and even native mussels, hindering the natives' ability to feed and reproduce. Their shells are sharp, making them a nuisance to recreation. The Minnesota Department of Natural Resources lists more than 270 water bodies as infested with zebra mussels.

Native to southern Russia, this small, striped mussel was first found in North America in 1988 near Detroit. It is believed to have arrived in the ballast water of oceangoing ships. In 1989 it was found in the Duluth harbor. It is unlikely it could have spread from Detroit to Duluth in a year, so this was likely another instance of stowaways from Europe. Today, it's pretty much everywhere in Minnesota from the big-river systems to northern recreational lakes. It is commonly known that zebra mussels spread by tagging along on boats moving from one lake to another. "Clean and Dry" has become a boaters' mantra similar to "Give

a Hoot, Don't Pollute." Many state and local natural resource and recreation departments have concerted campaigns to educate the public
and protect uninfested lakes. In Minneapolis, for instance, no boat may
legally launch on a city lake without an inspection.

In his Lake City lab, Mike is trying to replicate many of the conditions
found in metro rivers (unpolluted, undredged, un-zebra-musselled metro
rivers, that is) in order to better understand the threats and specific life
cycle requirements of various mussels. He is also rearing mussels for
reintroduction into the wild, to replace lost mussel beds now that the
rivers are cleaner. The snuffbox was one of his first success stories. He
began working with that species in 2008. His team developed a system-
atic way of producing a lot of snuffbox juveniles. Thousands of them
have been released over the years near Hidden Falls Regional Park in
St. Paul, in the Mississippi River gorge just below the Ford Dam.

The lab looks like a combination of an aquarium store and aqua-
culture facility, and in fact the setup uses principles of both. Rows of
shelves are home to aquaria stacked three high, each labeled with a tank
number and each home to different combinations of fish: creek chubs,
walleyes, bluntnose minnows, white suckers, northern pikes, sticklebacks, bass, and eels—forty different species. For some mussels—like
the spectaclecase—the host fish is not known, so Mike's team is doing
ongoing research by inoculating fish species with glochidia to see if anything takes.

In the middle of the room are large, circular tubs and long, linear
tanks with filter trays suspended below the surface of constantly flowing water. On the day of my visit, the tubs are full of largemouth bass
that have been inoculated with muckets. The glochidia come from the
Cedar River in Iowa, where muckets are plentiful. The resulting juvenile
mussels will be reintroduced to the Cedar River in south-central Minnesota, where they were eliminated by pollution many years ago. Three
dams block fish migration between these sections of the river, preventing natural dispersal of mussels upstream even though now the water is
cleaner. Inoculation is fairly simple. Mike's team releases the glochidia

from a pregnant mussel by prying open her valves using a syringe and needle and flushing the glochidia out of the gill chambers with water injected by the syringe. The dislodged larvae are rinsed into a beaker and then put into a tank with the host fish, where the team agitates the water for a while. They check the fish under a microscope to see if the mussels have attached, then leave them alone.

The long, linear filter trays are home to juvenile muckets and pocketbooks, which are being grown to a survivable size in the lab. The pocketbooks will then travel to the Minnesota Zoo and will continue to grow in enclosed pens under a pedestrian walkway that crosses a large lake. The water flowing through these tanks is piped from a thousand-gallon tank full of filtered river water sitting outside the lab's back door. The tank is refilled weekly from the Mississippi River in Lake Pepin. Yes, Mike's team drives a tanker trailer down to the river once a week to get more water. "This is our invention," says Mike. "The idea is you're matching what's going on in the river to the mussel, because that's what they would encounter if they were growing in the river. We're hoping to reduce artificial selectivity so that we are getting fit mussels to reintroduce."

He says that other labs that have gone with artificial diet to feed baby mussels have experienced a "bottleneck." The mussels do well for a while, then crash. The thinking is that nutrients in the river might change through the seasons—minutely, yes, but for a minute mussel larva the effect could be significant. After a year of trying this technique, though, Mike's team found it wasn't the perfect solution, either. Mike has hired a biologist who did her master's thesis on baby mussel nutrition and has added purchased algae food to the feeding regime. By harvesting river water weekly and supplementing with targeted nutrition, Mike hopes the mussels are getting as close to a natural diet as possible. They are coddled, but still provided a diet in sync with what's happening in the real world.

Near the front of the lab is a set of shelving with smaller tanks about the size of the bulk bins at grocery stores. The tanks mostly have red labels, and each is home to just a few fish. These were collected in the wild, from various places around the state. Bernard Sietman, a research scientist who works with Mike, describes this as the "gold standard" of mussel-host study methods. Each small tank is unusually blue and vacant except for the fish. Pipes and spigots move water in and out of the tank, and filters catch any transformed juveniles dropping off the fish. With bigger fish collected in the wild, the team can actually look at the gills in the field and see if larvae are present. For smaller fish, like the batch of Johnny darters occupying many of the tanks, they just seine a whole batch and bring them all in. This time, they got about a hundred fish and have seen fifteen or so larvae drop off. "Sometimes we just catch them and bring them in and see what comes off of them," says Bernard. Then they have to go through the process of identifying those tiny, transparent mussels. "It's not easy," he says with a chuckle.

The whole room feels (and is) a little do-it-yourself. Mike's team customized the system from a commercially available kit of parts. It doesn't always work perfectly. During my visit, Zeb was repairing some water supply pipes. He actually put a lot of these contraptions together and keeps them running with a mix of practical carpentry and plumbing, all while ensuring the team's findings can be empirically documented. Most of the mussel lab's funding comes from federal and state contracts, federal grants, or mitigation funds paid to the DNR. Mike and his staff are employees of the state, but the lab operates almost like an independent consultant.

In 2013 Mike was involved in required environmental mitigation associated with a new crossing of the St. Croix River near Stillwater. Attempts to build a new bridge had been mired in controversy for a decade. Concerns that it would open a gateway to urban sprawl in Wisconsin, coupled with a clash over adding another bridge to the St. Croix National Scenic Riverway, overshadowed the state and federally mandated process to assess impact on endangered species. The Lower St. Croix is home to a variety of mussel species, including the federally endangered Higgins eye. Because the Minnesota Department of Transportation often uses federal funds to reconstruct bridges, that agency has been hiring Mike and his team to do the required assessments under the rules of the Endangered Species Act.

The Stillwater bridge project was unique in that Mike advocated for and succeeded in getting a cash mitigation instead of a wholesale mussel relocation. "It used to be they would pay someone to move the mussels out of the impact zone. I made the argument that that wasn't a particularly effective way to protect the species. It would protect a few animals but not the rest." Mike and Rich Baker, the DNR's endangered species coordinator, developed a formula that looks at the area of impact and what it would cost to relocate the mussels as a way to set the amount of cash mitigation. A bridge project in the 1990s spent $200,000 to relocate mussels—and then the bridge didn't actually get built. Mike describes that as a windfall for a consultant but not very good for the mussels. In reality, he says, most mussels that get moved are common ones that are pretty much everywhere anyway. "I wondered what we could do with $200,000 to help recover some of these rare species," he says. The so-called "compensatory mitigation" now goes into an account with the DNR, and the funds can be used only for mussel work. That money helped Mike build the Lake City lab and fund staff and materials.

That story also has an interesting jurisdictional side note. Only one Higgins eye was found on the Minnesota side of the river, which led the federal government to not require any mitigation. The cash payment was possible because species listed by the State of Minnesota were found and because Minnesota has its own endangered species law that allows for compensatory mitigation. On the Wisconsin side, the federal government did step in because Higgins eye mussels were more plentiful. There, mussels were relocated and no cash was provided for further study and reintroduction.

Another ongoing project that brings funding to Mike's mussel research is a collaborative effort with the US Army Corps of Engineers and the US Fish and Wildlife Service. In 2000 the USFWS won what's called a "jeopardy decision" against the corps. This is a quasi-legal ruling between two agencies of the same government. The corps was held responsible for the introduction of invasive zebra mussels, which then affected populations of endangered Higgins eye mussels, particularly in the Mississippi River near Prairie du Chien, Wisconsin. In response, rather than fighting the ruling, the corps entered into a collaborative agreement to study and restore the Higgins eye. Since the ruling, the corps has put $7 million into the project. "The corps has a genuine interest in getting this all to work," says Mike. Corps money has paid for reintroductions of adult mussels in Minnesota and Iowa and of fish inoculated with mussels. The Wapsipinicon River in Iowa seems to be the most successful effort. Mike remembers corps and Iowa DNR scientists bringing host fish to boat ramps, inoculating them with Higgins eye larvae on the spot, and releasing them into the river. After a few years of these efforts, Higgins eye adults, absent in the river for many decades, started showing up again. And even more recently, juveniles have been found, indicating the original reintroduced population is reproducing. The Higgins eye was the first mussel Mike worked on extensively, largely because of the corps funding.

My second day on the river with Mike Davis, I see many more mussels. Mike's two boats start around 8:00 AM from the Hidden Falls landing and coast downstream to Watergate Marina. Mike, Zeb, and I are the team in the flat-bottom boat. Bernard pilots the other boat with Ashley from Mike's mussel team and a retired friend called Weggie. At Watergate we meet up with the other agency group. The corps' Dan Kellner gives some direction on who is going where, and the boats split up. Mike's boat heads downstream to Pike Island and site #210. The team is making good progress at moving through the sites, and Mike thinks they may not need all week.

Zeb dives and brings up a haul.

"A ton of mussels!" says Mike. "Different than upstream. It's a treasure trove!"

It almost seems there are more mussels than rocks. Now some actual sorting takes place. Zeb jumps in to help. Normally he has been resting near the front of the boat while others sort, but he's excited about this one. There is a three-horned wartyback, several pigtoes, a baby pimpleback, another pimpleback (these always have a green stripe).

We scrape and sort. We push the live ones into one pile, the shells into another, and the rocks overboard. It's the most exciting data entry we've had so far. Mike measures and calls out ages while I work the computer. Then we tip the table and return everything to the water. The river is still—not a whisper of breeze ruffles the surface. Dogs on the shoreline bark their echoes across the water. Zeb gets the country music going. Mike and I pull anchor, he sputters the motor, and we head to the next site. This day we see lots of wartybacks, a huge pocketbook, a threeridge, a paper pondshell, a few more pigtoes, and the shell of a pink heelsplitter—by far the most beautiful of all, and obvious in its naming, with its long, crisp edge.

Toward the end of the morning, the *Betsey Northrup*, a barge turned excursion boat pushed by *Ugh the Tug*, groans upstream from Harriet Island in downtown St. Paul. It's full of kids, all in bright pink shirts so their daycare leaders can keep track of them. It disappears around the bend above us, then soon returns back downstream, having turned around below the Ford Dam. At both passings the kids all wave and we wave back. I wonder if the teachers offer any guesses at what we're doing out here, dumping bags of rocks on a metal table, one guy in scuba gear. I wonder if they wonder about what's below the surface of this opaque river. At the beginning of the first day on this survey, when Zeb was pulling up quadrats full of sand and gravel and not much else, I couldn't actively believe there were "coral reefs" unseen down there. I can now, because I have seen huge hauls and significant diversity pulled from half-square-meter blips of the riverbed. I can assume that under us are vast landscapes of filtering animals, wedged in between rocks, waving their mantles to lure in fish. But it's still hard to picture. Maybe that's why historically we haven't cared very well for our rivers. The Mississippi, Minnesota, and St. Croix, at their best, are sluggish and brown. They feature no obvious fish migrations like the salmon rivers out west. They don't have the kind of crystal-clear water that begs for care. They hide their most interesting feature—those amazing mussel beds—beneath a curtain of suspended sediment. Maybe it was easy to dump sewage into these views because they looked muddy and dead already.

The Clean Water Act of 1972 changed that. By requiring municipalities to treat their sewage, and by placing restrictions on industrial discharge into waterways, the Clean Water Act has had a profound effect on rivers, especially urban ones. Improvement didn't happen overnight, of course, but if 1969 was a low point, water quality across the nation has been gradually getting better since. Mike Davis, in fact, gives more credit to the Clean Water Act than the Endangered Species Act for mussel conservation. His work reintroducing mussels to rivers is only possible because the rivers are cleaner again. Without the water-quality regulations, not a single endangered species rule would have any effect. The urban reaches of these rivers, says Mike, in part because of the extensive green network along their shores, "have become a refuge for endangered mussels where it used to be a dead zone."

Without the Clean Water Act we would never have hosted my son Ethan's seventh birthday on the shore of the Mississippi at Crosby Farm, facing survey site #210. It's June of 2015, just a few weeks after I visited Mike's Lake City lab and a couple months before I logged mussels on the river. The partygoers dig rivers in the sand, climb on the tangles of standing and downed trees on the shoreline, and occasionally fall accidentally or deliberately into the river. They are soaked, muddy, sandy, and happy. Wading into the water I can look up- and downriver and see no obvious trace of other people. Yet we are in the middle of the city on an industrial river. And to prove that last point, toward the end of the party a tug churns by pushing a pair of barges loaded with aggregate. The aggregate is arranged on the barges in a phalanx of pyramids. I call the partygoers' attention to the fact that this may be one of the last barges they will ever see at this spot on the river.

The barges were likely heading up through Lock and Dam No. 1 (the Ford Dam), then through the two St. Anthony Falls locks in downtown Minneapolis and up to one of the barge terminals on the upper Mississippi River. But on June 15, 2015, the Upper St. Anthony Falls lock was closed permanently by action of the federal government for reasons including preventing invasive carp from migrating upriver and the dwindling economic usefulness of the lock. Because the army corps will also cease dredging above the lock, the upper Mississippi River could return to a more natural state in the coming years, which would be favorable to mussels—if they could get there.

After my tour of Mike's mussel lab in May, he and I go out for lunch at a Chinese buffet in Lake City. We talk about Minneapolis parks. Mike has participated in a work group about a major project underway in downtown Minneapolis: the reconstruction of an island in the Mississippi above St. Anthony Falls called Hall's Island, which was removed in the 1960s to create more space for an onshore lumber yard. Islands can be good for mussels because they provide a variety of habitats and water speeds. The idea was part of a park board plan called RiverFirst, but the Army Corps and the DNR opposed it. A new island in the navigation channel? No way. An alteration of the Mississippi River shoreline? Huh-uh. Ultimately, the Minneapolis Park and Recreation Board had to go to the state legislature to get permission, citing, in part, the new islands the corps was creating elsewhere downstream in the name of habitat restoration.

Mike sees the potential to reintroduce mussels to the upper river, especially with the lock closure and the end of barge traffic. He gets a little excited talking about it, between bites of noodles and stir-fry.

He also has ideas about another stretch of altered river—ideas that seem a little crazy at first but make some sense when you hear them out. Mike is not the first to suggest this, but he adds a dose of practical reality to it. The pool above Lock and Dam No. 1 is a long, flat stretch of water reaching to the base of some rapids below St. Anthony Falls. Steep, forested hillsides plunge down into the river on both sides. The University of Minnesota perches on the east bank, while just a few street and railway bridges vault the entire valley from Minneapolis cliff top to St. Paul cliff top. Under the flat surface is likely a silty bottom that used to be one long stretch of rocky rapids cascading down to the confluence.

Why not bring back the rocky rapids? Why not remove the Ford Dam and let the river flow downhill all the way to St. Paul? With the Upper St. Anthony lock closed and the river-based industry going away from the upper river, the only need for Lock and Dam No. 1 is for excursion and pleasure boats and the limited power the dam still generates. Buy out the hydro power concession, the idea goes, remove the lock and dam (not cheap, but dream a little), restore the rapids. This is almost exactly what Columbus, Ohio, did in 2013 with its downtown waterfront. The city removed multiple low-head dams on the Scioto River, reworked 250 acres of mud flats as a major downtown greenbelt, opened the river to boating, and, yes, moved struggling mussels out of the mud flats and into more suitable habitat areas. And even the Columbus project took a note from dam removal projects in the Pacific Northwest, New England, and the Ohio and Tennessee River valleys, all of which demolished obsolete obstructions and restored free-flowing river habitat for salmon or other fish or mussels.

Clearly, the Ford Dam is not a low-head dam like those on the Scioto. Removing it would be a significant undertaking—but not nearly as significant as the Army Corps' "taming" of the Mississippi in the first place. Mussels would love living in the fast moving, de-silted, rock-bottomed river. Kayakers would love playing there. And lowering and narrowing the river would expose hundreds of acres of parkland at the base of the bluffs on both banks.

One thing I have come to love about endangered species scientists: they tend to think at a variety of scales at once. That resonates with me as a planner and landscape architect. At once, Mike is thinking about an individual mussel larva under a microscope and whether it will survive and also about transforming a landscape on a grand scale. He will keep working with numbered sites and buckets of lab-raised bivalves while at the same time feeling giddy to tear down a dam. That's what we'll need to protect and recover these species: a vibrant combination of big thinking and everyday action. Endangered species conservation is about the big-river habitat that laces the Twin Cities. It is also about that snuffbox Mike handed me in his lab, that smooth stone of an animal—individual, remarkable, and alive.

Piping plover

3

Plover

In May or June of 2014, a piping plover chick was born on the shore of an alkali lake in the center of North Dakota just east of the Missouri River near Turtle Lake. The chick was probably one of three or four that hatched from a clutch of sand-colored eggs in a nest no more elaborate than a divot in the sand. Its parents took care of it during its first weeks, snuggling it under their wings until it could regulate its own heat and leading it to and from feeding areas. It ran around on the beach—entering neither the water nor the inland grass. This is something it knew instinctively to do: stay in the open, on the sand, where it can easily see predators. This strategy, of course, has its disadvantages as well as advantages. See and be seen. Raccoons find it hard to sneak up on a plover family in the open, but merlins have great sight lines

The chick spent most of its time eating and resting—and growing. By July, it tripled its weight from about seven grams (the weight of a few pennies) to about thirty-six (just over an ounce, or the weight of a small head of garlic). Soon it was ready to fly. It took one last look around its birth beach, spread its roughly four-and-a-half-inch wings, and headed south. Most likely the bird made the trip solo, and probably nonstop. It found a mudflat around Corpus Christi Bay and settled in for the winter. Its North Dakota habits still drove it find an open beach or muddy shoreline and stay out in the open. Here on the Gulf Coast it had so much company: western sandpipers, willets, semipalmated plovers,

black-bellied plovers, sanderlings—shorebirds each with slightly different preferences for sand texture, proximity to the water, and degree of
openness. The North Dakota plover also gathered with other plovers in
the back bays and estuaries of coastal Texas, and likely never went out to
the sandy outer beaches as some other plovers would.

This Texas plover became an adult on the Gulf Coast. Even full
grown, it was still one of the smaller birds on the beach, around seven
inches from the tip of its beak to its tail, with a wingspan of about a foot
and a half. It had developed its striking black necklace, a single dark ring
highlighting its white and grey body. Its bright yellow legs propelled it
over the sand and mud in search of marine worms, small crustaceans,
and insects that it would peck out with its rather stout, black-tipped
orange bill. From time to time it would sing out the melody for which
it is named: a steady repeated whistle, clear and light. In mid-April, the
plover headed north. Arriving back in North Dakota, it decided, for reasons unknown, to fly past the beach of its birth and head farther north,
adding another hundred miles to its fifteen-hundred-mile trek. Perhaps
there were too many plovers already on the beaches near Turtle Lake.
Perhaps an initial scan of the environment turned up too many perceived threats. Perhaps at the very moment it landed on the beach a dog
turned up, unleashed by its owner for a jaunty run at the water's edge.
Perhaps during the winter the lake level had risen and flooded the beach.
Or maybe it searched its way northward, lake after lake, for a suitable
mate. Piping plovers can be few and far between.

The plover settled near the tiny town of Palermo. It must have found
another beach on another alkali lake like the one on which it fledged.
Here during the summer of 2015, chances are it did not successfully raise
chicks of its own. Piping plovers only rarely do. Maybe it never found
a good mate. Maybe its eggs were taken by a small mammal. Maybe its
chicks were killed and eaten by a bird of prey. Whatever stage of reproduction it achieved, our plover survived and, after just a few short months
in the north, flew south again.

In early fall our plover came to a place called Sunset Lake, at the
northern end of Corpus Christi Bay, on the central coast of Texas. It's

not unusual that it would land here. Texas has the highest population of wintering plovers anywhere in the United States. Piping plovers can be found in winter along the Gulf and Atlantic Coast from the Yucatan all the way up and around Florida as far north as the Carolinas but Texas is usually home to about half the total known population. And Corpus Christi, the self-proclaimed "birdiest city in America," has a complex shoreline of bays and islands and beaches and mudflats able to accommodate a wide variety of shorebird preferences.

I visit Texas in January 2016 to see this piping plover (*Characrius melodus*) and its winter home. Its generalized life history is culled from a series of sightings logged over the years into a national piping plover database. It is plover Z12. I see it and two others with David Newsteac, who works for the Coastal Bend Bays and Estuaries Program, an Environmental Protection Agency–originated conservation initiative. I meet him at a Starbucks on the north side of Corpus Christi Bay. He has been involved in shorebird monitoring since 2001, including some radio-telemetry work on piping plovers that found that tides mainly drive where plovers choose to winter. He also studies the red knot (another federally listed bird) and the long-billed curlew. About this last bird, we have a good laugh, as David notices maybe a dozen of them across the street from the Starbucks in someone's front lawn.

David has that lean, solid, calm look I have come to notice is common among Texas outdoorsmen. He tells me he just got back late last night from a hunting/management trip on a nature preserve site. He was targeting exotic ungulates that cause damage to native habitats. He got two exotic deer and a hog, which he had dropped at the meat processor just before meeting me.

David is spending the next two weeks, on and off, looking for plovers as part of the 2016 International Piping, Snowy, and Wilson's Plover Winter Census. This is a comprehensive effort to count as many plovers on as many sites as possible over a fixed period of time. It takes place every five years and involves multiple agencies, governmental units, and volunteers across the bird's entire wintering range. The Central Texas count is coordinated by Robyn Cobb of the US Fish and Wildlife Service, and she was kind enough to get me connected to David for a walking/ driving count and onto a boat trip the following day.

The overall task is Herculean, as the birds are spread out across thousands of acres of potential habitat in central Texas alone—habitat that changes constantly with the tides. In coastal Texas the tides are not predictable: they are driven mainly not by the moon but by wind. The actual amplitude of lunar tides here is tiny compared to other places in the world, just two or three feet in most places. Prevailing winds, however, can push water around in the big bays and lagoons, inundating some areas and exposing others depending on direction and speed. There can be variations across the Corpus Christi area. The tide rhythm is more seasonal than daily.

"The birds all have this wired, while us amateurs are just trying to understand it," David says, as we walk to the shoreline in Violet Andrews Park, a postage stamp of green descending down to Corpus Christi Bay. "There are times when [the plovers] are extremely limited in foraging habitat. There's just not much for them. And other times there's so much of it that your odds of finding them goes way down." Today's task for David is to cover a set of known plover sites on the northern edge of the bay. He describes this as an easier area to count because the habitat is limited by the surrounding city. "I'm pretty confident we'll find more or less every bird in here, but it's not really practical to cover every square inch of the Laguna Madre," he says. Then, with a smile: "But we must try . . ."

We arrive at the shore and David scans the very narrow mudflats with binoculars. To the east, homes perch above the bay, some of them with yards mown right to the edge of a rocky shore. To the west, thick vegetation chokes the shoreline. No birds. We drive through the neighborhood a short distance west, soft classical music playing on the giant pickup's sound system. We park at a gravel access drive at the end of a cul-de-sac and again walk down to the shore. The Corpus Christi skyline rises from the water across the bay.

Plover survey participant Beau Hardegree walks plover habitat in Corpus
Christi Bay, 2016

"We're having a very strange winter," says David. "Usually these flats
would be pretty well exposed, but now there's just a few little isolated
islands." This would become a recurring theme throughout this year's
census. The water was up across the area and plovers were not showing
up where expected—or at all.

Piping plovers need open sand-gravel or sand-mud beaches with hardly
any vegetation at all. They like to be out in the open, neither too close to
the water like the sanderlings that constantly run along at the wave edge,
nor higher up in the shore grasses like some sandpipers. Visibility is key:
plovers want to be able to see around them in order to avoid predators.
This is not a bird that runs and hides, instead relying on its coloring
to blend in with the sand or simply flying away when it sees danger. The
piping plover's preferred habitat isn't truly an intertidal zone, because
these areas stay mostly dry even at high tides, but they can be affected by

extremely high water. And the plover's idea of a perfect home is also most humans' idea of a perfect ocean-side playground.

The central Texas coast is full of beaches, bays, sand flats, and islands. In a word, it's complicated—and here I'm talking about both the human and the natural landscape. I'll start with the latter and save the former for later. Imagine yourself drawing a shoreline, a simple line in black ink. Make it a wiggly one, with lots of bays and bays-upon-bays, and peninsulas, and a few rivers reaching inward. Now draw gently curving lines across the front of it all. This is Texas: bays, lagoons, and barrier islands. Corpus Christi Bay is bigger than almost every lake in Texas, and at its upper end is another bay, Nueces Bay, that reaches even farther inland, bringing the ocean up into the arid plains. The city of Corpus Christi sprawls on the eastern and southern shores of its namesake bay, and from the waterfront you feel like you're looking out over the ocean proper. But way out there on the horizon is an island—a long, low, sandy rise called Mustang Island. And just south of Mustang is Padre Island, separated by a narrow channel barely two hundred yards across. And to the north is San Jose Island, with a channel that is wider (it's the main shipping route into Corpus), but still passable by ferry in about six minutes. These long, thin islands stack up end to end for roughly four hundred miles between Galveston and the Mexican border.

Between the islands and the mainland there are either bays or shallow, island-studded lagoons. Most of these are far saltier than the ocean itself (*hyper-saline* is the scientific term). The Laguna Madre, which sits between Padre Island and the mainland, is one of the saltiest ocean embayments in the world. The distinction between land and water here is subtle. What the maps call islands are often loose agglomerations of shallows from which the grasses and mangroves grow up above the waterline and give the impression of land, even though there is none. On some days, depending on wind and tides, it is possible to motor through islands. On others, vast mudflats seem to hover mere inches above the brown water. In addition, the waves and tides and wind are always rearranging things: adding sand here, taking it away there, finding a gap to worry themselves into and create a deep bay or a cut right through an island. A thousand-year time lapse of the coast would look less like stable land and more like the seasonal accumulation and melting of snows.

And yet, atop this transience—with the sand and mud and birds coming and going—so much permanent infrastructure has been built. The Intracoastal Waterway is like a dot to dot in the lagoons and bays. On your coastline drawing, take a ruler and strike straight lines between the wiggly shore and the linear but freehanded barrier. The waterway cuts off the edges of islands, gouges a line of depth through the shallows, and connects itself together with red and green buoys floating forever in place in the middles of bays and lagoons. The islands are popular because they are beautiful, and grand villas and condominium towers rise to many times higher than the landmass itself. Looking at Mustang Island from Corpus Christi Bay, the impression is of buildings floating on the ocean. Perhaps they essentially are.

In places an odd hybrid occurs. Housing developments seek to put every house on the water, and channels are cut through the forgiving sand and mud, then armored to keep them from eroding. A two-faced Venice is carved into the shoreline: roads at the front door, canals at the back. It is akin to the work of the wind and waves, but done even more quickly and then frozen in place.

And everywhere the highways must stay above water and out of reach of the hungry forces of nature. Built-up causeways, arrow-straight, sever one bay from another, leaping up into a bridge only where necessary to allow ships under them.

David and I follow one such causeway, Sunset Drive, along the narrow spit of land between Sunset Lake and the main bay. We park along the edge of the road facing a small oil production facility. These little bits of oil infrastructure are everywhere: fenced storage tanks on tiny islands of dry land surrounded by water, rickety wooden platforms by the dozens out in the middle of almost every bay and lagoon, and major platforms barely visible out in the Gulf, shining at night. David peers through his spotting scope at a group of small birds at water's edge. They turn out to be western sandpipers and sanderlings. No plovers.

* * *

The piping plover has a somewhat different legal framework than many other listed species (with the notable exception of the wolf). The federal government recognizes three separate populations: the Atlantic Coast, Great Lakes, and Great Plains. Science says that these populations don't normally interbreed and tend to stick to their geographic areas. All three migrate to the Gulf and Atlantic Coasts and some Caribbean islands in winter, but even on these wintering grounds they tend to stay separate—the Great Plains birds usually wintering in Texas and Louisiana, the Great Lakes birds in Florida and on the Atlantic Coast, and the Atlantic Coast birds merely moving a few states southward. Minnesota includes portions of both the Great Lakes and Great Plains areas; we'll get to that in a moment.

(Another shorebird, the rufa red knot, is listed as threatened in Minnesota, though sightings are exceedingly rare. This migratory powerhouse travels more than eighteen thousand miles each year between the southern tip of South America and the Arctic, where it breeds. Though it mostly flies along the Atlantic Coast, stopping to feed primarily on horseshoe crab eggs, some birds cross the central United States, hence its listing in around forty states, including the Upper Midwest. It was listed in December 2014 because of population declines related to, according to the Federal Register notice, overharvesting of horseshoe crabs, coastal development, and climate change. The latter may inundate the coastal flats where it feeds on migratory stopovers.)

The breeding (or summer) ranges of the piping plover all feature the sandy open beaches this species prefers, though in quite different environments. The Atlantic Coast birds spend their entire lives on ocean beaches, breeding from eastern Canada down to North Carolina. The Great Lakes population breeds on sandy beaches mostly on Lakes Michigan and Huron, though there has been some recent breeding success on Lake Ontario and birds historically nested on the shores of Lake Superior in the Duluth area. On the Great Plains, the birds find sandbars and beaches along big rivers like the Missouri and the Niobrara and their associated reservoirs. They also breed on the sandy shores of alkali lakes in the Dakotas and into Canada and on the shores of big northern lakes, like Lake of the Woods on the Minnesota-Manitoba border. The Atlantic and Plains populations, at more than two thousand pairs each, are by far larger than the Great Lakes, which has increased from just a few pairs at listing to a still concerning sixty or so today.

All three populations were listed in 1986: the Great Lakes as endangered and the other two as threatened. In addition, the species is considered threatened during migration and on its wintering grounds. Three years later, a recovery plan for the Great Lakes and Great Plains populations was prepared. In 2003 another recovery plan was prepared for the Great Lakes population only. This has been the most storied and managed population, and more is known about it than either of the other two, in part because it has the more restrictive listing, but also because there are fewer birds to study. In 2009 a five-year review was prepared that covers all three populations and their wintering range. This document, recognizing the complexity of three different migrating populations, runs to hundreds of pages.

The key threats to the plover identified in the 2009 review are largely the same as in the original listing. Put most simply, recreational development and use alters or destroys both breeding and wintering habitat and can also directly chase off and kill birds and destroy eggs and nests. On the wintering range, the study cites the excavation of new channels, hard armoring of shorelines, and beach nourishment and raking as key threats to habitat. Vehicles and pedestrians on beaches, particularly where dogs are allowed off leash, can directly impact birds. On the breeding range, development of marinas and other recreation areas affects habitat, while people and dogs on the beach have an even greater impact because plover nests are often out in the open but very difficult to see and can be easily crushed. Throughout its range, the plover is susceptible to increases in predator species like foxes, coyotes, and feral cats.

Minnesota sits in the gap between the Great Plains and Great Lakes populations. Plains plovers are found just to the west and northward into Canada, but Minnesota has fewer of the large, sand beach–edged lakes necessary for successful breeding. Great Lakes plovers have rebounded significantly in Michigan and to some degree in Wisconsin, but Minnesota barely has any Great Lakes landscape, so barely any Great Lakes plovers. The critical habitat picture in the state tells the best story. Just two habitat areas have been designated: one for the Great Plains population in Lake of the Woods, one for the Great Lakes population in the Duluth harbor.

And the numbers in Minnesota are dire. The oldest data on plover populations date to 1982, when forty-four birds were counted at Lake of the Woods. In 2011 the number was two. No plovers have been seen in the Duluth harbor for more than a decade. For all intents and purposes, the bird is or will soon be gone from the state. And little is being done by land managers to prevent that. The plover was likely never abundant here because of its edge-of-range location for two separate populations.

Minnesota doesn't need to have piping plovers in order for the piping plovers to survive. Rich Baker, the DNR's endangered species coordinator, told me bluntly that state and federal agencies have limited resources to protect and manage listed species and that Minnesota's priorities lie elsewhere: bats, butterflies, orchids. That's good science, but does it make sense ethically? Shouldn't Minnesotans have the responsibility for ensuring that the whole suite of species that once lived here still does, rather than pass along conservation duties to other places when it gets too hard? But on the other hand, as Rich explains, resources spent in Minnesota would draw down those available to Michigan, which has a far greater chance of success in reestablishing the endangered Great Lakes population. After all, state lines are a human construct about which the plovers care little. Can Minnesotans be willing to accept that they will not see a piping plover at Lake of the Woods or on Minnesota Point as long as the bird thrives at Sleeping Bear Dunes in Michigan or along the Missouri River in North Dakota?

On a perfect June Saturday, I leave for Duluth with a seventeen-foot, bright blue touring kayak on top of my car and absolutely no hope of seeing any piping plovers. It is breeding season, and the only critical habitat in the area is closed to human traffic—and hasn't been visited by plovers for well more than a decade. I launch the boat from Rice's Point in downtown Duluth and paddle over to Interstate Island, a wildlife management area split down the middle by the invisible Minnesota/Wisconsin state line. I am in the Duluth harbor, and industry surrounds me. My navigation chart says I have just crossed a major shipping lane. The shoreline undulates in a series of artificial fjords: docks for thousand-foot ore boats and trestles a hundred feet high with entire trains on top dumping loads of Iron Range ore through chutes into the waiting behemoths floating below. Above me the Blatnik Bridge carries Interstate 535 southward into Superior, Wisconsin, lifting lanes high enough above the channel to let the ore boats under.

I am mere inches above the water, nestled into the waves. A great flock animates the island. The birds rise and whirl and return. They call out in a never ending chorus. Ring-billed gulls, mostly, but also a great number of common terns (which are not in fact common in the Midwest). Double-crested cormorants perch on dead logs just offshore or bob in the waves, only their necks and heads visible.

Interstate Island is as unnatural as the harbor around it. It is a dredge spoil island, created during the periodic deepenings of the harbor. It seems to be placed awkwardly for big boat traffic, but it has the advantage of being far enough from shore to deter swimming predators like raccoons and coyotes. The narrow neck spanned by the Blatnik Bridge is one of several historic beach bars at the mouth of the St. Louis River. Though entirely industrialized and built up, it's actually a lens of sand not unlike a Texas coast barrier island. One more such bar lies farther out, to the east, and actually creates this sheltered Duluth-Superior harbor. Minnesota Point and Wisconsin Point together define the inland end of Lake Superior. They are the longest freshwater sandbar in the world. The Duluth harbor, in fact, has a lot of the geography of the Texas coast, just at a different scale—and it has the industry, too. The St. Louis River flows down from the forested north and backs up here behind the sandbars, creating a protected bay. This is the head of Great Lakes shipping. Bobbing there in the harbor, I am about twenty-three hundred miles inland and could easily see an oceangoing ship bobbing near me. Until

China built the Three Gorges Dam and made the Yangtze River navigable to Chongqing, Duluth was the farthest inland ocean port in the world.

As I approach the island, I notice four humans in hard hats standing within a fenced enclosure. Though Interstate is protected specifically for the plover, it has benefits for many other birds, like the common tern. The nesting tern colony there is one of the only ones in the Great Lakes. I assume those four are counting nests and/or chicks. The hard hats are necessary protection against the terns' aggressive parenting style. Signs on the island (which I can read through my binoculars) echo what I read on the Minnesota DNR website earlier in the week: no access allowed during the nesting season.

I circle the island and then spend a pleasant hour drifting downwind and paddling back up to the head of the island a few times. I use my binoculars to get close-up views of the gulls and terns pumping their wings against the wind. I can see their little heads scanning the surface for food, occasionally casting me a glance to make sure I don't stray too close to their territorial boundary.

After a while I let the wind cruise me back toward the landing, then along the massive bulkhead of the east gate basin and across the main harbor basin to Hearding Island. Plovers historically nested here, but a quick circumnavigation tells me why they don't anymore. Thick vegetation comes right down to the shoreline, exposing only very narrow sand beaches here and there. I paddle counterclockwise up to the northern tip of the island and pause on a little beach for a snack. The wind picks up. I weigh my options (wait for a calming or go now before it gets worse), then make a break for it across the harbor, hoping I don't see the aerial lift bridge rising, which would signal the entry of a massive freighter I would be hard pressed to outrun.

Safe beside the bulkhead, I rest, listening to the call of the gulls and the rhythmic *thuk-thuk-thuk-thuk* of the waves slapping against the corrugated harbor wall. Before European settlement, this spit of land beside me was a wide, sandy bar, and the estuary stretching out to the west was a complex interplay of sedgy bays, forested uplands, and sandy-gravelly islands and shorelines. It is impossible to know whether plovers ever nested here in great numbers, but it seems impossible now that they ever could return.

I strap the kayak back onto my car and drive over the Blatnik Bridge, through Superior, and out to the far southeastern end of Wisconsin Point, where the great sand bar begins to merge into the northern Wisconsin shoreline. From here, Wisconsin Point stretches three miles northwesterly, and all of it is parkland: a surprisingly oceanic endless beach, again not unlike those I saw on Mustang or Padre Islands in Texas. A harbor entry cut through the sandbar marks the end of Wisconsin Point and the beginning of Minnesota Point, which continues for another seven miles up into Duluth, ending at the Canal Park entertainment district and the steel aerial lift bridge. Minnesota Point is about half park and half residential, though the beach itself is all public.

I drive through sandy scrub forest to the road to Shafer Beach, the only location around the Twin Ports where plovers have recently nested. A gate blocks the access road: it is plover nesting season. I am actually happy to see the sign, even though I came here to see plover habitat. The beach itself is not closed—it is possible to walk along the water's edge from other access points, but the road closure is meant to make it more challenging to get there, in hopes fewer people will visit. I continue on to the next beach at Dutchman Creek. The northwesterly wind that made the harbor a challenge makes for a calm lakeshore, so I carry the boat down to the beach past families playing in the sand and wading knee-deep in Lake Superior.

As I paddle northwest, Shafer Beach soon becomes obvious. The narrow, rocky shoreline widens into a sandy beach about fifty yards wide. The inland slopes have been cleared of trees and shrubs in a swath that, compared to the adjacent areas, looks like a logging clear-cut. This is a deliberate effort to create preferred nesting habitat for plovers. I stay about thirty yards offshore and scan the beach with my binoculars. I know I would never find a plover this way, but I do view similarities to what I saw in Texas: fine sand, sprinkled with pebbles, gradually transitioning to sparse beach grass away from the water. I see white and gray driftwood—both weathered logs and dimensional lumber. I see gulls, crows, cormorants, and a swiftly running shorebird I cannot identify (perhaps a sandpiper of some kind—definitely not a plover: too brown). A father and two children walk slowly down the beach toward Dutchman's Creek. The little boy carries a bucket but collects nothing. The girl runs out ahead.

I beach my boat and walk up the gentle slope from the water, scanning the sand intently and watching my footfalls. I do it because there is no prohibition. I do it because others are here already. I do it because I doubt there are actually plovers here. I feel a bit guilty, and I wonder why access is permitted at all. Why must we be allowed to walk here during nesting season—plovers or not? Isn't there enough beach to go around? Sure, the gated access road probably prevents the daylong disturbances like those I saw at Dutchman's (tents, campfires, sandcastle building), but just one off-leash dog could chase off a pair of plovers finally deciding to nest here. All the good work (and money) that went into the clearing of vegetation could be for naught. Why go halfway

Restored piping plover habitat at Shafer Beach, Wisconsin, 2016

here, when sites like this one are so limited? I suppose people just love beaches, and it's hard to take any of them away from us.

~~~

While traveling in the Duluth area, I start posting images from my adventure on Instagram. Strategic hashtagging quickly links me into a community of birders and, specifically, some plover volunteers on the shore of Lake Huron in Canada posting as @ploverlovers. (I'm no genius—strategic here means sticking #pipingplover on all my posts.)

The summer's thread starts on April 26:
THE IMAGE: plovers on a sand-shell beach with small pieces of driftwood scattered about

THE TEXT: *They're back! Four plovers spotted at Sauble Beach this afternoon!*

MAY 2
three speckled eggs in a small depression in the sand, with some sticks and reeds on the ground and a single plant of beach grass at the edge of the frame

The Great Lakes Piping Plover Recovery Effort has discovered the first nest of the 2016 season at Sleeping Bear Dunes National Lakeshore! This photo shows one of the 2015 Sauble Beach nests, which we hope to see very soon.

MAY 3
a single plover beside an ATV track in the sand

Now that Piping Plovers have arrived, the most important thing is to leave them alone and to refrain from interfering with their nesting activities. A reminder that vehicles and dogs are not allowed on the beach.

MAY 5
two plovers on smooth sand, one of them standing tall and extending its neck, the other looking disinterested

Mating has officially begun, and the male Plovers are strutting their stuff in Sauble Beach!

🖛

I am not a birder. Rather, I *was not* a birder. I have studied plants all my life, have kept fish, have had orchids in the house pretty regularly throughout the years, and have been around enough cats and dogs to get the gist. But birds are foreign to me. The plover's story was the one I felt most uncomfortable with when beginning this project. I hardly knew a warbler from a sparrow, and every raptor was a "hawk," regardless of its actual hawk-ness.

So in the lead-up to that 2016 trip to Texas I buy a decent pair of binoculars and a Sibley guide and start poring through the latter to try to make sense of this new tribe. The binoculars give me pause, though. Perhaps philosophically, I have never carried any visual aids in the woods. I always felt intent on seeing the "real" landscape through "my own eyes." How silly.

Kerri comes with me to Corpus Christi. Yes, this is a research trip, but a vacation, too. Kerri and I have been married more than a decade, and travel has always been a part of our relationship. I am, of course, excited to be exploring someplace new in search of the piping plover, but Kerri, during the flight, also says she is excited to be traveling to see a little bird—flying south in winter, as it were. On our first evening in our Port Aransas condominium, while Kerri gets ready for dinner, I scan the beach from the balcony. A cotton ceiling of clouds stretches over the ocean to the horizon. The waves roll in low and regular onto a wide, flat beach. Near the inland edge of the sand is an endless line of posts, regular as links in a chain, denoting the edge of the Port Aransas ("Port A" to the locals) beach road. A motor home sits parallel to the post line, its pop-out sides extended. Wet towels and clothing drape over several posts.

On the beach side of the line, people stroll, with dogs, in ones and twos. Tiny white dots salt the sand, rising and settling again as the people move through. I put the binoculars to my eyes. The white dots resolve into gulls—with legs and beaks and wings that stretch as they threaten to take off. And the people have colored shirts and pants, with logos and words I can nearly read. I rotate my head to view up and down the beach from my high promontory, and the beach road posts tick away one by one. The motor home is giant; the draped towels all are printed with coral reefs and dolphins.

Coral reefs: Kerri and I honeymooned in French Polynesia, and we dove. She was the diver, not me; she has been to the Great Barrier Reef and the Red Sea. I learned in a Minnesota lake and took my first oceanic underwater breaths off a boat in a reef pass on the island of Fakarava. As I bobbed in the water, readying myself to go under, the surface was a blurry chop. But the moment I submerged my face, a whole colorful and detailed world exploded around me. I raised my head above the water again just to be sure of the extraordinary nature of the contrast, then returned under and descended.

The binoculars were like that. The next day at Padre Island National Seashore I go back and forth between magnified views of birds I don't know and the Sibley guide. I begin to see the differences in patterning size, and behavior that help me distinguish among birds. I learn about eye-rings, lores, underwings, primaries, and crests. I successfully (I hope) identify willets and sanderlings (birds I would have previously referred to as sandpipers, which they're not). I share this new knowledge with Kerri, who is contentedly reading in the sun. She is less than impressed, but she humors me.

We are about three miles south of the visitor center. We drove here on the beach. Yes, the National Park Service allows anyone and everyone to drive on the beach. It's a concession to Texas, where someone would tell me in the coming days, driving on the beach is an essential human right. As we lounged, a sparse parade of economy cars, jacked-up 4 × 4s, shiny SUVs, and pickups bristling with fishing equipment plied the "beach road." The beach road is wherever it's possible to drive. The NPS maintains it for all cars down to about mile five, then recommends 4 × 4s only to the Mansfield Cut at milepost sixty. The piping plover doesn't nest here, so there's no risk of crushing eggs, but vehicles are a disturbance nonetheless.

On the way back to the condo, we stop at Wilson's Cut. Then we walk the beach in Port A. I use the binoculars to look at birds just five feet in front of me; I am thirsty for detail. The names start to add up. More willets, a black-bellied plover, a ruddy turnstone, two kinds of gulls (there is more than one kind of gull??!!). I start to see the differences at a distance, verifying through my lenses. Once, I encountered woodland wildflowers this way and have never stopped stooping to see them up close, to name them in my head, and to store away their attributes in my memory. In Texas the birds are creeping in.

The next day I search for plovers with David Newstead, who provides context on which birds are everywhere and which are rare. I add dunlins (common), western and least sandpipers (sort of common), and avocets and stilts (rather rare, though when you see one you see many). David, whose eyes are trained for birds, stops suddenly on the way back to his truck to show me, through his scope, the fantastically named pyrrhuloxia, which looks a lot like a cardinal with a taller crest. I am sure I would have mistaken it for a cardinal three days ago (yet I would not have even seen it but for David).

Then I pick up Kerri and we go on a bird-watching boat tour. As the *Skimmer* pulls out of its Fulton dock and into Aransas Bay, Kerri and I open beers and the boat hostess hands out a birding checklist: the names of 171 birds arranged into categories. Grebes; ducks/geese/swans; kites/eagles/hawks; cranes; woodpeckers; owls; plovers. Each name with a little line beside it on which to put a check mark when the bird is seen.

I am a list person. I am writing a book about federally listed species. The book is arranged species by species. I hold the *Skimmer*'s bird list like a sacred text glowing golden with importance. I look over at Kerri. "Are you going to be a birder now?" she says, and sips her beer.

By the end of the boat tour I have twenty-nine check marks, none of them identified on my own, all with the help of the colorful captain, who drives and narrates in a gentle drawl. By the end of the Texas trip I have forty-three. Ten months later I am up to one twenty-five.

So am I a beginner? Of course. Am I birder? Well, I just went into my eBird app and logged the white-throated sparrow I saw the other day in my urban backyard and stalked for thirty minutes trying to positively identify. Birding has all the best parts of a scavenger hunt, *Where's Waldo* book, and matching game. Sign me up!

⁂

MAY 16

an image of a chick (presumably from a previous year)

First Sauble Beach Piping Plover nest of 2015 discovered this morning! We'll be seeing chicks on the beach in a month.

MAY 20

a plover laying in the sand, out in the middle of the beach, with no shelter whatsoever, seemingly so exposed, with the cobalt line of the lake in the upper third of the photo

A second nest was found on this beautiful Friday in Sauble Beach!

MAY 26

two plovers on the sand, black necklaces and topknots so vibrant and deep

Lots of excitement with courtship and nesting in Sauble Beach this week, but we are just as excited about the news of a nesting pair at Darlington Provincial Park—the first nest on the Canadian shore of Lake Ontario in 80 years!

MAY 30

a plover bedded down on a nest amongst sparse beach grass

As of yesterday morning, there are three piping plover nests in Sauble Beach!!!

JUNE 14

a sitting adult and jaunty, leggy chick, presumably from a previous year

Plover Lovers are anxiously awaiting the hatch of Sauble Beach's first nest of the season, which is expected later this week. With chicks on the way, it's about to get very busy on the beach!

JUNE 18

two pale, fluffy (impossibly cute) chicks, venturing out on the
sand with patches of beach grass in the background

*The first chicks of the season have hatched in Sauble Beach! Yesterday
afternoon, 4 brand new piping plovers emerged from nest 1.*

JUNE 19

a dapper adult male, four chicks, and a wooden tent-shaped
structure placed by volunteers to provide some protection

*Happy Fathers Day to all the dads out there, including the father of
Sauble's 4 chicks, Flag Boy!*

The most surprising beach in Minnesota is at Zippel Bay on Lake of the
Woods. This is the far north, as far as America is concerned. Farther
north than Maine, farther north than Canada's largest city. Arriving
on the shore of this sixteen-hundred-square-mile lake (that's big: more
than a million acres and the seventh-largest lake in the United States)
feels like reaching the end of a continent and staring out across an
ocean—complete with five miles of fine sand beach and shallow water
offshore, though the water is certainly not balmy. The sand in the state
park in places feels like ideal plover habitat, and plovers did historically
nest here, but not anymore.

I am at the tail end of a voyage through the northwestern prairies
visiting orchid and butterfly habitat. I walk the beach and add a twenty-
first new bird to my life list from this trip (common goldeneye). Then I
drive east to the small resort town of Wheeler's Point and look for a
motorboat so I can visit nearby designated critical habitat. The friendly
folks at Bugsy's oblige me with a twenty-foot Alaskan and an eighty-
horse outboard on a tiller (though they're a little mystified that I won't
be fishing), and I motor out into the big lake. I again encounter barrier
sandbars. Visible as smudges on the horizon are Morris Point, Pine and
Curry Island (which is actually just one island), and Sable Island. These

low sandy spits separate the main lake from Fourmile Bay, in the same way that Minnesota/Wisconsin Point separates Duluth harbor from Lake Superior and Mustang Island separates Corpus Christi Bay from the Gulf. The Canadian border runs down the middle of Rainy River and through the channel between Pine/Curry and Sable Islands.

I start at Morris Point, where a massive colony of common terns is sharing space with ring-billed and Bonaparte's gulls (this is the extreme southern edge of the latter's range, and when I put the dozens of Bonaparte's into eBird later, the app expresses skepticism and I need to provide additional descriptive information). I keep the motor low, or off, and enjoy the whirling and chattering of the birds through my binoculars. The area is posted "no admittance: plover nesting habitat," so I keep my distance. But distance can be deceiving under magnification, and I drift accidentally across the terns' invisible boundary. Dozens fly above my boat, shrieking and feigning dives. The ring-bills join in, emboldened by their brethren. I yank the motor pull as quietly as I can and move slowly away.

For the next few hours I cruise pleasantly around Pine/Curry and Sable Islands looking for birds. Pine/Curry is posted like Morris, except for a couple of designated shore lunch locations, where informational signage tells boaters why the rest of the island is closed. I occasionally encounter small groups of Bonaparte's gulls, their black heads and tiny black beaks distinguishing them easily from other gulls. White pelicans glower in groups of ten or so on tiny patches of gravel barely above the waterline. A small shorebird on Pine/Curry defies my best efforts at identification, though it stays visible for at least thirty minutes. Canada geese float in American waters and a bald eagle flies from a tree on a Canadian island.

Back at Bugsy's, the dockhand (with cocktail in hand) asks if I found what I was looking for. I tell him no, but that I didn't expect to. He seems puzzled but softly intrigued when I tell him this is a unique spot for birds. This is a fishing town, but maybe there's money in renting boats to birders. I let him ponder that and head back to my hotel for my own cocktail and a walleye sandwich.

a pair of plovers, one of them seeming to do a high-step cavort
behind the other

*This lovely pair of piping plovers is getting a second chance at a nest
after their first was washed out. In total, two new nests have been found
this week in Sauble Beach, which was a much needed boost after losing 4
chicks and two nests over the last 2 weeks.*

I feel surprised by this news, so I have to comment:

*Good news about the newly found nests. But oh no! How were the others
lost?*

We aren't sure, replied Plover Lovers. *Lots of ring billed gulls are on
the beach and could have taken the chicks. The parents are more of a
mystery; likely a Merlin or owl. Hopefully the two nests we have now
are successful.*

☙

One threat not identified in the original listing but discussed in detail in
the 2009 report is climate change. Climate change is likely to impact the
plover differently throughout its range. In the Great Lakes, the warming of the lakes themselves due to reduced snowpack (Lake Superior
is more than two degrees warmer in summer than it used to be) may
affect breeding patterns. However, consistently lower lake levels (again
a result of reduced snowpack) may expose more breeding ground as
beaches widen. In the Great Plains, predicted heavier spring rain threatens to inundate alkali lakes and river reservoirs and reduce breeding
ground. Sea level rise along the Gulf Coast is the greatest threat of all.
Those low-lying sand and mud flats where plovers spend nearly ten
months of the year may end up underwater. In fact, areas with low tidal
variation are even more vulnerable. The US Gulf Coast has seen sea
level rise greater than the world average (around 13 centimeters more
than the 10-to-25 centimeter range over the past century, as published

by the IPCC—the Intergovernmental Panel on Climate Change). In the Corpus Christi area specifically, 65 percent of tidal flats have been lost, and sea level rise has been cited as a contributing factor. In essence, the tidal flats of Texas, Louisiana, Florida, and North Carolina will be the first to go under, and that's where more than 50 percent of all the world's piping plovers winter.

The year 2016 seems to be a sample of things to come. The day after I find plover Z12 and its companions on land with David Newstead, I join a different plover census survey group and get out on the water. The eight scientists and volunteers who gather at the public marina in Aransas Pass are pessimistic but intrigued by the unusually high winter water levels. They don't think they will see many plovers in the usual spots, but even that observation provides some important data. Maybe this anomalous year is the new normal, explains Robyn Cobb, as the group readies the boats. Maybe this year's census will help managers understand what the implications of sea level rise might be for pipers and other shorebirds.

We embark around 9:00 AM. Robyn and a few others head northeast into Aransas Bay, while I join two men heading west into Corpus Christi Bay. Beau Hardegree, USFWS coastal program coordinator, pilots the boat. With us is Mike Lange, who used to be the senior biologist for the Texas Mid-Coast National Wildlife Refuge but who now buys land for the Trust for Public Land, a nonprofit that partners with government to secure parcels for conservation purposes. Mike is tagging along to take a look at some shoreline and part of an island. The eastern end of the bay is a strange mix of mangrove islands and industrial terminals. From moment to moment, I feel either in the midst of a borderless nature reserve or in the middle of a massive construction site. We follow the Intracoastal Waterway, which here hugs the mainland. On our right immense oil terminals and ship docks bristle with cranes hundreds of feet tall, standing like metal giraffes on land just a few feet above sea level. On our left are Dagger Island's mazes of mangroves, mudflats, and acres of grasses growing up from the water seemingly without land to support them.

We speed around the massive Flint Hills Resources oil terminal, where long docks extend a quarter mile out into the bay with tankers anchored at their outer ends. We enter the La Quinta Channel, which leads northward past the residential community of Ingleside on the Bay. Here homes stand just twenty feet from the water and boat garages turn the shoreline into a flat-faced parade of doors. Beyond Ingleside are other industrial complexes, fuel terminals, and a metal refinery with every surface seemingly painted rust brown from decades of iron dust.

We stop occasionally and scope the shoreline with binoculars, but see nothing. We return down the La Quinta and visit Pelican Island, cruise through the middle of Dagger Island, wander in and out of Harbor Island, and drive up the Piper Cut, a constructed channel leading into the backside of Mustang Island to the Island Moorings subdivision in Port Aransas, a Venice-like maze of canals fronted by big homes. At times we beach the boat and walk the sand flats. At times we anchor offshore and wade to islands.

At Pelican Island, the subject of the current conditions comes up again. Beau had checked in with the other boat. I ask if they have seen anything. "No," says Beau, "not in this mess."

"Nothing?" asks Mike, incredulous.

"They've seen some sanderlings," says Beau, and we all have a good laugh. I have learned by now that sanderlings are pretty much everywhere down here. "I don't know what they're gonna do when they go to look at this data. They're gonna have to qualify it and all. These tides are something. I don't know, some ice cap must have melted overnight or something." We chuckle again.

"If this is the new norm," finishes Beau, "this is bad."

It seems everyone knows sea level is rising. "You gotta be optimistic. You gotta hope we can slow it down a little," Mike says.

"But you gotta have room for [plovers] now," says Beau.

"And you should be preserving behind it," Mike replies, referencing the need to acquire and preserve the next layer of land higher, so the birds can move up as the sea does. There might be precious little of that, though, on the coast, because the islands are already so low and so much of the slightly higher ground is wrapped up in industry or waterfront housing.

I learn later that while we were toiling out on the water with no success, another scientist on foot was hitting the jackpot in exactly the kind of place Beau and Mike were talking about. The Port Aransas Nature Preserve protects twelve hundred acres of flat, sandy scrubland and open flats that are rarely inundated by tides. It's a prime birding spot, with trails and boardwalks introducing visitors to the complex barrier island landscape. The scientist on foot counted more than one hundred piping plovers there. A concentration like that is exciting, but could be dangerous for the species. A concentrated population is more susceptible to catastrophic disturbance: a few off-leash dogs, a family of foxes, or a raccoon run amok could stress or chase off the plovers. If the new normal is higher oceans, that will concentrate birds, and, as Beau said, that's bad.

We return to the boat launch and commiserate with the other boat's occupants, who, as suggested, saw pretty much only sanderlings. I admit to feeling lucky to have seen plovers with David the day before, because now the pressure is off. It would certainly have been disappointing to come all the way to Texas and not see a plover. With my expectations in check I am able to enjoy the other images: squadrons of white pelicans flying beside the boat at heights lower than our heads; a whirling mass of Forster's terns diving for fish ahead of and then all around the boat, one after the other crashing beak-first into the opaque green water; a reddish egret, an extremely rare bird (only a few thousand in the wild, says Beau), dancing in the shallows, creating shadows with its wings to herd small fish to within striking distance; walking across sand flats absolutely covered with perfect, unbroken seashells, almost as if no one had ever been there before to collect or break them; and dolphins rising in slippery arcs beside us, sighing gently and glancing our way as their eyes broke the surface.

The Plover Lovers Instagram feed goes quiet for awhile, focusing mainly on announcements for a series of educational beach talks. Then

JULY 25

an adult with two chicks—one much smaller than the other, and
nearer the adult—within a protective metal mesh enclosure

*Two chicks hatched from nest 5 last week, one on July 17/18 and the
other on July 20. It's highly unusual for chicks to hatch days apart,
particularly when no incubation was observed between. Sadly, the
younger chick (the tiny one in this photo) was taken by a crow while the
older sibling was taken by a juvenile gull, marking the end of piping
plover season in Sauble Beach, with no chicks fledged this year.*

I respond with condolences—the only thing that seems appropriate.
Others do, too, and offer advice. One shares a story from Crane Beach,
Massachusetts, where a nearby nesting colony of those aggressive, dive-
bombing common terns seems to protect the plovers.

The last post is a notice for the final beach talk of the season:

AUGUST 9

an expanse of wind-rippled sand, with not a shred of vegetation;
a line of tracks bisects the frame, heading upward, but no birds
are shown; no words are written

"We might have some here," says David Newstead as we work our way
through the park on the fringes of Sunset Lake. "See where those gulls
are—to the right, a few birds are moving like plovers." David uses behavior as his first clue. Plovers tend to run a few short steps, then peck
several times quickly into the sand. Other types of shorebirds may run
longer distances between pecks, or may peck a single time, then move on.
The differences are subtle, but David has watched these birds for decades
and can distinguish among their actions from a distance. He raises his
binoculars. "There are three pipers and a semipalmated plover there and
the three pipers are all banded. They've all got yellow leg flags: that
means US Geological Survey banded those birds, probably in North

Dakota." David moves in closer. He can see the colors from here but wants to read the text on the flags. The scope is better than our binoculars, but the writing is tiny on the tiny band on the bird's tiny leg. Once in a better location, David moves away and lets me look through the scope.

The bird appears in the circular frame like a portrait in a locket. I watch it run and stop, run and stop, then poke-poke into the sand with its little orange, black-tipped beak. It is adorable: a round white and light gray bird sprinting around the beach. Through the scope, I seem to enter its world. With my own eyes, the scene is scrub and highway and riffling water and a few tiny birds out there at the water's edge. In the scope, it is just the bird and the detail of the sand at its feet and the shells scattered around.

I look my fill, then let David put his eyes back to the scope. He writes down the numbers on the leg bands. He will report these sightings later, and they will be entered into the big database of bird movement. This is how I learn of their general life histories: 4G7, born in 2015 on a Missouri River beach in North Dakota; A08, banded as an adult in 2015 also on the Missouri in North Dakota; and Z12, the 2014 chick from Turtle Lake.

When I saw the North Dakota plover flagged Z12, during its second winter in Texas, its odds of survival were pretty good. The big question, though, would be if it could produce a next generation. So again in May of 2016 it returned north, resettling this time in nearly the same spot as the year before. Whether it mated, nested, and successfully reared offspring is not (and likely never will be) known. On the Great Plains, individual nests are not coddled and monitored by humans like they are along the Great Lakes. The landscape is too vast and the birds too numerous.

I can say with certainty that this piper was one of roughly five hundred counted in the Corpus Christi area during the 2016 international census. That's about the typical number, but Robyn Cobb notes that most of the birds were concentrated in the hundreds on a few exposed flats. Though there was no major census in 2017, Robyn tells me the tides were high again that year. She's not sure how this repeat will affect plovers long term.

Z12's admittedly generalized life history is a flight of fancy. There are of course innumerable possibilities for the bird's future. How many more times will it make those nonstop journeys north and south? Or, at risk of anthropomorphizing (note I did not give it a human name; however, as a great fan of Rachel Carson's *Under the Sea Wind*, I was tempted to), I wonder if it will feel the ache of spending a summer alone on a North Dakota lakeshore. Will it feel the pain of a return to an empty nest, raccoon tracks all around? Will it curse itself for its nest placement or feel frustration that its feigned broken wing did not lure the predator away?

At the end of a voyage, some year, it may find a breakwater or homes where its favorite beach used to be. It might be repeatedly chased or frightened by a two-legged or four-legged mammal or a mammal on four wheels. It might then be too exhausted to evade the next fox or owl or merlin. Perhaps one day one of its grandchildren or great-grandchildren will come down to Texas and find the land underwater, the mud flats and even the oil and gas terminals covered by a higher sea.

Leedy's roseroot

4

Roseroot

The valley of the North Fork of the Whitewater River is an Eden of hanging gardens. Cliffs rise more than eighty feet in a vertical wall from the south bank. Draperies of Virginia creeper swing in the cool air, ferns festoon the cliff's chinks and ledges, ash and hackberry trees lean out over the canyon from far above, gripping the thin soil with roots that look like balls of snakes. The rock itself is architectural: a reddish blocky foundation supporting a mass of gray. The gray is itself split horizontally by the long lines of slight overhangs shading dark cracks. In profile this cliff would appear gently sawtoothed, and a little top-heavy.

The North Fork cuts against this cliff with its slate-blue rush. Here, the river is a straight flume, one long stretch of rapids gradually undermining the rock. The pile of rubble and soil at the foot of the wall is evidence of the North Fork's success—and the failure of the rock itself to resist the intrusion of water from above. The rock is dissolving, its cracks widening until angled chunks drop toward the river and add to the talus pile below.

Which is why we are wearing bicycle helmets. You never know when a rock will fall, and also, as careful as we plan to be, we might accidentally dislodge one with the aluminum extension ladder Joel is carrying over his shoulder. Joel Olfelt is a biology professor at Northeastern Illinois University in Chicago. He is rail-thin. His gray hiking pants and denim button-down shirt seem two sizes too big for him. He is wearing a baseball hat under his likely decades-old Styrofoam bicycle helmet, brand name "Defender." Brian Teichert and Nelson Gonzalez are Joel's students. Nelson is the brawniest of all of us, and should probably be carrying the ladder. His chinstrap cuts into his chin, slightly. Brian is double-capped like Joel: red baseball under black helmet. His build is almost exactly like mine—that is to say, average—and he and I have worn almost exactly the same clothes: khaki-colored hiking pants and lightweight, long-sleeved blue-gray shirts. Someone else encountering our little group might have difficulty telling Brian and me apart. But Brian has a second layer, something I wish I had also copied. It's cold in this valley, even at the end of July.

The four of us are contemplating the vertical garden facing us across the North Fork. "All right," says Joel, "well, there's one. We're going to have to cross back over." We have waded the river once already, all of us rolling up our pants and changing into a second pair of shoes to keep our boots dry for the treacherous footing on the talus slopes.

Joel Olfelt's research team entering the Whitewater River valley for a Leedy's roseroot survey, 2012

"There's a couple right there," adds Brian, coming over next to me, leaning in and pointing at the cliff. "See that kind of sage green color? There are two of them."

"Some of them have yellow leaves hanging down from them," says Joel.

"Go probably about two or three meters up from the water," Brian continues. "Then there's another one about another meter or so above that. See, there's that little fern in that fissure there, then a meter up there's another set: one, maybe two."

"There's a whole circle of them up there," says Joel, bending to roll up his pant legs. "We'll get up close and personal with those."

They are pointing out a plant called the Leedy's roseroot (*Rhodiola integrifolia* ssp. *leedyi*), which Joel has studied since the mid-1990s, when he was a PhD candidate at the University of Minnesota. He makes trips once or twice per year to these river valleys of southeastern Minnesota to continue his ongoing survey of this extremely rare plant. I had never seen a roseroot before—few have. I knew they grew on cliff faces, but I never expected I would find them clinging to the rock, reaching their stems out into the void, ten, thirty, sixty feet above a rushing river.

Joel sends Brian and Nelson downstream to look for another group of plants he knows. He steps into the North Fork, ladder balanced on his shoulder, feeling for footing on the invisible riverbed. I follow him into the water, and the Leedy's-studded cliff looms above me.

The plant currently known as Leedy's roseroot was first found in 1936 in the Root River valley of southeastern Minnesota by the botanist John Leedy, his name forever linked to this cliffside succulent. Leedy thought the plant was simply a new occurrence of the already well-known eastern roseroots of Greenland and Labrador (then called *Sedum rosea*).

In 1975 another botanist, R. T. Clausen, published a more detailed analysis of 160 plants from twenty-three populations in Minnesota and New York. He determined that Leedy's was actually more like the far western roseroots, but different enough to warrant a subspecies name, which was nice for John Leedy, because the plant then became *Sedum integrifolia* ssp. *leedyi*. That "ssp." stands for "subspecies" and indicates the plant is sorta different from other roseroots, but not quite different enough to be considered a separate species. Clausen made his determinations based on the plants' appearance—leaf size and shape, flower type. This was long before molecular genetic analysis, so taxonomy primarily still relied on physical measurement and comparison of various specimens from different populations.

All the roseroot species in North America underwent another name change in 2010, swapping *Sedum* for the current *Rhodiola*. The latter was originally coined by the father of taxonomy himself, Linnaeus, in 1753. He saw significant enough differences between *Sedums* and *Rhodiolas*, but subsequent scientists tended to use the two terms as synonyms. More recently, botanists have begun using genetic analysis to verify Linnaeus's original hierarchies, and have found that he was exactly right about *Sedums* and *Rhodiolas*: the two groups do warrant separation. So the roseroots moved up one spot in the alphabet.

When Leedy's was renamed in 2010, it was already on the federal endangered species list. The name change necessitated an official Federal Register notice—one that Leedy's roseroot shared with the Missouri bladderpod and the Michigan monkeyflower, a trio that makes this particular register notice look a bit like a practical joke. The federal ESA listing happened pretty quickly, as these things go. It went under review in 1990, a proposed listing rule was put forth in 1991, and the plant was listed as threatened in 1992. Scientists felt that since Leedy's had such a disconnected and limited range—a range primarily privately owned—it was particularly vulnerable to disturbance, even though it was relatively stable where it did manage to occur.

When I visited the North Fork with Joel in 2011, the total Leedy's roseroot range was considered to be just six isolated sites in Minnesota and New York. Forty plants clung to shale cliffs near Glenora Falls, taking advantage of the cool, moist environment of a waterfall pouring down into upstate New York's Seneca Lake. The most plants anywhere—around four thousand—were found along two miles of that same lake's western shore. This population was shared by about fifty private homeowners, many of whom have constructed (or may one day construct) boathouses, stairs, and utilities down the cliffs or on the talus at the lake edge. Minnesota had four sites, in the Root and Whitewater River valleys.

I use the past tense here not because any of these sites have been lost. They're all doing all right (in Minnesota, one of the four sites is owned by the Department of Natural Resources, and two have cooperative private owners). Today, though, it is possible that the subspecies status of Leedy's roseroot may change, and there just might be more sites out there.

The stretch along the North Fork where I stand with Joel is the public DNR site, the 3,357-acre North Branch Unit of the Whitewater Wildlife Management Area. This work—wading creeks, carrying a ladder down a slippery side valley, and climbing thirty feet up dripping cliff faces— is one of three major studies Joel and his students are leading on the Leedy's roseroot. This is the field science. How many plants are here? How are they doing? How well are they reproducing? Joe is also performing two types of genetic analysis in the lab determining the plant's reproductive effectiveness and reconsidering once again its taxonomic relationships.

"The idea," Joel explains, "is that if we do this over a number of years, we begin to know how long-lived these are, and what their life history is. At the same time we get a sample of something like thirty to fifty individuals that gives us hopefully enough statistical power to start saying things about what proportion of the population is flowering and setting seed so that we can get at what we call an effective population size."

Effective population size is a glimpse at the viability of a population. It is based on a population's reproductive success. If a population cannot reproduce, it makes no difference how many individuals are living now, for there will be exactly zero once today's individuals die out. "We could count every one of them here," Joel tells me, "and say there are a thousand here, but that's pretty meaningless if only five of them are flowering every year."

Joel struggles mightily to get the ladder stable on the chunky rocks below the cliff. I help him find and place flat pieces of stone to build platforms for the ladder legs. Once he is satisfied, he hands me a bright-orange field notebook. "I'll climb the ladder," he says, "and I'll ask you to take notes."

Up he goes, step over cautious step. At the top he leans into the cliff, his body pressing closely to the rock, and grasps the nearest plant. Leedy's roseroots are unusual among perennials in that it is actually possible to track individual plants from year to year. Most perennial plants die completely back to the ground in fall, existing through the winter only as roots. Next year's shoots may not come up in exactly the same place. It is also impossible to scientifically verify whether a new year's plant in the same location is in fact the same plant or a nearby one, or a new one growing from last year's seed.

Leedy's roseroots die back to a perennial stem, or rhizome, which many perennials do, but Leedy's rhizomes remain exposed, peeking out

Joel Olfelt at the top of a ladder cataloging roseroots, 2012

of the cliff face like thin fingers of ginger. Part identification tags can be wrapped around this rhizome, so Joel can track individual plants from year to year. The one he holds now is named "230"—Joel reads the numbers out separately: 2. 3. 0.

He combs through the draping fronds and squints through his wire-frame glasses. He calls the data down to me. "We've got nineteen stems. And we have no flowers. So obviously no sex data." After a few clarifying questions on my part (I admit I'm a touch nervous to be "helping," for fear I might derail the study somehow), I find the row for 230 in the book and consider the five columns, separated by light pink lines and topped with headings.

Sex: blank
 # Infl [the number of inflorescences, or flower clusters]: *c*
Flowers / Infl [the number of flowers per inflorescence]: *blank*
 # stems: 19
seed filled: blank

I can't help but think this must be a healthy Leedy's: nineteen stems, after all (this would turn out to be one of the largest stem totals on a single plant all day). 230, however, was not contributing to the gene pool—at least not this year. This was the effective population principle made vivid.

"The next one is 231," calls Joel. "Five stems. And we have one inflorescence there. It is male. And we have five flowers. And now we have an oddly named one: D, as in dog, 2. This has four stems. And it has no flowers."

I put the data in the book.

231: Male, 1, 5, 5, blank.
D2: blank, 0, blank, 4, blank.

"Next we have WW0101," says Joel, reaching upward beyond the top of the ladder. "That has five stems. And two inflorescences. These are female. Twelve on the first—twelve flowers. Eight flowers on the second. And no filled seed, so in the last column, just put 'No.'"

A female. But no seed. Four other plants are within Joel's reach: 235, F2, F3, and F4. The number of stems ranges from one to twelve (Joel's comment on the one-stem F4: "there's hardly anything left of it"), but none of these have any inflorescences. As I jot down the numbers, I find myself thinking about the stories at play within this little society. Joel is careful not to anthropomorphize (though I do hear a slight catch in his voice whenever he says "no flowers"), but I can't help it, especially because they have sex—meaning they are males and females. Even the unknowns have a sex, we just cannot tell them apart until they bloom. I picture the five-stem male 231 waiting for the arrival of a hoverfly or a bee, always with an eye on the equally five-stemmed (and voluptuously named) WW0101. I expect he would be glad everyone else around has decided not to flower this year, or is too young to offer him any competition. Perhaps he is intimidated or titillated by F2, or by 230, with its nineteen stems: a veritable nest of potential, if it would ever flower. And what about that lone blooming female: WW0101? Is she frustrated that the only blooming male has relatively few stems? Does she wish 230 would unfurl grand male inflorescences for her?

Scientifically speaking, the data say this: eight plants in this first batch, with not a single seed set. Joel descends, moves the ladder slightly to check on WW0001 (a whopping twenty-seven stems but no flowers), then descends again and goes in search of others just up- and downstream. I climb the ladder.

Thirty feet up, my face inches from that bedrock, I am in a different world. Clumps of moss, wet as sponges, glisten and drip. Lichens in bronze and light gray speckle the rock face like an abstract fresco. It is noticeably cooler here, facing the rock, than on the valley floor, but humid. I am having a hard time keeping my glasses unfogged. Leedy's roseroots hang before me.

This is a succulent plant related to the very common sedums. It has a yellowish root that extends into the cliff face, and (as the data suggest)

A Leedy's tagged for ongoing study, 2012

any number of stems that reach out horizontally, most often dipping earthward, then curving out and up toward the light. The deep red flowers, when they occur, explode from the very ends of the stems in tight clusters. The flowers are either male or female, not "perfect" like many plant species, though rarely a plant may have both male and female parts in their flowers. Together, the stems and flowers rarely exceed eight inches in length.

The whole plant appears sculpted from light green putty. The stem and the many thick leaves arranged along it are exactly the same color. Many-stemmed individuals like WW0001 are miniature prehistoric forests, smooth round stems arching every which way, heavy leaves overlapping to create even darker shade within the dimness of the valley.

I turn my head from the cliff. Upstream the North Fork emerges from a mist cloud. The shoreside vegetation grows ghostlier the deeper I peer into the distance. I allow my mind to transport itself back in time. The picture that comes to me immediately is some classic natural history museum rendering of the age of dinosaurs. Thick-leaved plants. A humid, hot, dripping landscape, waterlogged and swampy. Vegetation almost like what we know, but not quite. In that time, the Jurassic, these rocks would have been buried under layers and layers of other rocks, though this dolomite, this future cliff, would have already been built in the seas of an even earlier time.

But the Jurassic would have been too hot for the Leedy's (not to mention there were no flowering plants in the Jurassic), so I project forward. The Pleistocene ice age: roaring silt-laden rivers, bracing winds, very few if any of the stiff trees that arch over me, saber-toothed cats hunting mammoths. And this cool vertical wall standing here, just like now, with the valley below eroding slowly downward, flooding up as the ice melted, dropping to a trickle as rock or ice dams cut off the flow from upstream.

If I could focus on this wall of roseroots in a time lapse from twenty thousand years ago to the present, the trees would grow, then die, then grow again, the river would drop from my hips to its current place thirty feet below me, and these plants would persevere. This cliff is their terrarium, their conservatory, their protective bubble of cold.

"I tend to feel Leedy's is a relict," says Joel. By *relict*, he means an ice age leftover, a holdout, a hanger-on. In southeastern Minnesota, the roseroots are lucky enough to be growing on rare geological formations called algific talus slopes. *Algific* means "cold-making." Talus is that rubble at the bottom of rock cliffs. To understand this relict theory, how exactly rocks can be cold-making, and why Leedy's roseroots have such a limited range, we have to look at two aspects of geological time: the formation of the bedrock that is right now inches from my nose, and the reason why there are cliffs in the Midwest.

In central Minnesota, about 160 miles west of the Whitewater, some of the oldest rocks on earth are exposed in the wide valley of the Minnesota River. The roughly 3.6 billion-year-old Morton gneiss is the basement of the continent, some of the earliest volcanic crust spewed upon the earth in the very first days of land creation.

From then until about 600 million years ago—the Precambrian era—
the land that would eventually become the midwestern United States
saw mountain ranges rise to heights rivaling the Himalayas. A deep rift
began to cleave the continent in two (as a rift is now doing to Africa),
then abruptly stopped, leaving a deep valley that became Lake Superior.
Erosion was rampant, as no plants yet existed to hold the soil. The continents moved about, with North America spending millions of years
right on the equator.

At the end of the Precambrian, a low-lying North America (though
of course it had nothing of the shape of today's North America) began
a gradual cycle of rise and fall. This land had highlands and lowlands,
and over time it subsided downward, then rose again as tectonic forces
buffeted its edges. It was as if the land were breathing, slowly and deeply.
And with each exhale, the ocean would wash up over the land. With
each inhale, the sea would retreat and the rains would pound the bare
rock and wash it, grain by grain, into the shallow bays.

A height of land called the Transcontinental Arch reached southwest-
erly from the heavy granite in present-day Canada all the way down into
New Mexico. Southeast of this arch, covering southeastern Minnesota
and extending to the south, was a low spot that remained flooded with
seawater for hundreds of millions of years. This calm shallow arm of the
ocean—not unlike today's Gulf of Mexico—was called the Hollandale
Embayment, after a Minnesota town about fifty miles southwest of the
Whitewater River valley. The formation of rock in this shallow sea over
a very long time created a stack of sandstones, limestones, and dolo-
mites. One layer in this cake is the Shakopee Formation, seventy meters
of mostly dolomite with a prominent band of sandstone near the very
bottom. This is the rock against which Joel propped his ladder and to
which the roseroots cling.

Dolomite is a type of rock formed from the mineral calcite. It's different from the more commonly known limestone. Limestone is pure calcite. Dolomite has been transformed by the replacement of about half
its calcium by magnesium—a process that happens when older limestone is resubmerged in magnesium-rich seawater. Calcite rocks cannot

form without one crucial thing: life. The Cambrian period, which began 541 million years ago, signals the beginning of an explosion of life in the sea. Tiny creatures began to build tiny, hard shells to protect themselves from larger shelled creatures, like fifteen-foot-long cephalopods with shells that tapered to points. When these animals died, their shells fell to the seafloor, piled up, and, over millions of years, became stone.

The dolomite in the Shakopee Formation was created during the early Ordovician period, around 490 million years ago. For the next nearly 400 million years, more rock was deposited on top of the Shakopee as the sea gradually advanced and retreated. Then the area saw a gradual erosion of all that rock during a relatively stable period of approximately 98 million years. Then the first glaciers came.

The cliffs on which the Leedy's roseroot lives are an oddity in the Midwest. The landscape roughly flanking the Mississippi River in south-eastern Minnesota, southwestern Wisconsin, northeastern Iowa, and northwestern Illinois features deeply cut valleys and gorges, few lakes, and plentiful bedrock outcrops. In much of the Upper Midwest, the soils are tens to even hundreds of feet deep, but in this riverine region they cover the rock with the merest blanket of sustenance. Geologists call this the "Driftless Area," referring to the general absence of glacial drift: the rock, sand, soil, and gravel deposited over much of the northern United States during the most recent glaciation. These sixteen thousand square miles in four states were not visited by the four primary glacial advances spanning the roughly two million years of the Pleistocene ice age.

That's not to say the Driftless Area was completely unaffected by the ice age. Surrounded by glaciers, the area's climate was harsh, akin to the northernmost alpine tundra of Canada and Siberia. Cold winds blew incessantly, and meltwater rushed across the landscape. The winds covered the bedrock with a fine dust, picked up from bare soils left by glaciers in retreat. This so-called loess (pronounced "luss") blanketed the landscape like dunes.

So the rock on which the Leedy's roseroots grow was created eons ago in a shallow sea. Then while the rest of the Midwest was being obliterated and buried by glaciers, that rock was mostly left alone, but was cut through by melt-swollen rivers and exposed. And that is the last piece of the Leedy's habitat puzzle. Dolomite is easily dissolved, relatively speaking, by water that is even slightly acid—as most water naturally becomes when it touches soil. Water trickling down into the cracks so common in this stone widens those cracks, sometimes expanding them into caves, sometimes creating sinkholes on the surface. Aerial photographs of southeastern Minnesota look dented, as if a ball peen hammer had been taken to the croplands.

This is called a karst landscape, and it can give rise to algific talus slopes. Water needs a way out once it is done wandering about underground, and it escapes through the faces of the cliffs or through the talus rubble. As these water-made passages widen, they invite air in and work like an air conditioning system. In winter, any warm air in the caves rises upward out of surface sinkholes. This draws cooler river valley air into the caves through the cliff face or talus slope passageways. Water in the caves freezes. In summer, the process is reversed. Cool air drops from the caves into the river valley, sucking more air down into the sinkholes to be cooled by the ice. The dolomite is making cold.

The result is that cool air wafts from the cliffs all summer. Shady river valleys are already usually cooler than the surrounding flatlands, but an algific talus slope is cooler still. It is a little bit of ice age in the middle of the Midwest. Algific talus slopes occur throughout the Driftless Area, usually on north-facing slopes, and are home to plants and animals normally found much farther north, like balsam fir and showy lady's slipper orchid. Also found in these unique habitats are two other species on the endangered list. The northern wild monkshood, a showy purple-flowering perennial, occurs only in the Driftless Area, in Ohio, and (like the Leedy's) in New York. The quarter-inch-long Iowa Pleistocene snail was considered extinct. Fossils of this tiny creature had been found in young rocks, but in 1955 a scientist discovered a snail contentedly eating leaves on a northeastern Iowa algific talus slope.

Though neither the monkshood nor the snail are found in Minnesota (and the Leedy's is not found in Iowa, Wisconsin, or Illinois), all three are completely dependent on the cliffsides of the karst landscape. Their presence together also bolsters Joel's theory about Leedy's being an ice age relict. The snail, the monkshood, the fir, the orchid, and the roseroot most likely did not blow in together from the tundra in the Rockies or the Canadian Arctic. They were here all along, weathering the ice age in the Driftless Area and clinging to those few special spots where summer temperatures stay between 45 and 55 degrees.

Joel envisions a world, sometime during one of the long intervals between glacial advances, when *Rhodiolas* spread out across North America, likely dispersing across the Bering land bridge from the mountains of Asia, where there are fifty species in the genus. They dispersed within the cold, windy tundra, their ranges likely expanding southward as the glaciers grew and retreating back north as the glaciers shrank. In theory, then, at the end of the last glaciation around twelve thousand years ago, *Rhodiolas* growing throughout the Midwest would have expired in the new, hotter environment. But in Minnesota's Driftless Area and New York's Finger Lakes it found an environment that remained ice-age-like. Of course, Joel offers the caveat that this is "not the sort of thing that is easy to conclusively show one way or the other."

Though this limited tolerance makes these species' ultimate survival precarious, it also makes conservation efforts quite straightforward. It is unlikely the range of the Leedy's roseroot, the Pleistocene snail, or the monkshood will expand. We must therefore preserve and protect what we have.

Easy, right? Just buy the land and set it aside.

Unfortunately, just as the land itself creates the perfect, limited environments in which these relics can live, it also links them to the outside world, with all its agriculture and cities and subdivisions. In a karst landscape, water moves underground very quickly, across long distances, and in unpredictable ways. What goes in a sinkhole might come out in a creek miles away. What sinks through farm soil into the dolomite might drip out of the face of a cliff somewhere else. Fertilizers, pesticides, soap from car washing, dog waste, raw sewage: into the ground, through the rock, and onto the algific talus slopes. Leedy's roseroot and its cohorts sit at the center of a vast watershed. They are beneath the funnel into which society pours its waste.

I descend the ladder and Joel and I edge our way downstream to meet Nelson and Brian, stepping gingerly from rock to rock at the river's edge, and often through the fringes of the North Fork itself. Joel has left the ladder behind, since the other Leedy's sites are accessible by walking atop much bigger talus slopes. It was a wet spring, with much flooding throughout the Upper Midwest and soon we encounter a muddy flume stretching from the top of the cliff all the way down to the river. There is no water in it now, but it is quite recent.

"These are some of the hazards of being a plant on the cliff face " Joel says, understating the obvious. A fan of soil crosses our path, and chunks of rock with bright faces freshly cleaved from the cliff rest at uncomfortable angles on the talus slope and in the water. "Obviously this has gotten wet and pulled away."

Though there aren't any roseroots right here, this channel is nevertheless a dramatic lesson. Joel reminds me of the gravel road above along which we parked our cars. "That road runs right along the cliff top here. I've been gently prodding the DNR to see if they couldn't do something, but somehow they don't seem to think that they politically can. But that seems to me to be something that is sending more wash over the edges here."

Joel chooses his words carefully. He has ongoing relationships with the DNR managers here and the three private owners—relationships that are important to his work. He also has not officially studied whether that road, or any other road, increases cliff-face erosion.

I can speak more directly. Historically, forests and grasslands would have buffered the cliff edge, just like they would have buffered prairie streams in which live endangered Topeka shiners, or major rivers that are home to five species of endangered freshwater mussels, or moist prairie wetlands where the endangered western prairie fringed orchid thrives. One of the private Leedy's owners actually removed a bluff-top farm road, replanted prairie, and slapped a conservation easement on the whole thing. Another—one "suspicious" of Joel's work, who has not permitted access—has no vegetation above his cliff. His population of Leedy's is the smallest.

Soon I find that getting to the roseroots, physically, can be even more precarious than climbing a ladder propped against a cliff. Joel and I scramble above the river on a trail no wider than my two feet side by side. We are on the top of the talus slope, which here rises at more than a forty-five-degree angle up from the river to the cliff face. The reddish sandstone, so notable at the first site, is completely buried. The slope is covered with shrubs and trees, for which I am thankful, because we have climbed about fifty feet above the river at this point, catwalking between the steep slope and the vertical stone wall. There isn't much room to move around. We encounter Nelson and Brian, who have been recording tagged roseroots on the exposed section of the dolomite. They're a little stumped, because some of the tagged plants are way beyond their reach.

"I don't know how you tagged those," says Brian, "unless you have Inspector Gadget arms."

"I'm Spiderman," says Joel, smiling (and offering no actual explanation for the high tags). There are lots of roseroots, and Joel tells me to get comfortable, because we'll be here a while. He climbs as high as the little ridge will go, braces himself against the cliff, and starts calling out data to Nelson. WW0807: three stems, one inflorescence, four flowers, male. 238: one stem, one inflorescence, male. WW0808: forty-six (!) stems, one inflorescence, male. Joel does move a little like Spiderman. He has one leg on the ground (that is, the top of the talus slope), another on a tiny rock ledge, an arm splayed backward, and the other arm pawing the roseroots. Brian gets in on the act, ascending like a rock climber and plastering his body against the slope.

The first one he finds, 213, has four inflorescences. That brings out another important piece of scientific equipment: the List of Random Numbers. It would be inefficient and time consuming to count the number of flowers on every inflorescence (imagine if the forty-six-stem big boy were really flowering), so Joel and his team randomly select three inflorescences to count. To eliminate any deliberate or unintentional bias (at the end of a long day, wouldn't you pick the one with the fewest things to count?), they generate a list of random numbers, one through ten, printed out in neat columns on a piece of white paper. Joel looks at the first number on the list. Brian counts the inflorescences aloud, starting over with the first one (but continuing to count up) when he has counted them all. When he reaches Joel's number, Joel stops him. That's the inflorescence for which he counts the flowers. When that one's done, he counts again, skipping the inflorescence he just counted. Joel stops him when he reaches the second number on the random list. Once used, a random number is crossed off, so the entire counting day is randomized.

Because Brian doesn't know which number he's counting to, and because Joel can't see which inflorescence Brian is on, this system creates a truly random selection—it's double blind. Such randomization is necessary for statistical analysis, and Joel must document that he used this (or a similar) technique when he writes papers for publication. It wouldn't be so bad to count all four of 213's inflorescences, but Brian's next find, 212, has seventeen (though randomization doesn't save him from having to—or perhaps it ensures he must—count the inflorescence with twenty-eight flowers, the highest of the day).

As the counting continues, this wall becomes a bit peculiar. WW0807, 238, 213, 212, 211, WW0104: all male. Many of them are flowering, but perhaps in vain. (208 has given up entirely. All that's left is a tag around a dried root. "We don't need to follow that one anymore," says Joel.) Again I am reminded of population dynamics. This cliff face is Edenic. It is clearly isolated—that is, protected—and full of roseroots. A casual observer (like me) would be thrilled at this find. However, based on what we have counted so far, there is no possibility of a next generation here.

But then, Brian finds a couple of untagged specimens, close together, one on top of the other. Joel creates new numbers for his book. WW1103 is male. It sports a modest two stems, but both have inflorescences, with a total of eighteen flowers. A good showing. WW1102 is female. Joel and the students remain sedate and businesslike, but their spirits seem to lift, just slightly. This lady also has eighteen flowers.

"Is there filled seed in it?" asks Joel. He directs Brian to pull off a single flower and pass it to him for examination. The flowers are tiny, about the size of a rice grain, and the seeds are smaller still. Joel pulls the flower apart with practiced fingers and announces that yes, there are filled seeds. I would hope so. WW1103 is mere inches away, and this female roseroot is in the middle of a whole colony of flowering males.

Brian collects one-half of WW1102's seeds. The seeds are the color of milk chocolate. Joel tells me that under a microscope minute ridges and wings are visible. He believes these allow the seeds to waft on drafts rising from the river. Leedy's roseroot can likely colonize upward, which makes sense. If the seeds only fell, the general location of these plants would descend the cliff from generation to generation, but from where we stand we can see roseroots quite near the top of the cliff, clinging to tiny cracks and fissures like their nearby brethren.

This seed collection is allowed only because Joel has a permit from the Minnesota DNR for scientific study. Without such a permit, it would be illegal under federal law to alter or disrupt these plants in any way, or to take any plant, in part or in whole. Over the years Joel has also taken leaves and brought them back to his laboratory for genetic analysis.

The science building at Northeastern Illinois University is a Brutalist hulk of concrete and brick, set at an odd angle to the rest of the gridded campus on Chicago's north side. It looks like an abstract erratic, dropped in place from glacial heights. Or an eroded cliff face, with strata of different stone types exposed. Even the interior reminds me of the southeastern Minnesota karst landscape. Concrete ramps with concrete walls switchback up through a central atrium and link lecture halls entered through dim, close openings. The faculty offices are stacked in quads that hang off the main hallways like suspended rocks about to become talus. Narrow stairways descend to one pair and rise to another sitting directly above. As I follow Joel to his office the February after cataloging roseroots with him in Minnesota, I can't escape the feeling that I am moving deeper into a cave, into the dissolved insides of a mass of dolomite. The passages narrow from the grand ramp to the hallways in the office wings to the little stairways and catwalks that lead to Joel's tiny office. One vertical slit of a window looks out on the flat greensward about thirty feet below.

I visit Joel here to learn about genetics. Joel has spent years considering whether *Rhodiola integrifolia* ssp. *leedyi* is due for another name change. "The work I've been doing," Joel explains at the beginning of our conversation, "suggests that Leedy's is a separate species." That work includes two very different undertakings: the collection of tissue samples from all North American *Rhodiolas* ("I have traveled thousands of miles to obtain samples," says Joel) and the laboratory analysis of the *Rhodiola* genome. The first means days on cliffsides in the rain and wind. The second means walking down the hall to the university's genetics lab, which we do, and Joel explains his process to me.

Unlike the taxonomy of Linnaeus and the early describers of Leedy's today's taxonomy peers deep into a specimen's DNA, sequences its nucleotides (designated with the letters A, C, G, and T), and compares different specimens in a computer database. Joel doesn't have to sequence the entire genome, however. Vast amounts of any living creature's DNA are exactly the same as many other more distantly related creatures (humans, for instance, share about 99 percent of our DNA with chimpanzees), and other portions vary from individual to individual, governing things like leaf thickness and length, the number of stems, and whether an individual is male or female. "We are looking for a region of DNA," explains Joel, "variable enough to be informative" but not so variable that it may differ from plant to plant within a population. The basic idea is to find the differences in DNA (if there are any) between multiple individuals at different Leedy's sites and at different *Rhodiola* sites across the continent.

Specifically, Joel and his students have been looking at DNA from the cell nuclei and from the plant's chloroplasts. Most of this work is done chemically, and the first thing that greets us as we enter the lab is a home refrigerator–sized deep freeze unit full of various enzymes and other chemicals. The freezer is choked with frost; again I am reminded of an algific dolomite cave. The lab is no bigger than a kitchen.

In order to get enough DNA to sequence, scientists have to, essentially, run a copy machine. Once the target DNA is extracted (by smashing the plant tissues and then squirting them with various salts and detergents), it goes into a thermal cycler. This machine—located just across the hall in a separate laboratory—incubates the DNA in an enzyme soup by raising and lowering the temperature of the solution rapidly, thirty-five times. Each temperature change triggers the enzyme to copy a targeted portion of the DNA. It splits open the DNA like a zipper and corrals all the random nucleotides floating around in the soup, arranging them according to the original pattern. This is how all life works: pattern on one side, enzyme fluid choked with nucleotides, organization according to the pattern.

After this step (the "polymerase chain reaction"), Joel has enough of his target DNA to actually test it. This stuff is miniscule. Sections of countertops in the lab are devoted to racks of pipettes, turkey baster–like tools that measure in fractions of microliters (a raindrop, incidentally, is about 20 microliters). First, he tests for purity. To do this he uses a gel electrophoresis box, a small plastic tray with trapezoidal black sides. Joel mixes a type of special gel, pours it into the tray, and lets it harden (a process he describes as very much like making Jell-O). A plastic comb makes a number of small pits at one end of the gel, into which DNA samples are placed. DNA has a negative charge, so the whole box is put into a machine that generates an electrical charge, and the DNA moves across the gel from one side of the box to the other, pushed by the charge because of differences in polarity.

This gel is thick, and DNA molecules have certain masses. Depending on how heavy they are, the molecules can move only so far across the gel until they get, essentially, stuck in the mud. To visualize it, imagine exactly that: a patch of muddy ground, and you are standing at the edge with a variety of balls—ping-pong ball, golf ball, baseball, bowling ball. Roll each ball across the mud with exactly the same arm strength, and the ping-pong ball will travel the farthest from you. The bowling ball may very well stay right at your feet.

What matters with the DNA purity test is not how far the balls travel, but whether all the balls are the same. If there were more than one snippet of DNA involved in the polymerase chain reaction, many copies of each snippet would be in the resultant solution. It would be like having a million baseballs and a million and a half bowling balls—except you can't actually see which balls are which, nor sort them by hand. If Joel is sequencing a baseball, he wants no bowling balls at all in the mix. He wants all the resting places of all the balls to be the same distance from where you rolled them. In the electrophoresis box, a pure sample will show up as a single line across the gel. An impure sample will show a long smear, as many different DNA molecules get stuck at various points in the gel. An impure sample means back to step one: extraction. When Joel gets a pure sample it is sent to a commercial lab, which can return the DNA sequence, letter by letter, within twenty-four hours for about three dollars per test—and deliver the results to Joel's email inbox.

Joel shows me what looks like an Excel spreadsheet on his computer screen. "For example, here I've got a Leedy's roseroot from Minnesota, and we've laid that next to something from New York, then we've set that next to some of the western subspecies, and we ask is that the same?" Most squares, each with a letter inside it, are black. White highlights some difference in the sequence between any of the specimens. A total at the bottom of each column shows how different the various specimens are.

Put simplistically, if most Leedy's specimens have little difference in their DNA sequence but differ markedly from another population, that suggests these are different species.

So what's the verdict? Is Leedy's a separate species? Joel initially thought it was, and submitted a paper to that effect. Upon peer review, however, the theory fell short of some desired thresholds. Joel had been sequencing two DNA regions and other taxonomists wanted a third. They also wanted a broader range of Leedy's roseroot's close relatives sampled. In the midst of that additional sequencing and sampling arose a twist in this family history.

One day, Joel happened to be browsing some of the online government gene banks. As scientists everywhere sequence the DNA of living creatures from horseshoe crabs to pine trees to elephants, they often post these raw sequences for public view, primarily so scientists can use them for other comparative research. Joel was surprised to find sequences posted from another *Rhodiola* subspecies in Canada (*R. integrifolia* ssp. *integrifolia*, or, commonly, king's crown). He had never seen any roseroot postings other than his own before—such an obscure species, an obscure line of work. He ran some comparisons. "These were rather surprisingly close to Leedy's," Joel tells me, with a mix of shock and curiosity. The results turned all of Joel's thinking on its head. Suddenly, he began to wonder not whether Leedy's was a separate species, but what other *Rhodiolas* it was really related to. He went back into the field with students on a collecting trip across the Great Plains and up the Rockies. He secured permits to snip leaves from Leedy's to bring back for genetic analysis. One of his students procured preserved king's crown tissues from Alaska and Russian Siberia.

His first stop was the Black Hills of South Dakota, where a small population of the western ssp. *integrifolia* huddled near the cold summit of Harney Peak, now known as Black Elk Peak. "We imagined we were getting more [samples of] western Rhodiola," Joel tells me by phone years after my visit to his Chicago office, "but we got there and said, 'Wow, this looks like Leedy's.'" Returning home after the trip, Joel and his students sequenced the Black Hills *Rhodiola*, and it looked a lot like Leedy's genetically, too. So another outpost population of this threatened species has been found—hidden in plain sight because everyone thought it was the western subspecies.

But that's not all. In this new study, Joel was able to get roseroot genetic data from up and down the Rockies and even into Siberia, some through his own collecting and some through collaborations with other botanists. He found distinct differences between roseroots in the southern

Rockies (the American portion, roughly) and the northern Rockies and Alaska, the latter ones being much more similar to Siberian specimens. Leedy's appears to be far more closely related to the northern (Arctic) version than to the *Rhodiolas* in the southern Rockies.

In 2014 Joel published these findings in the journal *Botany*. This time the peer reviewers agreed with his theory. Previously, all the western *Rhodiolas* were considered one big subspecies (*integrifolia*), and Leedy's was a separate outlier. But now it looks like there might be two separate western species—an Arctic and a southern Rockies—with Leedy's being a subspecies of the Arctic one. "There's a very deep split there," between the two western types, Joel says. He believes Leedy's is still a separate subspecies. The conditions in the Arctic and in Minnesota and New York are just too different for the plants growing there to be interchangeable. But those distinctions are nuanced.

"What we're trying to do when we name species," says Joel. "is we're trying to put things into specific boxes because humans like to do that. It's a judgment call. We're trying to put something in a category that varies along a continuum. How far along a branch of the tree of life do you have to be before you're a separate species?"

After our tour of his lab, Joel and I walk through his neighborhood to a restaurant he likes. I can't help but notice that he, too, has a small and specialized habitat: his university job, his home. and his church are all within a five-minute walk of each other. Following some time teaching in Minnesota after earning his PhD, he and his wife decided to settle where they did because the small area met all their needs. They have two children, one of whom attended a different nearby university. These few blocks are Joel's and his family's perfect microclimate.

As we walk I ask him the question I ask all the rare species scientists I talk with: why does this little thing matter? Most often, the reasons fall into one of three categories: religious, biological, or beneficial. The religious reason features the classic "God put it here so we must preserve it, as stewards of His creation," or some similar iteration. The biological reason is promoted by scientists who believe in preservation for preservation's sake, simply: it is and therefore should continue to be. The beneficial reason is usually pharmacological: there might be medicine in there!

In our earlier conversations, Joel had touched on the biological and the beneficial. He also has a practical reason for studying the roseroot that doesn't have much to do with the fact that it is rare. He likes that his students get to contribute to basic scientific knowledge. These are undergraduates, after all, and they write credible scientific papers that broach new knowledge about a little-known species. It's basic science, for sure, but the lack of competitiveness (they're not studying wolves, for example, or humans) means they can learn the basics and still discover new information in an environment primarily focused on learning rather than on great breakthroughs.

With regard to the importance of the species itself, and its threatened status, Joel admits, "It's not one of the major conservation questions of our time. It's a really sweet little story, interesting distribution, interesting microhabitat, but we're not going to set national policy based on this alone." That's a refreshing and honest perspective. I question him on the hard reality that both in-field study and associated molecular study have found that the effective population size is only about 10 to 20 percent, not atypical for a listed species, but low, in general, for vital populations. Isn't Leedy's perhaps destined for extinction, I ask, especially considering its limited habitat, its failure as a breeder, and its likely status as a relict from a former age?

"At this point in their evolutionary history," Joel corrects, "they don't reproduce well." He suggests that Leedy's may be a species still in its infancy, and that we cannot know whether it will die out or become the next millennium's dominant plant. The same could be true, he says, for the prairie bush clover, the dwarf trout lily, and any other endangered species. This is a completely new idea for me. I had always pictured endangered species as being in decline, but here Joel was saying they may be on their way to success. After all, mammals looked doomed to fail when they first scurried about under the feet of the dinosaurs. And humans were a small offshoot of a thriving hominid family—an offshoot that reproduced very poorly because its infants had such big heads and were so completely helpless at birth. Had we peeked in on humans during one fifty-year timeframe way back then, we might have listed them as endangered.

However, the reasons Leedy's is threatened have nothing to do with the natural order of things. Joel is comfortable with the idea of extinction in general, but not with one species' responsibility for the extinction of another. Pesticides, deforestation of bluff edges, and climate change itself are threatening Leedy's populations. We humans are modifying the evolutionary timeline, not just of Leedy's but of hundreds, thousands of species. That, says Joel, is unacceptable. "Who are we to squish whatever has been brought forth?" he asks.

If that statement sounds like it has religious undertones, it most certainly does. Joel is a devout member of the Evangelical Covenant Church, a Christian congregation that, according to its own literature, affirms the Bible as the only true word of God. Joel's affirmation of evolution, therefore, puts him slightly at odds with his church (though Covenant also believes in "freedom in Christ") and wholly at odds with the prevailing "Bible is true" philosophy of most of today's evangelical churches. Some years ago he wrote a paper for the church's magazine in which he argued that belief in God and an acceptance of evolutionary theory are compatible. The congregation was split on the matter, with some considering the paper to be tantamount to sacrilege.

"I am good with creation *and* evolution," he explains. "I would say that God created through the process of evolution, but nevertheless this earth is a gift to us and its pieces are gifts to us—whether you're looking at the machinery that was used to put it together, or the perhaps more poetic or literal (in some people's belief systems) idea that this all was created as a potter makes a pot and plopped down here."

In either case, he says, we need to guard the "evolutionary potential" of what's here. Joel believes there should be no disconnect between devout Christians who interpret the Bible literally (seven-day creationists) and scientists. "A seven-day creationist ought to value all of the pieces of creation as a gift from God that should be lovingly stewarded," he says.

One outcome of that belief, according to Joel, could be someone protecting Leedy's populations by buying land—something the scientists
are also advocating. Whether one believes in the Garden of Eden, in all
its literal verdancy, and the idea that everything present now on earth
was present there in that garden, or whether one believes this is all just
chemicals and random chance, Joel argues that the moral imperative—
to be good stewards—is the same. And that the situation is critical.

"In terms of conservation," says Joel, his voice serious and low, "we
should be very concerned about this species winking out."

And that would be, what? Sin? A desecration of creation? A turning
away from God? Or, less loftily, a poor commentary on a certain big-
brained bipedal species?

Joel, Brian, Nelson, and I, still in our bicycle helmets, amble farther
downstream on the narrow talus trail. Ferns brush our heads and the
river whispers below. Brian, at the head of the line, finds an old metal
tag looped to a Leedy's root about hip high on the cliff face.

"Let's see," says Joel, crouching to peer at the plant. "WW6. Do we
have that one?"

Nelson looks in the field book for that name. "Nope. I don't have
anything like that in here."

"Okay. Let's see," Joel repeats, obviously a little puzzled, or perhaps
touched. "This is one that I did DNA fingerprinting on for my thesis
work. This is one that I sampled in 1993." He points to the bottom of
the list of names in the field book Nelson is holding. "In that space at
the end there, if you could write down a few notes: First labeled 6-18-93.
And it's just hanging by a few threads."

Joel reaches out to touch the plant as he says this, cradles it in his hand.
A long pause is filled only by the river and the windblown trees. It's not
scientific to say this, I know, and perhaps I am still in a ruminative mood,
but I can only describe this moment as affectionate. Most ecological or
biological study involves populations, statistical analysis, extrapolation.
The individual rarely matters. But all the Leedy's roseroots we have
bothered with today, exactly thirty-two so far, have names—odd names,

to be sure, but names. They have their own lines in Joel's orange book, and personalized data sheets on Joel's computer in Chicago. Joel knows the detailed life histories of F3 and WW101 and 211 and all the others. True, in his scientific work, these individuals are statistically subsumed into the overall dynamic of the population, but all day long we have been, as Joel said early on, getting up close and personal. Getting personal with a perennial plant.

As Joel holds this one roseroot, I suppose he is being flooded with memories—memories of nearly two decades of coming here, counting the plants, counting their stems, inflorescences, and flowers, collecting their seeds and leaves. He has devoted a career to an obscure plant that feels almost hopelessly outmatched by pollution, a precarious living arrangement, mostly unsuccessful reproduction and the very climate. And here, at the edge of its habitat, with the steep cliff face petering out just around the next bend: WW6, at least eighteen years old, a bookend to Joel's time on these cliffs.

Brian has walked ahead, and Joel calls to him to ask if he sees any more. A few, he says, but small and without inflorescences.

"Well," says Joel, "we're at the end of the line. I think we should head back."

Prairie bush clover

5

Bush Clover

James Nowlin stands in chest-high prairie grass, facing due north. Chest-high prairie grass stretches away as far as he can see in every direction, except for a few scraggly willows in the valley of the Cottonwood River. Five other men stand near him, complaining of the heat, perhaps, or reminiscing about home. The six are about to walk due north, in a straight line, for exactly one mile. They are surveyors for the General Land Office of Minnesota, and they have been out here on the prairie for a few weeks now. It is July 29, 1858. They are here in the midst of the twelve-year-long eviction—through broken treaties, forced dependency, and war—of the land's former inhabitants, the Dakota. They are here to map the land so it can be given to white immigrants flooding across the prairies in search of farmland.

The compassman, Edwin Kilborn, takes a final reading. One of the chainmen, the hindman, either George Fisher or Henry Raymond, holds one end of the survey chain, and the rest of the party starts walking. Ira Crum and Joseph Vanace, the axmen, lead the way, but there's little for them to do on the open plains. The chain measures exactly sixty-six feet long and is composed of one hundred links, each exactly 7.92 inches. When the crew reaches the end of the chain, they stop, pull the chain tight, and set a tally peg. The hindman begins walking north, soon arriving where the lead chainman and the rest of the group stands. Edwin takes another compass reading and the group heads north again, leaving the hindman behind. They reach the end of the chain again, set another tally peg, and repeat the process.

The crew's work is detailed and repetitive and mandated by law—specifically, the Land Ordinance of 1785, an unprecedented delineation of millions of acres that allowed for the movement of Europeans into the western United States and all but eliminated one of the world's great natural landscapes. James and his men lead and follow like this forty times, which gets them exactly one-half mile. At this point, while the hindman catches up, Ira and Joseph the axmen dig a few trenches into the prairie soil. That's tough work, because the earth is more root than dirt: these prairie soils, thickened with hundreds of species of deep-rooted flowering plants and grasses, have been building for thousands of years. The big bluestem that tickles the surveyors' chins has roots that plunge up to twelve feet into the earth. Ira and Joseph pile the excavated soil into a small mound and set a wooden post into it. They're sweating in the prairie summer, with no shade to be found.

Another forty chain lengths and again they pause to dig trenches, build a mound, and set a stake. James opens his red leather surveyor's book, the three-inch-by-five-inch tome that he guards carefully to protect it from rain and snow and rushing rivers. It is the only record of the crew's work. It and the wooden stakes will become official legal documents, the boundaries of parcels for sale by the federal government in this part of southwestern Minnesota. James found no landscape features of note along this northerly mile—no bodies of water, no marshes, no settlements, no wagon roads or Indian trails—so he notes nothing but the post his crew set at forty lengths and this, the corner of sections 25, 26, 35, and 36 of Township 109 North of Range 35 West of the 5th Principal Meridian.

The crew is making good time through this treeless country. They have probably heard horror stories of their colleagues hacking their way through the bogs of northern Michigan and the "laurel hell" of the western slope of the Appalachians, places where surveyors could advance as little as a single chain (sixty-six feet) per day. James's crew has been covering about six miles per day before camping for the night. They will finish this township—thirty-six square miles—by mid-September.

While the men set the post, James scans the landscape the crew has just crossed and writes, in exuberantly looping script: "Land is slightly rolling. Soil first rate quality."

I am reading James Nowlin's survey notes not out on the great American prairie, but indoors, in downtown St. Paul, at the Minnesota Historical Society's reference library. Moments ago, a young librarian delivered to me a cart with a banker's box full of little manila sleeves. I unfolded one like a Christmas gift to reveal James's red book, cinched delicately by a white length of string tied with a dainty bow. As I leaf through these 150-year-old pages, I notice both a mind-numbing repetition—each placement of a stake is described exactly the same way—and an elegant simplicity to the prose.

"Soil first rate quality" appears frequently in the description of the six-mile-by-six-mile piece of the Louisiana Purchase originally and officially called Township 109 Range 35. Today it is known as North Star Township, and it sits at the far western edge of Brown County, Minnesota. I am reading these notes because I want to get a sense of how much the prairie has changed in the last century and a half. A few months before, I walked in James Nowlin's footsteps on a survey of my own. I was in search of the prairie bush clover, one of the many prairie plants James may very well have seen but not recognized, one of many never mentioned in his survey book, concerned as he was with the straight edges of the big picture frame, not the intricacies of a strange landscape.

I went to a place in Section 33, three miles west of James's starting point, called Cottonwood River Prairie Scientific and Natural Area. In 1858 this was prairie with some fairly steep topography. As the crew followed the eastern line of the 160-acre Section 33, they mucked through marshes, dropped down into a river bottomland, set their quarter-section stake practically on the bank of the Cottonwood River, then rose back onto the highlands. Along the western section line the crew crossed the Cottonwood and two of its tributaries. James wrote: "Land is hilly in the center of the section. The balance level and first rate quality of soil."

The prairie landscape at Cottonwood River Prairie SNA, 2010

That soil, which James and hundreds of other surveyors found as they fanned out across Arkansas, Iowa, Missouri, Minnesota, and the Dakotas as part of the 5th Meridian survey, would feed the world. Its sale, in perfectly square sections and quarter sections, brought cash to this young, strapped nation. It became the literal foundation of the Heartland, a mythical place that still today drives political thinking and rhetoric—a mythical place that has all but erased indigenous people from the landscape.

Although men could plow the prairie, as they have done across the entire Louisiana Purchase, they could not move the hills in the center of Section 33, nor farm them very well. That is why the prairie bush clover (*Lespedeza leptostachya*), a federally endangered species, can be found here and in places like this—the rare acres not touched by plow.

Section 33 is square; it is one of millions of squares that march across the Midwest, hardly breaking their rhythm even for rivers and lakes.

This creates a landscape unlike any other in the world. It's so organized, legible, easily navigable, boring, some say. For this, thanks is due Thomas Jefferson, an architect by avocation, a scholar by background, an inventor by nature. Jefferson's father was involved in early surveys of some of Virginia's large estates, and the younger Jefferson was fascinated throughout his life with architectural and mathematical regularity. When he became Virginia's delegate to the fledgling Continental Congress in 1783, he began to consider several critical measurement issues facing the newly independent republic. He proposed three things: a common currency called the dollar, the vacation of the eastern states' claims to the Northwest Territory (the land between the Appalachian Mountains and the Mississippi River, won from Britain in the 1783 Treaty of Paris—notwithstanding its current inhabitants) and a process for surveying and measuring all that newly claimed land.

In 1785 Congress declared the dollar as the exclusive currency of the new nation and also passed the aforementioned Land Ordinance, which called for surveyors to "proceed to divide the [Northwest Territory] into townships of six miles square, by lines running due north and south, and others crossing these at right angles. . . . The lines shall be measured with a chain; shall be plainly marked . . . and exactly described on a plat." (Though it took some years, Jefferson did eventually convince the eastern states to give up their claims to the Northwest Territory, paving the way for the creation of new states like Michigan, Indiana, and Illinois.)

To understand the groundbreaking nature of the Land Ordinance (sometimes called the Northwest Ordinance), it is important to understand how things were measured before the 1800s. Surprisingly, weights and measures once varied from place to place, changed depending on whether a commodity was being bought or sold, and were almost always designed to benefit those higher up on the social ladder. A bushel of vegetables, say, was always the same price, but not always the same size. This variability was also true of land measurement. An *acre* originally referred to how much land a farmer could work in a day, so it varied in size from place to place, depending on the toughness of the soil, the presence of rocks and trees, and steepness. This type of measurement required long tenancy on the land and eliminated the possibility of land as a commodity, since nothing could be bought or sold without extensive research and understanding of the terrain.

In the Northwest Territory, the land had never been worked, so there was really no way to measure it in the conventional practice of the time. Certainly surveys were performed, both in Europe and in the original American colonies, but they relied on a "metes and bounds" system. Describing property by metes and bounds is like standing in the middle of it and pointing out landmarks, as if someone said, "I'll take everything on this side of those three big oaks, down to the creek over there, and all the way up to that big gray rock near the top of that hill." The problem, of course, is that the oaks can die, the creek can cut a new course, and the rock can be moved in the middle of the night by unscrupulous neighbors. It's also nearly impossible for anyone to easily measure the area of the irregular parcels created by this system. Even with the standardization of the acre, it takes some mathematical backflips to calculate the area of an irregular multi-sided shape. An ordinal system like the one Jefferson proposed largely ignores the landscape. It resists the temptation to go just a little farther north to the edge of the river, to give that bit on the other side of the lake to the next section, to put the line at the top of the ridge instead of just beyond.

The same year the Land Ordinance was passed, the first survey crew set out to mark the very first east-west line, beginning where the western boundary of Pennsylvania met the Ohio River. By all accounts, this first survey was an abject failure. The lines weren't straight; members of the party, working for land speculators, fudged distances; and after two years only about seventy townships were surveyed, a mere 0.2 percent of the Northwest Territory. And to make matters worse, no one bought the land, not even the speculators. The survey was abandoned.

Then, in 1803, President Thomas Jefferson bought the vast Louisiana Territory from France. This created three more big problems for the fledgling nation: the United States ended up with even more unmeasured

land, the contents of which were entirely unknown to the new nation—
though these lands were occupied and well understood by the various
indigenous tribes that lived there; the nation was nearly bankrupt from
the Revolutionary War, previous failed surveys, and the Louisiana Purchase itself (the latter a fact not lost on the press and Jefferson's detractors); and this new free democracy was attracting more and more
people, who were crowding the already cramped coastal plain between
the Appalachians and the Atlantic. The solution: restart the survey, apply
it to the new territory, and while at that, include the unsurveyed parts
of the Northwest Territory (Illinois, Indiana, and Michigan), as well.

The Public Land Survey is fractal; it begins at state-sized scale and
narrows down to the smallest unit, the quarter section. When James
Nowlin's crew placed their wooden post after one-half mile, they were
noting the finest level of the survey's detail; and that post's exact position had been determined by different survey crews delineating ever
smaller boxes on the landscape. The largest tracts of the survey are
organized around a north-south Principal Meridian and an east-west
Baseline: the crossing axes, the origin of the graph. The 3rd Principal
Meridian runs the length of Illinois and organizes most of the section
squares in that state. The 4th takes care of Wisconsin and parts of Illinois
and Minnesota. The 5th and 6th together handle most of the Great Plains
states. Many western states, like New Mexico, Utah, and Idaho, have their
own meridians, while some, like California and Nevada, share one.

Surveyors began at the intersections of meridians and baselines (so-
called "initial points") and surveyed those lines. Then they surveyed other
vertical and horizontal lines called guide meridians and standard parallels, which are between twenty-four and thirty miles apart. Next came
the township lines, which run in both directions six miles apart. Each
thirty-six-square-mile township was given a numerical code referencing
its distance from the initial point. When I visited North Star Township,
its official identifying numbers told me I was 109 townships (or 654
miles) north of the baseline (which happens to run through the center

of Arkansas), and 35 ranges (or 210 miles) west of the 5th Principal Meridian, which doesn't actually touch Minnesota (the line runs too far east).

Once the township lines were surveyed and all corners marked in the
field—this had been done for 109 North 35 West by another surveyor
named Jacob Myers the autumn before James Nowlin's crew appeared—
the way was open for groups like James's to do the more detailed work
of marking the corners of every 160-acre quarter section and describing
the landscape. And then, because an acre was always an acre and a section was always a section, the land could be sold sight unseen.

The United States bought the Louisiana Territory in 1803 for $15 mil-
lion—less than three cents per acre. In 1864, when land started selling
in North Star Township, the going rate was around $1.25 per acre. By
the 1880s, the price had risen to around two dollars (though by that time
Americans could also homestead the land, meaning they could farm it
for five years, then own it free and clear, so not all the land was actually
sold). Acre for acre, the land value increased a whopping 6,600 percent
in eighty years. In 2015 the median going price for Minnesota farmland
was $4,600 per acre (153,000 times more than the 1803 price).

Though the land value increase was great, the scale of the survey
undertaking was truly mind-boggling. The Louisiana Purchase alone
included 828,800 square-mile sections. The Northwest Territory had
another 260,000. Even at prairie pace, that's about 540,000 survey days.
It would have taken one crew nearly fifteen hundred years to complete
it all.

Strangely, despite its inherent focus on the landscape and the fact that
it was undertaken on foot, the Public Land Survey taught people to
ignore the landscape. Its perfect lines and easily described parcels put
less emphasis on the nuances of slope, wetness, and forest cover than on
acreage. And that's where the story of the prairie bush clover begins
to end. Between the 1860s and the 1930s, more than 99 percent of the
750 million acres of native prairie in the United States was converted to
cropland. There used to be about half as much tall-, medium-, and short-
grass prairie as there is Amazon rainforest today. Imagine even half of the
Amazon rainforest gone. That would be considered an environmental

catastrophe. But the prairie went under the plow rapidly and without anyone suggesting any kind of preservation.

The prairie bush clover is endangered, and so is the prairie itself.

Shelley Olson is an amateur photographer. "I love to come out here on my own time and take pictures," she tells me gazing wistfully at the waving grasses of Jeffers Petroglyphs historic site. Shelley is a guide here, and through her photography she taught herself to recognize different prairie plants. She staffs the visitor center and takes people on tours of the site's namesake, a collection of rock carvings, some of which are seven thousand years old. Shelley has the bright smile and soft form of the farmer's daughter and small-town mother that she is. Her auburn hair flips in the prairie wind, making her look as glamorous as if she were piloting a convertible. Her photo albums sit behind the front desk, populated with prairie denizens: leadplant and wolfberry, blazing star, red clover, showy goldenrod and Canada goldenrod, big bluestem, little bluestem, Indian grass, sideoats grama grass, aster and pasqueflower, round-headed bush clover, prairie bush clover.

Half of Jeffers's eighty acres—half a quarter section—have never been plowed. The rock rises up here like a russet whale breaking the surface of the sea. It's hard Sioux Quartzite: the eastern end of a million-year-old magma upwelling that is quarried for building stone in South Dakota, topped with wind turbines in far southwestern Minnesota, crushed for gravel just across the road to the west, but preserved here, considered sacred to the Dakota, the Ioway, the Otoe people. This land is two Public Land Survey townships directly south of North Star Township. At almost exactly the same time James Nowlin was running his chains, this land was being described by another crew led by John Bruniun. John made no mention of the quartzite. He called this first-rate soil, which it isn't.

Patches of bare rock draw streaks across this land, and the meager grasses grow in shallow soil underlain by that same rock. Or the soil is too wet because rainwater can't percolate into the earth, again because of the rock. The earliest European owners of this land probably noticed the carvings but likely didn't particularly care about them. They left the

A petroglyph at Jeffers Petroglyphs historic site, 2010

land alone. Decades later archaeologists began to study the petroglyphs. In 1966 the state bought the land.

The portion Shelley and I are standing in was plowed. The soil here is deeper, better, first-rate quality. It used to grow corn. But in the 1970s the state tore out the stalks, tilled up the land, and seeded one of the first prairie restorations. Prairie bush clover was not part of that original seed mix, but Shelley casually points it out to me. A few dozen plants are growing just feet from the trail. Once the tilling stopped and the native grasses and flowers took over, the prairie bush clovers came back on their own.

We walk out into the prairie—not chest-high grasses, because the big bluestem hasn't yet begun to flower here, but a textural knee-high pool of stiff gray leadplant, bright goldenrod, thick-leaved mountain mint, and two kinds of bush clover: round-headed (*Lespedeza capitata*) and prairie. Bush clovers are spindly, hip-high sentinels at this time of year.

Their single stalks rise straight from the ground, with the leaves and flower heads becoming weightier as they ascend. They are top-heavy; they bend in the wind.

I easily spot the round-headed bush clover, the more common of the two. Its flower clusters are cat paws, fuzzy and tan, like bits of teddy bear. Its wide green leaves are arranged in familiar shamrock triads all along the single stem. The prairie bush clover, the rare one, is also the more delicate. Its flowers are hardly noticeable and its leaves are narrow, still arranged in groups of three, but more silver than green. Several short arms sprout from the main plant. Only on close inspection do the tiny flowers become apparent: white funnels with pink throats, each no bigger than a pea. They are loosely spaced and casually arranged, so unlike the furry masses of its cousin. The two bear only a passing family resemblance. The round-headed bush clover is the athlete, the letterman, the football captain, while the prairie bush clover is the ballet dancer.

Shelley heads back inside the visitor center and leaves me to contemplate the prairie on my own. The wind is up and wafts across the landscape like gusts on a small lake. And as sailors learn to read the winds by their effect on the water, I begin to learn the plants from the wind's effect on them. I stand on the trail and try to pick out the prairie bush clovers as they move. The round-headed clover is easy. Its stems lean down in stiff lines and stay down; it reclines from its feet with its body straight. The fine grasses that surround it bend and flex rapidly. The burly leadplant nods its shaggy shrubbiness all at once, bowing politely. The milkweed flips up its broad leaves, as if raising its hands against the wind, while the spike gayfeather wiggles stiffly back and forth like a mast in the gale. Prairie sunflowers bob their bright heads on stems rendered invisible by the movement leaving only yellow dots floating above the prairie.

The prairie bush clover is graceful. It bends at its feet, like its cousin, but more rapidly, then drops its top farther downward. It executes a deep, formal bow followed by a playful dipping head flick even lower. In a group, they are a chorus line at curtain call, slightly out of synch, lithe and confident.

* * *

The prairie bush clover is a legume, like soybeans and other clovers, and all legumes have the ability to take nitrogen from the air and put it into the soil. Most plants take their nitrogen from the soil, which could rapidly deplete the stores of this nutrient. Legumes, with their ability to perform "nitrogen fixation," are therefore a critical component of the prairie. The prairie bush clover could be grown today in cattle pastures, to help fertilize the other grasses and to feed the cows with nutrient-rich seeds.

Prairie bush clovers don't reproduce well. The plant sports two kinds of flowers: the pink and white ones that are open to pollinators, like most flowers, and ones that remain closed throughout their entire lives. The open flowers do set seed, but how they are pollinated is not well understood. The closed flowers always set seed, for they pollinate themselves, inside their protective sheaths. This is a genetic issue, since all the seeds are clones of the parent. Even specimens that touch each other when they bow in the wind cannot cross-pollinate. Perhaps because of that self-breeding, only about ten percent of prairie bush clover seeds are viable.

Strangely, though, round-headed bush clover populations, which are far more successful reproducers, seem to be hybridizing with their prairie cousins. Round-heads growing near prairie bush clovers, like those at Jeffers, are starting to grow arms; their leaves are becoming more slender. This shift suggests a pollinator at work, but again, it is not well understood.

The Jeffers prairie trail leads me to the quartzite outcrop. Ropes threaded through concrete blocks mark a path across the stone, dodging the sacred carvings. I wind between etchings of hands, turtles, and bison pierced with spears; squiggly lines called "lightning snakes" and crowds of human forms called "family groups"; constellations; thunderbirds; circles, squares, and horned men with circles for feet and circles for hands; and later settler texts: "1924 R E Harrison," "LW 1948." Half of the rock face is covered with black plastic, in place to kill the lichens that are slowly creeping across the stone and threatening to obscure the petroglyphs.

It is just before noon. The sun is high and the subtle carvings are hard to see. The manager of the site, having just finished giving a tour, makes them more visible for me with a mirror and a big piece of plywood. The mirror reflects sunlight in a low, raking angle across the stone, simulating dawn or dusk. The plywood shades the surface from the direct overhead sun. Seen in this certain light, the glyphs jump from the blood-red stone.

I continue along the trail as it loops through the prairie behind the outcrop. I am tuned to a certain movement in the wind, a way of seeing that will make the prairie bush clover jump from the chaotic grassland. I want to find one on my own, to identify one particular plant out of this mass of biology. This prairie has been here for nine thousand years. People began moving through here sporadically seven thousand years ago, making their way down through the plains from Alaska and the Bering land bridge. Five thousand years ago more permanent residents hunted elk and bison, sometimes dressed in the skins of wolves. They marked these rocks with pictures from their prairie world.

When the first Europeans came across this land, just more than three hundred years ago, the Dakota were here, hunting the bison, sometimes setting fire to the grasses to clear views or to drive animals to slaughter. The Dakota found medicines in these plants; they gathered wild rice, berries, and edible roots; and they grew corn in small gardens. By the middle of the nineteenth century, as immigrants poured into the region, territorial leaders focused on gaining title to the land and began to force treaties on the Ojibwe and Dakota. Relations between the Dakota and the newcomers became increasingly difficult. In 1851, a few years before the survey crews began to put their orderly European stamp on this complex land, the Dakota signed the Traverse des Sioux Treaty and moved to reservations along the Minnesota River.

But the United States reneged on its agreements, offering just a fraction of the cash it promised and allowing white farmers to take up land within the Dakota reservation. In August 1862 the Dakota attacked military outposts and towns in the Minnesota River valley, including the city of New Ulm. The US–Dakota War lasted just a few months. Dakota warriors killed more than six hundred soldiers and white settlers, including entire families; no one counted the Dakota dead. Federal reprisals were fierce: Dakota women, children, and elders were marched to a concentration camp at Fort Snelling, at the confluence of the Mississippi and Minnesota Rivers—at Bdote, the place sacred to many Dakota. The men were marched down the Minnesota River to a prison camp in Mankato. More than three hundred were convicted of murder and sentenced to hang. President Abraham Lincoln intervened and halted the executions of all but thirty-eight, who would die to appease the angry settlers. The day after Christmas, 1862, thousands of the newcomers turned out in Mankato to witness the largest mass execution in US history.

I stop at a knob of quartzite hidden in a gulley overgrown with stunted trees. It's a bison rub, polished mirror-smooth by perhaps ten thousand years of giant prairie beasts scratching away their winter coats. I have never seen my own reflection in rock. I look like a petroglyph.

I don't see any prairie bush clovers, though I do see plenty of their cousins. I worry, after this mere hour-long hike, that I have already forgotten how to see them, so I return to the patch Shelley showed me. I spot them immediately, delicately bending and dipping in the wind.

In my desire to find a rare bush clover on my own, I drive due south, staying in Range 35, and the townships tick away, descending in number, as I slip ever so slightly closer to the Arkansas baseline. I walk up the steep bluffs above the Des Moines River, in Township 104. This hillside used to be pasture, but the Nature Conservancy bought it and gave it to the state. Now it is called Des Moines River Scientific and Natural Area. The valley of the Des Moines River is considered the core area for prairie bush clovers, and the sign near the grass parking lot helpfully informs me that the plant is here, somewhere, among the thirty acres of seven-foot-tall big bluestem. I walk uphill into the vegetation. I focus specifically on the north-facing slopes because all the scientific literature tells me this is the clover's preferred habitat. I am enveloped by grasses.

The ocean was the favorite metaphor of the early explorers, settlers, and poets, who often drew parallels between the disorienting character of both grassland and waterscape. "A great sea of grass," said Meriwether Lewis with simplicity during the Lewis and Clark expedition in 1803. In 1877 the army man Richard Irving Dodge (namesake of Fort Dodge and Dodge City) wrote, "The first experience of the plains, like the first sail with a 'cap' full of wind, is apt to be sickening." Author and traveler Eliza Steele, in 1840, described grasses "rising and falling in gentle undulations, as if an enchanter had struck the ocean swell, and it was set at rest forever." And one of the earliest European explorers to set eyes on this landscape, Spanish gold hunter Francisco Vásquez de Coronado, wrote this in 1541 to his king: "I reached some plains so vast that I did not find their limit anywhere I went with no more landmarks than if we had been swallowed up by the sea.'

The Europeans feared this landscape. It was a wilderness unlike anything they had ever seen in the Old World. A tallgrass prairie manages to combine both vastness and closeness into the same moment. Walking through the tallgrass at Des Moines River is like being not so much on a great ocean but under the surface of the sea. Whenever I stop moving the big bluestem closes in around me, touches my face, the backs of my hands, my neck. The prairie allows me to occupy only as much space as my physical body needs. An arm's-length away, I can see nothing but a green and amber wall.

At the same time, the sky above is unrelentingly huge. There are no tree branches to break the monotony. Cloudlessness erases all sense of distance. And when I move through the grasses, they seem to go on forever. Every step is identical, like an endless video loop of the same few seconds. I put my hands in front of me to part the stems, and there are always more stems, always the shushing that crowns out the sound of my breathing. The prairie feels, ironically, almost lifeless—so uniform, so legible.

But even this is a deception. I stop again and look down into the grasses and see ten different species at first glance. There can be dozens in a square meter, all with their own forms, colors, and tricks for eking life from the crowded landscape. The prairie is at once overwhelming in its simplicity and frightening in its complexity—at once belittling in

Tallgrass prairie at Des Moines River SNA, 2010

its vastness and nerve-wracking in its closeness. It is a place difficult to comprehend.

I return to my car and drive south again, thinking of the surveyors walking in straight lines through these terrestrial kelp beds, thinking of farmers arriving to lay eyes on their 160 acres for the first time. I know the first thing I would do is clear a space, plant something familiar.

The recent history of the land that James Nowlin marked in his little red books can be found in another set of books, thick heavy ones, also bound in leather, stored at the Brown County Courthouse. I enter the room through a bank-vault door. The giant books rest in stacks of floor-to-ceiling cubbyholes, each with a bottom of stainless steel rollers, to allow the books to slide easily from their perches. Land title abstracts, marriage and death certificates, and land deeds are compiled here, evolving through time from handwritten pages to printed forms with typed data to microfiche to scanned PDF files accessible on the room's lone computer. I spend the better part of two cold January days here in New Ulm, learning about the landscape of the prairie bush clover in pages and pages of script.

The first moment in the recorded history of Section 33, Township 109 West, Range 35 North involves Ojibwe women, not the Dakota who occupied this prairie immediately prior to European settlement—and this is a key fact in the anglification of this land. When the United States and several bands of Ojibwe people (a tribe primarily of the northern forests) signed a treaty in 1854 at La Pointe, Wisconsin, every Indian head of household became entitled to a then-unspecified eighty acres of land. They probably didn't expect that land would be swaths of prairie hundreds of miles to the south.

Once James Nowlin and others completed their surveys in the late 1850s and the land in the rich Minnesota River valley was sold quite literally from under the feet of the Dakota, despite their own 1851 treaty, and after the Dakota War, the Minnesota prairie became the property of the federal government. In March of 1865, Catharine Brunette, Nancy Stilwell, Margaret Bastian, Margaret Bruce, and Alexis Roy, Ojibwe women all, were given free title (a "patent") to their own halves of quarters of Section 33—eighty acres each. The same day, they signed their powers of attorney to white lawyers. They signed with Xs, next to which a scribe wrote their names and the words "her mark." Also on the same day, those lawyers sold the land to the Redwood Coal Company for $100 per eighty acres. It is unknown how much the Ojibwe women got for the land, but likely less than $100. In January of 1866, three other Ojibwe women did the same thing, transferring the remainder of Section 33 to Redwood Coal. At the time, to an Ojibwe woman, money must have been more important than eighty acres located a hundred miles from her home in Minnesota's north woods.

There isn't any coal in this part of the world (though people looked for it), but a stream still bears the name Coal Mine Creek today. Redwood Coal was therefore either a doomed venture or a landholding company. The Ojibwe women (pages and pages of their original patents clog the early Brown County land register books) probably never saw the land. Redwood Coal could have been banking on the value of the land for agricultural purposes, since, thanks to the surveys of James Nowlin and others, it was well known this was rich prairie earth. In 1892 the company dissolved and transferred its holdings to its executives and associates, often for just one dollar for hundreds of acres. The southwest quarter of Section 33 went to Henry Rice, whose widow, Matilda, sold it in halves to Friedrich Meine in 1898 and 1902 for a total of $1,587.74. She also deeded a hundred-foot-wide railroad right-of-way to the Minnesota and Iowa Railway for $300.

Meine's name suggests he was part of an influx of German immigrants who came to southwestern Minnesota (hence the name of Brown County's largest town: New Ulm) from the 1850s through the 1870s. It wasn't an easy piece of land: steep in places, marshy in others, snipped at the southwestern corner by a railroad, cut irregularly along the north edge by the Cottonwood River. But the Meines managed to hang on to the half section for the next ninety years, while around them other German Americans—the Kettners, Blankenburgs, Seidls, and Jeunemanns—struggled through the Great Depression and beyond, often taking out extra mortgages on the land or simply migrating farther west where land was cheaper.

The prairie bush clover was listed under the Endangered Species Act in 1987, and a recovery plan was adopted in 1988. By then, the locations of key remaining clover populations were well known, and the Meine property's untilled hills were a priority for preservation. In 1990 the great-grandchildren of Friedrich Meine, James, Rita, Roger, and Janice, sold 125.82 acres of the southwest quarter of Section 33 to the State of Minnesota for $83,750 ($665 per acre), to be designated the Cottonwood River Prairie Scientific and Natural Area.

I arrive at Cottonwood at midmorning, on my way back to the Twin Cities from points west. After leaving Des Moines River natural area unsatisfied, I camped at Kilen Woods State Park, home to yet another scientific and natural area, this one named for the prairie bush clover.

The prairie grasses there were not as tall, and were surrounded by oaks and maples coating the sides of deep gullies that ran down to the Des Moines River. The wind was blowing, so I tuned in to the movements of the plants. I walked back and forth across the hills and found no prairie bush clover.

The next morning I headed west, over the high ridge of the prairie coteau and down into the watershed of the Missouri River, where the endangered Topeka shiner minnow lives. Over the next few days I explored this similar landscape. In far southwestern Minnesota I hiked down the face of the sixty-foot-tall upwelling of Sioux Quartzite known as the Blue Mounds. I visited nearby Pipestone National Monument, where the quartzite is underlain by the only occurrence in the world of a soft red stone that indigenous Americans from many tribes have been quarrying and carving into pipes and figurines for thousands of years. Then I returned east, to Cottonwood River: Section 33, Township 109, Range 35, 5th Principal Meridian.

There's no parking lot here, so I edge my car onto the grassy shoulder, glance at the interpretive sign, and promise myself that this time I will find the prairie bush clover, dancing somewhere in these 125.82 acres. If I find one, I'll just look. The law wouldn't let me pick any part of the plant anyway. My interest is esoteric. This elegant plant is symbolic for me of another time, when nature and culture were more in balance. All of Minnesota's federally listed species strike me this way. They are touchstones. Though according to DNR biologists I spoke with the prairie bush clover may have always been rare due to its narrow habitat preference, and was likely eaten to the ground by bison, it wasn't grazed into oblivion by cattle penned in small pastures or cut for prairie hay. It was left alone here—wild.

I climb the hills at Cottonwood and peer down into the grasses. I move slowly, stopping and scanning the landscape with each wind gust, hoping to pick up the telltale bending and dipping movement of my quarry. I pay particular attention when the slopes face north and the grasses are shorter, the latter indicating the slightly more nutrient-poor soil where the clover tends to grow. I see many round-heads

The grasses here are hip-high, so I can read the landscape. I continue north to the highest ridge. The undulating summit reminds me of a woman sleeping on her side beneath a dun blanket. I climb to the shoulder, the highest point, and scan the slope below. There are leggy plants there with three-part leaves, but they have gone to seed, so are probably not prairie bush clovers. But as I move among them, I begin to think they might be. The grasslands I have seen over the past few days were all at different stages of development. The bluestem here is not yet flowering, as it was at Des Moines River. Perhaps, due to minute differences in soil, sun exposure, and water, these are bush clovers that have already bloomed and set seed. The leaves look the same, though not as silver. They bend similarly in the wind, but not exactly. They are everywhere here, their seed heads like ground black pepper sprinkled on the prairie. I waver. At one moment I decide they are prairie bush clovers and I rejoice halfheartedly. The next I decide they are not. Whenever I convince myself they are, I am a little disappointed. I wanted to see one, know for sure on sight, and experience the thrill of the find. This uncertainty tempers my excitement.

I sit down in a small patch of these doppelgangers, partway down the northern slope of the ridge, and survey the landscape. It is August 19, 2010. At a pace of about six survey miles per day, James Nowlin's crew would have arrived here in this section 152 years ago on almost exactly this date. The scene has changed so much since then, but I can almost watch the surveyors inch across my view. Their original lines are still here, in the wire fences that divide properties, the gravel roads between farms, the perfect rectilinearity of every piece of land.

I imagine them coming out from behind the ridge to my left, moving north. They ford the Big Cottonwood River and set a stake in the ground on the opposite bank: the quarter section. They follow the wire fence that separates the corn on the Juenemann farm at the foot of this ridge from the beans on Ken Groebner's land to the west. They cross the railroad tracks and pass just east of Groebner's white farm buildings. They walk the dirt road that leads north from the Groebner homestead, flanking the beans the Juenemanns planted north of the tracks. Where those beans give way to Kelvin Bast's pasture, the axmen set another stake, the section corner. Now moving eastward, Nowlin's crew inchworms their way along another wire fence line separating Jeunemanns' from Bast's, then, a little farther along Jeunemanns' from Ron and Peggy Groebner's. They finish their mile and return west, along the true line, the final line, the north line of Section 33, the square in which I sit. Occasionally, James bends to scrawl in his red notebook. The crew turns north and is lost from view.

Whether James and his crew were fascinated by, annoyed by, interested in, or ambivalent toward the prairie is lost to history. All we have is that little red notebook and some hand-drawn maps, which are empirical and say nothing about prairie species. It is unlikely, even if James saw prairie bush clovers, that he would have known what they were—they would have been one more grassland plant to him. My own interest, in fact, arises only out of the clover's legally recognized rarity. There are many fascinating plants here, but I want to find this one, and on my own. Though this certainly isn't obsession—I've been out here for only a few days, after all—I am not satisfied with the trailside specimens at Jeffers. Somehow they don't seem "wild" to me. Shelley pointed them out, as she does for hundreds of visitors each year. That was like seeing tropical birds in a pet store. But here at Cottonwood—seeing a bush clover here would be like the swoosh of parrots through the Peruvian jungle: birds we've all seen but never so free.

But I've seen the prairie. I've been over my head in it. So, why this plant? Why does it matter so much? Wouldn't the prairie be fine without it? It's only a minor player anyway, isn't it? It's not the only nitrogen fixer—every site I visited had an abundance of round-heads, which provide nutrients as well as nectar for insects.

Then Shelley Olson's words echo in my head. "It's a gift from God," she told me back at Jeffers. "It's on earth for a reason. Sometimes humans will be able to figure out the reason for something, and sometimes we won't." She figures we should protect everything because if there is a reason we're meant to discover, we better not eliminate the plant before we can benefit from it. This statement is an old saw in the endangered species community. Medicine is often cited as the likely "reason," with plenty of examples from the rainforest and elsewhere to support the case.

But then she chuckled and said: "And also I think it's really pretty."

Shelley's right. There's something uniquely elegant about the prairie bush clover. It's a certain color of silver-green that manages to blend in with the vegetative chaos until I notice it, then the color suddenly stands out and draws my eye back again and again. The way the plant moves describes the essence of the prairie: the uniformity of the stiff-backed bow and the intricacy of the little head-flick at the end. It stands tall, straight, alone, but would look strange and isolated if not surrounded by its cohorts.

I come out of my reverie and look again at those dark seed heads all around me. They are not prairie bush clovers. I am sure of that now. I don't know what they are, but they lack the elegance, the singularity of the clovers.

The wind blows. Something taps against my right shoulder. I turn my head in time to see a tall, thin plant recoil back to its upright position. Another gust and it dips again, touching my back with a downward flick of its head. And now I scan the slope once more and there are dozens of prairie bush clovers. They have been here all along: graceful lines bending and dipping, so suddenly obvious, so unmistakable amongst the grasses, in the wind, in the prairie, bending and dipping.

Three rare butterflies,
from left: Dakota skipper,
Poweshiek skipperling,
Karner blue

6

Butterflies

Of all the amazing things that happen in nature—the growth of a redwood tree from a seed the size of a grain of mustard, the annual Arctic-to-Antarctic journeys of some birds, the likely ability of cephalopods to see with their skin, the fact that some frogs can freeze solid and then thaw out none the worse for wear—the most incredible may be the metamorphosis of butterflies and moths. Yes, a water-breathing tadpole sprouting legs and lungs is cool, and the gradual transition of a beetle from a wormy thing to a grub with legs to a hard-shelled flier is an exceptional feat. But as transformations go, the caterpillar is king. I know you're mostly up to speed on this, having watched the process in your kindergarten classroom or mail-ordered a few painted lady butterflies to nurture on the kitchen table, but for the sake of staring at the same point of incredulity, let's narrate the feat.

A tiny caterpillar chews a little hole in a soft-shelled egg and inches its way out onto a green leaf and starts eating. The caterpillars purpose is to generate energy and body mass. So it eats and eats. Typically, a species has a particular preference for food, and in many cases does not stray from its favorite. It gets bigger, longer, plumper. It might sprout fluffy tufts or golden horns or extra appendages of all sorts of colors. Caterpillars alone would be a wonderful addition to our vibrant world of life. But caterpillars can't mate—they don't have the parts. Plenty of tube-shaped animals do, and they are perfectly content to stay tube-shaped their entire lives: worms, slugs, sea cucumbers. Caterpillars, however, get the rare opportunity to experience what it might be like to be two species in one lifetime.

They make a chrysalis, maybe hanging from a leaf or branch, maybe in a little hole in the ground, maybe nestled into the base of a clump of grasses. This chrysalis is made out of themselves—they use their own body fluids to make a hard shell around their tube-shaped body. Then (here's the true wonder of it) they dissolve. Everything inside that shell becomes a uniform soup. Scientists have cut open chrysalises at various stages of metamorphosis and found that this is universal. It's soup in there: caterpillar soup. Let me restate that, because this is why I think the caterpillar-to-butterfly magic trick is the best in nature. The caterpillar is not gradually transforming into a butterfly in there. It is not sprouting wings and long, thin legs. It is not gradually changing color, as leaves do. It's not dropping off those colorful appendages and leaving them on the floor. It is quite literally starting over. It is breaking down every structure, every membrane, every foot, eye, mouth, bit of skin, and organ into an undifferentiated swirl of cells.

And then out of the soup a butterfly materializes. Somehow, within that cozy sheath, feet are made—feet that can taste flowers. A tongue sometimes as long as the whole body is formed—a supple spiral conjured from the liquid. A body often thinner and smaller than the caterpillar's congeals—imagine emerging from sleep smaller than you were. And wings! Broad, soft, micron-thin wings with patterns and colors and iridescence. That the wings are made inside a watery space several times narrower than those wings is a true marvel.

We know the rest: the chrysalis splits open and a fully formed butterfly or moth climbs out, waits for its wings to stiffen, then flies away on winged errands. Some begin eating ravenously, sipping nectar with agile tongues. Some fly incredible distances. Some (moths mostly) don't even have mouths and can't eat, so they mate, starve, and die. Some live a few days, some a few months. In many cases, the animal spends far more time as a caterpillar than as a butterfly or moth. To us humans, the butterfly is the climax, the beautiful version of the species. We call the caterpillar a "larval stage" of the butterfly. But maybe to the animal, the winged stage is the scary final moment, the death throe, the last gasp. Butterflies are mostly caterpillars.

And butterflies may remember being caterpillars. A 2008 study by Martha Weiss, Doug Blackiston, and Elena Casey published on PLOS ONE exposed caterpillars to a strong smell in conjunction with an electric shock. Essentially, the researchers taught caterpillars that nail polish was bad for them. They set up a little Y-shaped tube and put the caterpillars in the stem of the Y. The little wrigglers had a choice of paths: nail polish smell and a shock, or no smell and home free. After awhile, they began to regularly choose the scentless option. Then, metamorphosis. Out came the moths (in this particular study, tobacco hornworms), their entire existence recombobulated, no caterpillar neuron nor ganglia preserved. Into the Y-tube they went, with the acetone on one side. The moths chose the odor-free (and presumably shock-free) side 77 percent of the time. (A control group chose sides more or less equally.) Granted, this was one species of moth, the results were far more conclusive on larvae that were closer to metamorphosis, and scent aversion does not exactly mean actual memories are retained. But how any memory— even vague dreamlike recollections of a scent that once caused pain— can be preserved through the complete breakdown of bodily structures is unexplainable. It is almost like remembering a past life—if you believe in the idea. It becomes somehow spiritual: as if there is something operating the mechanics of life that is beyond cellular function. After all, what makes something "alive" or "sentient" is an open debate, and the butterfly raises some fascinating questions. Does the caterpillar know it will become a butterfly? If the butterfly doesn't remember its caterpillar days, is it the same individual or an entirely new one? Is the animal alive in the cocoon?

There is no equivalent of this miracle in nature. Not even close. Assuming a typical caterpillar/butterfly life cycle of about six months, imagine this: a human baby is born, eats nothing but spinach for forty-six years, lies on the floor and covers itself in a shroud of spit, and stays inert that way for twelve years. Then out comes a bioluminescent twelve-armed starfish able to teleport to the moon. It's really that odd.

Sometimes I wonder if all the butterflies and moths are the result of a truly clever and artistic Creator. Or the randomness of evolution gone absolutely haywire. It's nearly inconceivable that an animal can do this. I think that on some distant day when we encounter life (intelligent or not) on some other planet, we will be amazed, of course, by what we find, but we'll also say, "Eh, well, on Earth we've got butterflies."

Unless we don't.

Unless we don't have butterflies on Earth.

"[The Poweshiek skipperling] was an unremarkable butterfly until it remarkably disappeared," says Erik Runquist. Erik is the butterfly conservation biologist at the Minnesota Zoo, where he leads the effort to conserve two federally listed species: the Poweshiek skipperling (*Oarisma poweshiek*) and the Dakota skipper (*Hesperia dacotae*). I am getting a crash course in butterflies from Erik and his colleague Cale Nordmeyer at the cheekily named Chrysalis, a converted shipping container on the back trails of the zoo's 485 hilly forested acres. Their work is away from the public eye, so though I have been to the zoo countless times, I feel like I'm getting a backstage tour. In the Chrysalis, Cale and Erik raise butterflies. This is a climate-controlled space where they can shepherd their tiny livestock through the winters. Next door are two hoop-style greenhouses: one for the skipperling, one for the skipper.

Erik is clean-shaven and tall, his casual air reinforced by his gray collared sweater and khakis. Cale is a little more tousled, with a short-cropped beard and hair that creeps around his ears and the back of his neck. On this brisk day he wears a slightly worn, dark-green Minnesota Zoo zip-up sweater and shorts. A tattoo of a pileated woodpecker takes up most of his calf. Both men are in their early middle age, and both grew up around nature.

"I'll admit to thinking that this was a really boring butterfly when I was a little kid looking for butterflies in southwest Minnesota," says

Cale. "I got excited when I found a giant swallowtail." He pauses for effect. "I was such an ignorant ten-year-old." The Poweshiek skipperling (its first name comes from the county in Iowa where it was found, which in turn is named for a Meskwaki chief) was once one of the most commonly found butterflies on the prairies of the Midwest. Erik says it was rare to visit a prairie and not find them. They were as ubiquitous as robins or squirrels in the forest. In fact, for a long time, Poweshieks didn't appear in naturalists' records because they were so plentiful. It could be assumed, the naturalists were saying, that one would nearly always find Poweshieks on the prairie.

Then, suddenly, in the mid-2000s, amateur and professional naturalists started realizing the Poweshieks were no longer around. Now, one can expect some localized fluctuations in population from year to year and site to site—this is a pretty fragile animal, after all. But then those naturalists started comparing notes. The notes were dire. Historical record searches revealed that Poweshieks have not been seen in Minnesota, South Dakota, and Iowa since 2008, and in North Dakota since 2001. In the late 2000s scientists fanned out across the Midwest and prairie Canada to look for Poweshieks. None were found in Minnesota, Iowa, or the Dakotas. None. Those four states constitute 95 percent of the butterfly's range. Minnesota includes 48 percent of the Poweshiek's range—that's the greatest proportion of any butterfly species' range contained in the state. Minnesota was the core habitat area of this insect, once home to individuals too numerous to count. They are all apparently gone. The total known world population of Poweshiek skipperlings resides now in a few sites near Flint, Michigan, and in Manitoba just a few miles north of the Minnesota border, and one site in central Wisconsin where just a handful of individuals are seen per year.

Based on the late 2000s survey work, scientists estimated the world population at between five and ten thousand individuals. But another population crash happened in 2012–13, just as Erik was starting up the butterfly program at the zoo, and the current generous estimate is five hundred. "We think it's lower this year," says Erik, "maybe a couple hundred individuals left. Which makes it one of the most endangered animals on earth. And one that pretty much nobody has heard of. And it was in our backyards in Minnesota. And now this species is in serious risk of extinction within five to ten years." He seems visibly shaken.

Erik has been in this place before. He grew up in southern Oregon, an only child whose companions were the butterflies in the yard and the trout in the creeks. "I was chasing butterflies when I was a little kid, and I never let go," he says. He got his degree in ecology while studying and propagating the Schaus' swallowtail butterfly in Florida. Once wide-ranging throughout south Florida, that three-and-a-half-inch brown-and-gold insect was eventually limited to a single island in the Biscayne National Park in the Florida Keys, and was threatened by habitat loss and an increase in spraying for mosquitoes. Erik participated in a captive breeding program, which had been initiated just months before Category 5 Hurricane Andrew hit in 1992. The storm all but destroyed the island, and the butterflies with it. "The entire world population [of Schaus' swallowtails] was in a few grad students' kitchens in Gainesville," Erik smirks. The program increased the captive population and was able to reintroduce them to their home island and several others nearby. After Erik moved on, the wild population declined again due to drought, but the captive breeding program has continued, creating an ongoing safety valve for the species.

Erik came to Minnesota in 2012 to start the breeding program for the Poweshiek and the Dakota skipper. The same surveys that exposed the crash of the Poweshiek also revealed the Dakota skipper population was at a historic low.

Cale has been at the zoo since 2008 working on a variety of species, but shifted full time to butterflies when Erik came on board. Cale grew up in the Twin Cities, but his family is from southwestern Minnesota, and he visited the prairie often. He was born with a caregiver's heart. "I always wanted to find all the little things and raise them," he says. He did his undergraduate work in Oregon at Lewis and Clark College and is currently pursuing his master's from the University of Minnesota on Dakota skipper ecology.

An adult Poweshiek skipperling in Michigan, June 2016, and male and female Dakota skippers raised at the Minnesota Zoo and released at the Nature Conservancy's Hole-in-the-Mountain Prairie in southwestern Minnesota, 2017 (courtesy Cale Nordmeyer, Minnesota Zoo)

It is important to recognize that Erik and Cale's work is not about reintroduction. They are creating, in essence, backup populations to the wild ones of both species. Theirs is an annual cycle that begins around the Fourth of July with a cross-country road trip. When the butterflies emerge from their chrysalises to mate, observers at various Poweshiek and Dakota sites notify Erik and Cale. In the case of the Poweshiek, the zoo researchers quickly drive to Michigan and set up in a hotel room, reserved ahead to ensure it faces southwest. They rearrange all the furniture. They answer questions from the perplexed owner. Venturing into the prairie, the ecologists find and capture female butterflies, which are typically hanging out on the tops of flowers. The females, presumably already pregnant, are brought back to the hotel room in portable enclosures. For the next forty-eight hours, each expectant mother is carefully watched as she basks in her advance-planned sunlight, until she lays eggs.

Once the eggs are in the container, each female is whisked back to the prairie and returned to the exact flower from which she was taken (the ecologists use GPS, but, they say, most of the sites are so small it is easy to remember individual flowers). This whole rigmarole is designed to have the least disruption on the population. They capture only every fourth individual they encounter and only up to ten females from each site. As they describe this sequence of events, I can't help but think of alien abduction stories: the strange capture, the return to the exact same spot two days later . . .

The eggs are driven back to the Chrysalis at the zoo to rest in climate-controlled happiness until they hatch. The caterpillars live in little clumps of grass growing in pots with tall white nylon socks on frames over the top of each pot. The hoop house, where the caterpillars spend most of the year, looks populated with tiny futuristic white skyscrapers, a virtual city of condominiums inhabited by insects.

Skippers and skipperlings are actually in the same broad group of butterflies, which happens to have the most individual species of any type of butterfly. They are often mistaken for moths because they fly strongly in one general direction with more power than other butterflies. This

"Condos" for overwintering caterpillars at the Minnesota Zoo, 2015

quick "skipping" from one flower to the next gives them their name. Perching, they tend to hold their wings at different angles: forewings out and back wings up, rather than all four closed above their backs or open to the sun, again like most more familiar butterflies. They look a bit like an F-14 jet fighter.

Unlike the monarch, neither the Poweshiek nor the Dakota adults migrate, tending to not even cross tree lines or hedgerows, so they are generally content to stay in the hoop house all year. Both species spend most of their yearlong lives as caterpillars. Instead of feeding out in the open and crawling about on leaves like the monarch caterpillar, the Dakota skipper is a shelter builder. A dark brown Dakota caterpillar spins a little home of silk at the base of a clump of grass and stays pretty much in there out of sight. To feed, the Dakota peeks out its head, reaches up as high as it can without leaving the shelter, grabs a blade of grass, and pulls it back down into its silk sanctuary. ("It's adorable!" says Cale.) This feeding activity had never been seen in the wild, and the full life cycle of the Dakota skipper was not well understood until the zoo's breeding program began. The Poweshiek caterpillar stays higher on the grass and weaves a very minimal silk shelter. Its green color and longitudinal stripes help it blend in with the blades. Both species overwinter as caterpillars inside these little spun houses, and both species make their chrysalises inside them.

The zoo has around 650 Dakota larvae at the moment. The word *around* is an unusual one for a zoo-managed population. Typically, zoo curators know exactly how many penguins, tigers, monkeys, or snakes they have. But not every shelter has a living caterpillar, and the whole contraption is so tiny (hibernating Dakota caterpillars are a little less than a centimeter long) that actually peeking inside could kill the animal. "Schrodinger's caterpillars," Cale calls them, and pauses to see if I get the joke.

The butterflies emerge in late June or early July. This is a pretty intense time for Cale and Erik, who lament that they never, ever get the Independence Day holiday off. The Dakotas and Poweshieks are both emerging at the same time in the hoop houses, and both species are also emerging in the wild. Erik and Cale grab personnel from other zoo programs and get all hands on deck for "the mating game." This year, Erik and Cale figured out how to tell male and female caterpillars apart (the chrysalises of the different sexes look different, but the caterpillars are nearly identical, except that it is possible with a hand lens to see the male genitalia through the skin). Once the caterpillars begin metamorphosis, they are taken out of the white skyscrapers and placed into hatching cups. During this time, the scientists decide who will mate with whom. They have detailed lineages on every butterfly. They know the interrelationships between individuals and clutches. All of that is important to ensure the greatest genetic diversity even within what is in reality a very small population.

Within hours of emerging, the butterflies are put into larger enclosures with lots of flowering prairie plants, from which they can drink nectar. "The breeding piece is hard," says Erik. "You would hope that you could put any two butterflies in a cage or just touch their bodies together and mating happens, but that doesn't happen with these." (Only Dakotas are being bred at the zoo; Poweshieks are strictly about egg collection—more on why in a few moments.) Through years of trial and error, they have learned how to get the insects interested in each other. "It was a rude awakening for us the very first year we had adults here at the zoo," chuckles Cale. "I have this perfect pedigree lined up, I'm pairing up one male to one female . . . and they're just sitting there." But because they had many more males that first year than females, Cale set up a kind of holding pen ("the bachelor cage") for those extra boys. The behavior in there was drastically different than in the one-male-one-female cages. They were far more active, combative even. What Cale and Erik do now is deliberately create that boys-only environment. To keep the pedigree traceable, once the males are in the cage, they are anaesthetized for thirty seconds through a process developed in collaboration with the zoo's veterinarians. The males are marked with Sharpie pens with dots of different colors. Then the female is introduced into that cage. "It is not what you are picturing this now looking like, where they all swarm her," Cale says, reading my mind. "There seems to be some kind of pre-selection, either by the female or the males themselves, but the human observers aren't sure. Once the butterflies mate (yes, zoo staff and interns watch the whole proceedings closely), the colored dots become the key to the lineage.

Before I meet Cale and Erik's butterflies at the zoo, I visit the butterflies' real-world home. Clay County is one of the few remaining places where the Dakota skipper can be seen in the wild. Buffalo River State Park is about fourteen miles east of Fargo/Moorhead on the flat ground left by ancient glacial Lake Agassiz. Just to the east the old beach ridges rise up. Driving US Highway 10 through the eastern half of Clay County is an ecological journey from flat grassland to rolling savanna to lake-studded forests. The state park and two adjacent reserves—the Nature Conservancy's Bluestem Prairie Scientific and Natural Area, and the Minnesota State University Moorhead's Regional Science Center—together protect around seventy-five hundred acres of tallgrass prairie cut through by the twisting course of the park's namesake river.

Morning on the Wide Sky Trail at Buffalo River State Park, 2016

I arrive at Buffalo River State Park as the evening light fades in the northwest. It is high summer, just days after the solstice and night falls slowly. Humps of rock in the prairie are lit like the phases of the moon, depending on my angle. Every tree casts a shadow that goes on forever. Signs at the park visitor center say the Dakota skipper is here. Bluestem Prairie is designated critical habitat for both the Dakota and the Poweshiek skipperling, though the latter hasn't been found here for a decade.

Hoping for a miracle sighting but mostly interested in enjoying the prairie in summer bloom, I set off the next day on the Prairie View Trail. Thick woods flank the river, but as the trail heads south, the grassy flatness of the landscape takes over. Bobolink couples chase each other about. I see two kinds of milkweed in bloom, gray-headed coneflower, and leadplant. Butterflies are here, too: pearly crescentspot and pearly eye. I don't see any skippers.

Later that day I drive to the Bicentennial Prairie, a little farther north but still in Clay County. Officially known as Felton Prairie Scientific and Natural Area, this state land has no trails, so I park under circling hawks and amidst swirling tree swallows and tromp off into the waist-deep grasses. This roughly 160 acres was preserved first by the county in— you guessed it—the bicentennial year of 1976, after the local Boy Scout troop led a year-long environmental education program and petitioned the county to buy the land. The sign in the overgrown parking area has a picture of a Dakota skipper perched on a purple coneflower. Bicentennial Prairie is on the edge of a historic Lake Agassiz beach ridge, so it's slightly rolling, with a slash of wet areas through the middle. The knee-high grasses are punctuated by the red flash of prairie lily, tiny yellow hoary puccoon, and the surprising silver and purple of scurf pea. And purple coneflower. When I spot one of those rising up from the prairie, I approach as slowly and quietly as I can, hoping to spot a skipper perching there, awaiting a mate. I might be a bit early in the season, though. I do see pearly eye and viceroy butterflies—the former a lovely suede with dots the color of dark leather, the latter a monarch lookalike, but smaller.

Felton Prairie has the distinction of being critical habitat for three listed prairie species: both butterflies and the western prairie fringed orchid, though none of them are believed to be here. Still, I am content to hunker down at the edge of the wetlands and watch the sedge wrens. My breath catches when a northern harrier glides a mere hundred feet from me and no higher than my head. Later, near the end of my circular ramble, I sit on a little rise and am honored by the bubbling call of an upland sandpiper. It flies frenetically across the prairie, gurgling in soprano, then settles somewhere out of sight in the grasses, then flies again, settles, and flies again.

I return to Buffalo River State Park and take a dip in the swimming hole, which is quite literally a hole dug in the sandy ground for the purpose of swimming. It is a glorious summer Saturday, and the hole is busy with families day-tripping out from Fargo/Moorhead. The racial and ethnic diversity surprises me in this mostly white part of the country. Large extended African American and Latino families find space on the grass around the WPA-era stone bathhouse and enjoy the day, their different languages and inflections and food aromas filling the air. That night, I sleep with the rain fly off the tent, the grassland strangely still and the stars overhead astounding.

In the morning I hike the Wide Sky Trail, and it is as it says. I check my field guide to identify several butterflies, but they won't alight long enough for a good look. I marvel at the thickness of the leadplant and the prickle of the purple coneflower's seed head.

I drive farther north to Lake Bronson State Park, in remote Kittson County, the most northwesterly state park in Minnesota. The eastern half of the park is critical habitat for both endangered butterfly species, but this is the aspen parklands, and that's the main reason I go. Aspen parklands is a Level 1 ecoregion, according to classification systems put in place by both the Minnesota DNR and the EPA, meaning it is as distinct as prairie is from woods. Minnesota is the only US state with any aspen parklands, a biome that reaches north into Canada. This unique landscape is savanna-like, but without the oaks and maples most often associated with landscapes of open grass and patches interspersed with copses of trees. Here, as its name suggests, groves of aspens rise up from the prairie.

What I notice most here is the way the wind acts on the landscape. Aspens vibrate with the wind not unlike grasses and flowers. A gust moving across the parklands sets everything a-whir. Above me, the silver-green aspen leaves flash and hiss; around and below me, the grasses bend and sway. Even the skinny trunks of the aspen move, metronoming lazily back and forth. The whole landscape is buffeted to motion, the aspen almost more like a tribe of grasses than one of trees. Lake Bronson is remote and quiet on weekday evenings. I share the nearly two-hundred-site campground with one small group. Whippoorwills trill me to sleep.

The Dakota skipper and Poweshiek skipperling were listed together as threatened and endangered, respectively, in October of 2014. The next November, the US Fish and Wildlife Service listed critical habitat in four states: thirty-eight sites for the Dakota and forty-five for the Poweshiek. In many instances, the two species' critical habitats overlap. Because the listing for these two is very recent, there are no other official government actions, like status updates or five-year reviews.

There are plenty of ideas on why the Dakota skipper and Poweshiek skipperling populations have crashed, though none is absolutely conclusive. The Minnesota Zoo's Erik and Cale think it is probably a combination of factors—many of which are also stated as the official factors for federal listing. An overall reduction in habitat over the past century certainly can be blamed. The conversion of prairie to row crops, and the gradual evolution of those row crop farms to being more and more "weed-free" (weeds, here, meaning those little strips of flowers and grasses that used to poke up around the edges of fields and in the roadside ditches) has reduced available food and shelter for these and other prairie species.

Grazing and haying are less straightforward stressors. Though row crops provide practically nothing in terms of butterfly habitat, haying and grazing can take place on landscapes with native grasses and flowers. Those activities have even been used with some success to restore and manage prairie landscapes. And in fact the most reliable Dakota populations in South Dakota live in hayed prairies on tribal land that has never been plowed—the haying being done at times and at cut heights that don't harm the butterflies.

Though public comments in the Federal Register feature significant concern that the federal listing will restrict cattlemen's rights (the North Dakota Stockmen's Association officially opposed the listing), there is an out. In the case of the Dakota skipper, which is listed as threatened, not endangered, the USFWS has written what's called a 4(d) rule. This is a tool available in the Endangered Species Act—only for threatened species—that allows for "incidental take" of a species under certain conditions. Essentially, a 4(d) rule lets people accidentally kill animals or plants if doing so might benefit the species as a whole. Grazing and haying might kill butterflies, but rather than restrict these activities entirely (or require them to undergo a lengthy permit process), the rule allows them under certain conditions. According to Rich Baker, the Department of Natural Resources' endangered species coordinator, the argument here is that grazing and haying, under any circumstances, is better than row crops when it comes to preserving habitat for butterflies. By making it easy under federal rules to continue grazing and haying, the hope is that ranchlands won't be converted to corn and beans.

The federal listing also specifically highlights mineral exploration and mining and energy extraction as potentially significant habitat impacts. The development of North Dakota's Bakken Formation for oil and gas is identified in the report (and vehemently defended in the public comments submitted to the USFWS). The federal listing notes that oil and gas exploration has taken place in every county in North Dakota except one, and that two key counties for prairie butterfly habitat—McKenzie and McHenry—are within the active oil extraction area. Because skipper butterflies are very localized, rarely crossing even a gravel road, the fragmentation that comes with oil and gas well pads, access roads, staging areas, and even the associated residential ("man camp") development makes suitable patches of prairie even smaller, thereby limiting butterflies' habitat area and access to each other.

Overall habitat loss doesn't explain, however, why populations within protected prairie areas are also crashing. Conspicuously, the crashes of both butterfly species coincided with a significant increase in the use of pesticides—including neonicotinoids—in farm fields. Neonicotinoids, or neonics, are insecticides applied as seed coats to control various agricultural pests. A mid-2000s invasion of soybean aphids was met with increased aerial spraying of another set of insecticides: broad-spectrum pyrethroids and organophosphates. Many scientists and members of the public have concerns that these chemicals are drifting into prairie remnants and killing native butterflies, bees, and beetles. The USFWS recently established a work team called the Poweshiek Skipperling Contaminants Group (on which Erik and Cale participate), which is studying chemical drift on sites in Minnesota, South Dakota, and Michigan. Samples of grass and soil are receiving full-spectrum chemical analysis.

Besides the Dakota and Poweshiek, there is one other federally listed butterfly in the state. In 1992 the Karner blue (*Lycaeides melissa samuelis*), a tiny iridescent beauty, was deemed endangered. This is not a prairie butterfly; rather, it inhabits open patches within the forests of far southeastern Minnesota and eastward into Wisconsin. The Karner blue needs wild lupines, for nectaring as adults and as forage for caterpillars. In the mixed forest of the so-called Driftless Area, lupines once grew in abundance: in road ditches, at the edges of pastures and farm fields and along hedgerows.

The Karner blue is well documented: a recovery plan in 2003, a recovery plan update in 2011, and a five-year status report in 2012. The five-year report does not recommend reclassifying the species overall as threatened nor delisting, but it says that twelve populations in New York, Michigan, and Wisconsin are near or have met the main criterion for doing so: six thousand individuals per population for five years running for reclassification or ten years for delisting. Since the Karner's listing in 1992, overall losses have been minimal, and the butterfly has been reintroduced to Ohio (where it had likely been historically but was not found in 1992) and has increased in both population and range in Michigan and

Wisconsin. In Wisconsin, the Department of Natural Resources has led the creation of a Habitat Conservation Plan involving forty-two partners that seeks to improve Karner blue habitat on more than 240,000 acres of nonstate land. At the table are forest and mining companies, local highway departments, county forestry departments, and power companies. It appears to be working.

Though scientists are optimistic about populations in other states, the combined resources of the state and federal government couldn't stop the free fall in the land of lakes. The major Minnesota population area for the Karner was at Whitewater Wildlife Management Area. Karners haven't been seen there since 2006. Rich Baker profoundly regrets this loss. "It's gone from Minnesota," he laments, "and we tried hard." Federal protection as early as 1992, comprehensive conservation efforts on state land, collaboration with landowners on management practices—none of that worked. Says Rich: "We were successful in documenting their decline and extirpation from the state." There is some interest in removing the Minnesota recovery unit from the federal recovery plan, in order to ensure resources are allocated to other parts of the range or to other species with a continued chance of survival, but, according to Rich, that probably wouldn't change anything.

Pollinator insects have been generally hard hit over the last decade, and mysteries still surround their decline. The Dakota, Poweshiek, and Karner blue are on the federal list, of course, but eight other prairie butterflies appear on the state list, and it is quite possible that six or seven of those are already gone from Minnesota. Honeybee colonies are collapsing coast to coast, jeopardizing billions of dollars of agricultural revenue and threatening the very food we eat. In 2016 seven bee species were listed in Hawaii, the victims of habitat loss, invasive species, and pollution. And in January of 2017, the USFWS listed the first continental bee: the rusty-patched bumble bee (*Bombus affinis*). This fuzzy insect was commonplace in most of the eastern United States, including most counties in Minnesota. Unfortunately, almost immediately after that listing became final, the Trump administration barred federal agencies from spending any money on research and recovery efforts (which are required under the ESA). Apparently, this bumble bee is a potential hindrance to agriculture, mining, and energy extraction.

And then there's the monarch (*Danaus plexippus*). The king of butterflies, flying into our imaginations with its epic four-generation journey between Mexico, the Upper Midwest, and the eastern United States. The butterfly everyone knows: striped, fat, yellow, black, and white caterpillar; orange and black adult. Once seen seemingly daily in backyards and any old grassland you could find. Now being considered for listing under the Endangered Species Act.

Of late, the monarch has risen to the level of the polar bear and the rhino in terms of people's concern for its welfare. Though the rhetoric now is about "pollinators," which encompasses bees and allows for an economic justification for the alarm (Crop failure! Economic impact! Food shortage!), the monarch has a special place. Those other big animals are often called the "charismatic megafauna" of conservation. How do you get people to care about poaching? Show an elephant with a gunshot in its skull and its tusks sawn off. How do you get people to care about the health of oceans? Show bloodied whales or sharks speared and cut and left to die. How do you get people to care about climate change? Show an emaciated polar bear stranded on a tiny ice floe. The monarch might be the first charismatic microfauna.

Why? For starters, I'll go back to the amazing life cycle. Last fall, my son Mason's kindergarten class was host to twenty-three monarch caterpillars. The kids cared for them, fed them leaves, and, sadly, watched them die off one after another. Just one completed its life cycle and was released into the schoolyard. Most kids get that same science unit: the amazing metamorphosis of the caterpillar. Books are written (I'm sure we can all recite *The Very Hungry Caterpillar* nearly by heart). The idea of seemingly impossible transformation is embedded in our culture—our American culture in particular. We make something new of ourselves, we reinvent, we go quiet, shed our skin, and come out more beautiful on the other side. The fact that our aggressive and ongoing transformation of our national natural landscape is killing the uplifting symbol of that transformation makes us question things a little.

We also care deeply about the monarch because along with the twinge of guilt there is the ability to self-absolve. In the case of the Topeka shiner, the dwarf trout lily, and even the prairie butterflies, it's all on us Americans. So to some degree we put it out of our mind. But the monarch can also be Mexico's fault. Everything I read in the literature about the monarch says the reasons for its decline include possibly pesticide use and habitat loss throughout the United States and on its wintering range in Mexico. Usually, that statement is followed immediately by stories of illegal logging in the Sierra Madre and the Mexican government's inability to protect the few remaining wintering grounds.

The monarch is a species we love and can feel guilty about, but not too guilty. Same as with elephants and rhinos and polar bears: I didn't buy any ivory, we say, that's the Chinese. If only Asian countries would ban rhino horn powder. I keep my heat turned down in the winter; I drive a hybrid. I made sure that deck I built used certified lumber, so it's not from illegal cutovers in the Sierra Madre. But consider this: the route from Mexico to Minnesota roughly follows Interstate 35 through lands that were once rich with prairie flowers. What do we expect the monarchs will eat on their arduous journey? And it is becoming increasingly obvious that what there is to eat is already poisoned by neonicotinoids. That's not a Mexican problem—it's about American corn and soy fed to American cattle and sold in our local supermarkets.

The administration of President Barack Obama took the issue seriously. In 2014 Obama issued an executive order to address the plight of pollinating bees, bats, butterflies, birds, and other insects. The order established the Pollinator Health Task Force, a working group of federal agencies charged with creating (within 180 days) action plans for research and public education. It also charged federal agencies with improving pollinator habitat on federal lands—potentially a major step, because between the Departments of State, Interior, and Defense and the General Service Administration, well, that's a lot of land. In May of 2015 the action plan was released (a little late but not bad, as it goes with the federal government). There is quite a bit of detail, but the essence is this: more money for habitat programs, along with comprehensive research on neonicotinoids to be led by the Environmental Protection Agency—research which was completed in 2016.

Of course, as a directive from the president to the agencies, it can all be reversed when administrations change. Within two days of the inauguration of President Donald Trump, the *National Pollinator Health Strategy* had been removed from the White House website. It remains available on the archived Obama White House website, and the Trump White House website does include the *Pollinator Partnership Action Plan*, a 2016 document that highlights possible federal/nonfederal partnerships.

In the official Federal Register document listing the Dakota skipper and Poweshiek skipperling, public comment number 111 offered support for the USFWS and the Endangered Species Act in general, saying that it provides a great benefit to society. The commenter, however, "did not believe that listing the butterflies was one of [these societal benefits]." The commenter questioned why these two butterflies "are of such importance that they should be listed."

The response includes the basic finding that, under the preamble to the ESA, any species, if endangered, should be listed, regardless of benefit to humans. And it could have stopped there. But it doesn't. Buried deep in the eighty-somethingth page of a necessarily dry government document is this:

> [T]hese butterflies are important and do provide a societal benefit. Humans depend on the variety of life for food, clothing and medicines. When we lose species we lose their potential for the future and we lose their effect on other species which, in turn, have ecosystem roles and future value. Continued degradation of our lands and waters that reduces our biological diversity—the variety of life—is important. Habitat and water degradation, and maybe even climate change, can be reversed, but the loss of a species and its genes is irreversible.

Further, the prairie ecosystem is not completely gone, yet, but it will be if we do not take measures to save its plants and animals. Protecting these small butterflies means protecting their habitats, so that some of this ecosystem, with all its variety of life, remains. Humans depend on the variety of life for food, clothing and medicines. The variety of life that we have in this country, including functioning ecosystems, is our natural heritage.

This little essay says "variety of life" five times. In literary terms, it is poignant and unexpected writing, considering its source. It has em dashes. It has sentences made complex with exquisitely used commas. It repeats verbatim its key message: an echoing mantra. It has this poetic phrase: "the loss of a species and its genes is irreversible." It's a powerful whisper. This reminds me of Rachel Carson toiling in a government publishing office with a mind full of connections and a heart full of care.

Rachel Carson, before she became a household name for her 1964 book *Silent Spring*, was an in-house writer for the US Fish and Wildlife Service. If there are latter-day Carsons out there in government service, then neonicotinoids are this generation's DDT. We seem to be about at the equivalent moment as when Rachel Carson wrote her condemnation of DDT. There is significant community concern and quite a bit of circumstantial evidence to show that neonics are harming pollinators, but the government has yet to take firm action because, in essence, the science is not yet clear. When Carson's world-changing book came out in 1964, she and it were vilified. Today some honeybee advocates are called alarmists overstating the hazard. In most cases like this where something *seemed* hazardous (dirty drinking water, cigarettes, lead paint, DDT), the public was often way ahead of the regulation—and turned out to be right. There has rarely been a case when something so ubiquitous and widespread about which there was a health concern turned out to be safe after all. The facts always play out the other way.

Unfortunately, if this is the case with neonics, they will continue to be used for a long time before they are finally banned—and then, they won't be banned overall but only restricted. It's an ugly secret that though Carson's book famously led to a DDT ban, that ban is only on use in the United States. The chemical is still manufactured here for export to other countries where its use is legal. Cigarettes are still legal. Why? There is too much money at stake.

Neonicotinoids get their name because they are cousin to tobacco, acting on the central nervous system to produce paralysis and death in insects. The first commercially available neonic, Imidacloprid, was patented by the mega-corporation Bayer in 1985, and is still the biggest seller. Neonics have been in development, though, since the early 1970s (the DDT ban went into effect in 1972—maybe the big companies saw the writing on the wall . . .). Today, seven different neonics are in the marketplace under a variety of brand names, like Gaucho, Platinum, Assail, and Venom. The main "improvement" the neonics have over the organophosphates that Carson spoke out against is that they don't seem to affect mammals and birds the way pesticides like DDT do. But, remember, the science isn't settled.

Neonics are water soluble and are taken up by plants, so seed coating applications put neonics into the pollen and nectar of plants. According to the Environmental Protection Agency, nearly 100 percent of corn seeds and 75 percent of soybean seeds have a neonic coating. The EPA estimates that 3.5 million pounds of neonics were applied to 127 million acres each year between 2009 and 2011. The European Union and several European countries have restricted or banned certain neonics specifically because of negative effects on bee colonies. The EPA, though not required to do so by rule, has initiated a review process for all the neonics. All assessments are expected to be complete by 2018. A preliminary EPA and California study released in 2016 found that neonics are bad for bees, but only when applied on cotton and citrus. The EPA was sued in both 2012 and 2013 by environmental and food safety groups for failing to regulate or ban the insecticide. As of June 2016 the case was still moving through the system, tangled in paperwork. In 2013 a pair of US representatives introduced the "Saving America's Pollinators Act," which would ban the use of four neonics until the EPA study is fully complete. The bill died in committee.

Now to the circumstantial evidence. Neonicotinoids are insecticides: they are designed to kill insects. Over the past fifteen years, they have become the most widely used insecticides in the world. Over the past fifteen years, honeybee colony collapse disorder has spread worldwide and begun to threaten the livelihoods of farmers everywhere and the very availability of food. Over the past fifteen years, the monarch, which travels the Great Plains feeding on nectar, has gone from an abundant and regular visitor to an occasional and remarkable sighting. Over the past fifteen years, the Poweshiek skipperling, once so common that naturalists didn't even make notes on it, has been absolutely eliminated from Minnesota.

Thankfully, Erik and Cale are edging toward reintroduction of their Minnesota Zoo butterflies into the wild, which is a more difficult and controversial task than you might expect. The work with Poweshieks has been limited to raising butterflies from eggs to adults and re-releasing them back where they came from. But with the Dakota skippers, the zoo has several generations that have no direct connection to the wild. This brings us to a fraught and ongoing discussion in the scientific and conservation community. "So what do you do when you're working with something that's on the edge of extinction? Do you intervene or not?" asks Erik. "Do you take a California condor approach and get everything out of the wild and do a Hail Mary with breeding? Or do we do the opposite, stay totally hands-off and help populations recover through management of the landscape?"

To consider this question with regard to the Poweshiek and Dakota, Erik convened a workshop at the Minnesota Zoo. It took place over three days in October 2015 and involved fifty scientists from across the country. The so-called "structured decision-making workshop" used an International Union for Conservation of Nature protocol to determine the best approach for these two butterflies. The group decided that the Poweshiek would be best handled through a "head start" program. Poweshieks have never been seen breeding in the wild, nor have they been successfully mated in captivity. Therefore, the eggs that are collected each year in Michigan overwinter at the zoo as caterpillars and, when they emerge, are brought back to that same site in Michigan. In essence, the zoo program is trying to put more adults in the field by creating a higher survival rate through the controlled conditions of the lab. In the wild only a few percent of all eggs survive to adulthood. "At this point it's a bit of a triage," says Erik. "We don't want to lose any more populations. We're just trying to stop the bleeding."

In the case of the Dakota skipper, the breeding at the zoo has always been seen as an insurance population, but discussions have turned to reintroduction. "We're excited," says Cale. "But I'm a little nervous. These are my babies!" And in fact some of those babies went out into the world in the summer of 2017, the first reintroduction of any skipper butterfly in North America. The working group recommended and supported reintroduction of Dakota mainly because it's in better shape than the Poweshiek. The Dakota is gone from about three-quarters of its historic range (compared to 96 percent for the Poweshiek). At sites where they persist, the populations appear fairly stable.

It seems counterintuitive to me to focus on reintroduction of the less-threatened species. I ask: wouldn't the one in more dire straits be the one we would want to bring back more quickly? The experts give me a few reasons. There are very few Poweshieks to work with. There are only several hundred in the world, and they haven't been bred in captivity. That's the technical reason. The philosophical reason is this: reintroducing them to a different site, therefore, is in fact a relocation of a portion of one site's potential population, which could affect the population at the first site. Several hundred is barely a viable number, and splitting that would make two less-than-viable populations. At the core of these discussions is the edict to do no harm to existing populations. Any reintroduction program with the Poweshiek could jeopardize the world population. Thus the head start program instead of reintroduction.

Also, put simply, less is known about the Poweshiek. In order for a reintroduction to be successful, more must be learned about the animal's life cycle, its habitat needs, and the threats to its survival. "It's not just about the need to be there; we need to be smart about it," says Cale.

To that end, along with the head starting and the ex-situ breeding, Erik and Cale are exploring other avenues of research. They are looking at the optimal number of larvae per plant, trying options from one to seven. They have been using mainly prairie dropseed grass as the host plant for both species, under the assumption that this is a common native plant in the sites where the butterflies occur. It's been successful, but it's really hard to grow, so this year they have larvae living on big bluestem, little bluestem, sideoats grama, porcupine grass, and even nonnative Kentucky bluegrass and smooth brome. "As a conservation biologist," says Cale, "it's odd to spend time and resources growing smooth brome," but if successful in the lab, it will be far easier and cheaper to grow the host plants necessary to raise butterflies, which is the end game, after all.

One morning when I was young, I can't remember exactly what age I was, I woke up and all the bushes in the backyard were alive and moving. A big storm had come through the night before, and as the morning broke misty and damp, we looked outside at a world coated in butterflies. The house where I grew up in the suburbs of Chicago was set near to the back lot line, and a tall hedge of honeysuckle divided our yard from the neighbors'. The hedge was full of monarchs. They hung like an orange and black carpet, with blips of motion here and there as individuals pumped their wings in the growing warmth. Breezes ruffled the tapestry like laundry drying on a line.

We see monarchs in our city yard—not as many as thirteen years ago, when we first moved in, and we rarely see caterpillars, but they are still here. Our yard features a not-too-well-kept patch (we have two young kids, mind you) of leadplant, coneflower, butterfly weed, poppies, sedum, and flowering herbs like chives and oregano. This area is rich with bees and butterflies because we have a sequence of blooming throughout the spring, summer, and fall. Planting organic pollinator gardens is the most important advocacy action Americans can take if they want to keep species like the monarch, the prairie skippers, and the rusty-patched bumble bee around for the long term.

Every fall now, my family attends the Festival de la Monarca, in a park near our house in Minneapolis. This one-day multicultural party is put on by the Minneapolis Park and Recreation Board and a few partners. It is meant to bring awareness about the monarch and pollinators in general, and also cultural awareness about the city's Latino population. The migration of the monarch is the link. Aztec dancers, a kids' fun run, taco food trucks, art projects, and a monarch release are highlights. We go into a shady tent where recently hatched butterflies rest on potted prairie plants. With the careful help of naturalists, we affix a tiny, nine-millimeter polypropylene disk with microscopic lettering to each butterfly's rear wing. The butterfly's total weight is around half a gram and the insect may travel three thousand miles before it dies, so these tags have to be airy light—they're about two percent of the butterfly's weight. We carry the butterflies, still woozy from hatching, out into the nearby patch of prairie savanna, which has been carefully cultivated by neighbors for well more than a decade. We set them down on bee balm or a coneflower and watch them. Somewhere far away, a naturalist, probably in New England, will capture this same butterfly, read the lettering under a microscope, and catalog this individual's journey.

We—my small family and the network of people who care—are mapping the voyages of this species in order to better understand and protect it. There is no more miraculous life-form on earth than the butterfly—and it's at a tipping point. We are losing this life-form through our own direct actions, namely habitat loss and chemical use. Unlike climate change, these are not problems that can be too overwhelming to solve. There are things we can do in our backyards. We humans, we Americans have done this before: the eagle, the wolf, the alligator, the manatee—all were species suffering from direct persecution, habitat threats, and chemicals. All are species back from the brink.

If we act now, another generation of kindergarteners will be able to marvel at the most unbelievable feat in all of nature.

Unless we act now, butterflies will be just a story we tell.

Canada lynx

7

Lynx

The boreal forest is the world's largest terrestrial biome, covering about 29 percent of the world's land area. It circles the globe, generally above 50 degrees latitude, and covers nearly all of Canada, Scandinavia, and Russia. It dips down into the United States along the western mountain ranges, in the upper reaches of New England, and in the Midwest, where it is commonly called "the north woods." It goes by other names, too, depending on geography and subtle differences in plant and animal species. Russians call it taiga. Canadians use that word, too, when referring to the northern reaches of the forest, up near the tundra where the trees become sparser and plant diversity is low. Ecologists like "Laurentian mixed forest" for the combination of conifers and maples and oaks that covers much of northern Minnesota, Wisconsin, and Michigan.

Anyone who owns or has visited a cabin or lodge "up north" can picture the boreal forest/taiga/Laurentian mixed forest. It's about conifers and birches and rock-edged lakes. It is marshy depressions where beaver and moose and otter use dry places and wet places interchangeably. It is loon calls and the aurora borealis; granite outcrops and vast soggy bogs turned golden in the fall by the only needle-leafed deciduous tree: the tamarack, or larch. The commonality in all this is low temperature, low availability of nutrients for plants and animals, and significant variation in the amount of light by season.

The boreal forest of northern Minnesota, 2017

The boreal forest is one of the world's youngest landscapes, and it is built on some of the world's oldest rock. To understand this we need another name: the Canadian Shield. In the earliest days of earth's existence, more than 4.5 billion years ago, the molten magma that covered the entire earth began to cool into hard crust. The earliest great chunks of crust are known as *cratons*. These are the proto-continents, and they have existed since the beginning of hard land on earth. There is one under south Africa, another under western Australia, and one under central Russia. The Canadian Shield is under central Canada, stretching from Hudson Bay southward to the northern reaches of Minnesota. The oldest minerals on earth are in Australia and date from 4.4 billion years ago. But the oldest consolidated rock on earth is in the Canadian Shield, on the eastern shore of Hudson Bay: 4.2 billion years old.

Since their formation, these cratons have been moving about the earth, crashing into each other, breaking apart again, and collecting other bits of land to their edges. Earth was always and still is a volcanic world, and the edges of the cratons are tortured complexes of lava flows, ancient mountain ranges risen and re-eroded, and newer sandstones and limestones transformed in the heat of even newer volcanic events. But through all those billions of years of torment, the cores of these cratons remained stable—geologically speaking. Some of the earliest granites in the world exist largely unchanged in Canada and northern Minnesota. (The oldest rocks in Minnesota, interestingly, are not in the north, but in the Minnesota River valley, which was part of an even older micro-continent that collided with the Canadian Shield around 3.5 billion years ago.)

The floor of northern Minnesota is ancient, but this landscape has been wiped clean over and over again by glaciers. The boreal forest is young because periodically, over millions of years, mile-thick carpets of ice have scoured the life off the bedrock. Farther south, in the tropics, in the southern prairies, and even in vast swaths of the deciduous forest, trees and grasses have had time to build a comfortable existence. They have created their own fertilized bed in which to grow. They have cracked the rocks and incorporated the minerals and their own dead tissues into deep, rich soil. Not so in the north. On the Canadian Shield the glaciers have been gone only about eight thousand years. That's an eyeblink in ecological time.

Time in the boreal forest is never straightforward. The age of the rock defies our concept of age, while the forest itself came into existence when there were already humans in North America. A swamp of spindly black spruce looks like a young nursery planting, when in actuality each tree could be more than a hundred years old. Seasonal change is nowhere more dramatic, and animals rush in the summer and sleep through the winter. Hurry up and wait; wait and then hurry up. Some frogs spend fully three-quarters of their lives literally frozen solid. In summer, the evening seems to go on forever, while in winter the hearth fires are lit at three in the afternoon. On a windless winter morning, time stands as still as is possible, while the black spruces try to become as old and weathered as the rock. Amongst this, wild rabbits change color to match the season, and the hunting cats float silently on the snow.

"The lynx *is* the snowshoe hare," says Dan Ryan, in the mode of some kind of Zen koan. "And the hare *is* the boreal forest." Dan is not the kind of man from whom you might expect a Zen koan. He is a wildlife biologist for the US Forest Service, based in Aurora on Minnesota's Iron Range. He is midwestern through and through: born and raised in the suburban Twin Cities, schooled in rural Wisconsin, and now working among the woods and lakes of Minnesota's far north. I am riding beside Dan in a forest service truck. He is taking me lynx tracking.

As Dan's koan suggests, finding lynx (*Lynx canadensis*) is all about finding the right landscape. The boreal forest is a sere land with little to eat. Animals must be ready either to eat anything that comes along or to specialize and get really good at finding that one thing. In winter, the snowshoe hare (*Lepus americanus*) eats the branches, twigs, and small stems of deciduous trees and shrubs. The lynx is also a specialist. It eats snowshoe hares. Around 95 percent of a lynx's diet is snowshoe hare. Find the hare, find the lynx. Find the boreal forest, find the hare.

The area where Dan works—and the area we are exploring on a bright, comfortably cool February day—is perfect. In fact, it is the epicenter of the lynx discussion in Minnesota. This cat was trapped for fur up into the 1970s, right along with other furbearers like fox, bobcat, and beaver. It's not that trappers wanted lynx specifically—a lynx is not actually that much different, as a fur commodity, than bobcat—it's just that they were there, too, in the forests trappers were working. But lynx numbers dropped off. There were very few sightings in Minnesota in the 1990s, leading to the belief that this was a long-traveling feline migrating down occasionally from Canada. Its full common name is the Canada lynx, after all. Most people doubted that the lynx was reproducing in Minnesota, and because of this, it wasn't considered for rare or endangered status. But in the late 1990s, a pair of kittens was found near Isabella, and scientists began to question the old thinking. The forest service and others (most notably Ron Moen of the University of Minnesota Duluth) began studying the animal, found it was in fact resident in Minnesota and recommended it be placed on the endangered species list, which it was in 2000.

The same year the lynx was listed, Dan came to northern Minnesota and started tracking the cat. He goes out dozens of times every winter, a few days after a fresh snow, when lynx tracks are most visible. When we were planning this time in the field together, we both watched the forecast and kept in touch several times a day, so I could travel north at just the right time.

We drive east from Aurora into the Isabella area, the state highways hemmed in by high plow-drifts, snow still clinging in clumps to the trees. Dan talks in a matter-of-fact monotone (but without pause) until some subtle difference in the landscape makes him quiet. I can see the change, too. The aspen and white pine give way to scrubbier conifers. This area on either side of the St. Louis / Lake County line is a southern finger of the great northern boreal forest. It feels more harsh somehow. The trees are less majestic, but individuals have their own twisty, strange characters. Thick groves give way to white, open fields studded with seedlings barely breaking the surface of the snow.

Dan begins scanning the roadsides. He slows, and his eyes dart across the road ahead—the left shoulder, the right shoulder. Where the land drops down away from the road, he sits tall in his seat and peers over the drifts. Where the land rises up, he scans the edge of the forest at the top of the road cut. Every so often, the pristine plain of white is laced with prints. Sometimes they wander out from the forest edge, then return back into cover within twenty yards. Sometimes they make a direct line for the road and continue on the other side. Sometimes they come to the road and end—the animals often follow roads and may plunge back into the snow some distance farther along.

Dan stops the car and we get out. Tracks come right up to the pavement. "You can kind of see they're always pretty much in a straight line," Dan says, pointing at the paw prints near my feet. "They're always floating on top there, not really punching down like a wolf would do. You can kind of see here, the four pads, nice and big and round. This is a real nice easy one to see." The print is huge, nearly as large as my hand, and makes barely a divot in the snow. The depressions created by the pads are spread wide apart, with little ridges of snow between. Dan explains how the lynx, in deep snow, will widen its feet, much as we humans can spread our fingers apart to catch a basketball. Foxes can't do that. Bobcats can't do that. The lynx is built to hunt in the snow.

I raise my eyes to the line of prints heading into the forest edge. But Dan doesn't want to follow this one. Over the past fourteen years of following tracks and identifying individual animals, he knows pretty well which cat is which and who is where. He was also out tracking yesterday and has already been out many times this winter. He is looking for a complete picture of this year's population, and he's pretty sure he has already accounted for this cat. So we get back in the truck and drive on.

After another ten minutes or so of driving, Dan spots two sets of tracks, not unlike that first set, leaving the road edge and making a beeline for the woods. These he wants to follow, so we gear up for the snow. Dan, as usual, tells stories about unusual lynx sightings from his years in the winter woods. Perhaps counterintuitively, we won't try to be like the lynx and wear snowshoes. I had assumed we would, so I brought a pair, but Dan warns me off them. The brush is often very thick, and under

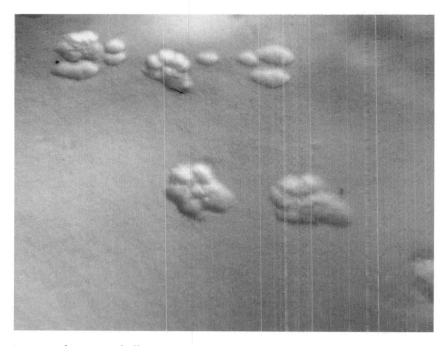

Lynx tracks near Isabella, Minnesota, 2016

the snow is a mass of branches that in summer are thickets and in winter are snowshoe entanglers and ankle breakers. Best to wear sturdy warm boots and waterproof pants and just post-hole down into the snow.

We stand at the road edge and survey the two lines of prints. "I guess right now, if you want to just follow this one," Dan directs me to the left tracks, "they'll come back together. We'll just make sure we stay within sight of each other. Lynx are normally solitary but females with kittens usually stay pretty close to each other. If we can find where they killed a hare, then we have a better chance of finding a scat."

Yes, we're looking for poop. Though it's wonderful to see actual animals (the day before, Dan encountered a mother and two kittens that just stared lazily at him as he cruised by on a snowmobile), it's not necessary. The best way to identify individuals and family relationships is through genetics, and there is plenty of genetic material in poop. Dan can find out which cats are in the woods without ever seeing one.

I verify my mission: I'm looking for poop. "Yup," says Dan, grinning, "yup."

"And in a moment," he says, heading off along his line of tracks, "you'll find out how deep the snow is."

I take two steps alongside my designated set of tracks, careful not to mess them up, in case Dan needs to check my work, I guess. Pretty easy going, actually. Then about the fourth step I plunge down up to my hips. I nearly bury myself in the snow face-first. The awkward foot placement feels like missing the bottom stair. I can't help but exclaim, and Dan laughs good-naturedly.

I post-hole through the snow, the lynx tracks beside me barely making a dent. My tracks suddenly split. Are there two animals? Hare tracks also muddy the picture. Dan comes over to help. "Do you want to follow that one and I'll follow this one?" Dan suggests. "Sometimes when they get into the really thick hare areas, it gets hard to follow them." We are in a low, snarled thicket, and I am performing acrobatics to simultaneously get over the waist-deep snow and under the neck-high branches, all while trying to keep an eye on the sequence of prints coursing effortlessly beside me. "You don't have to follow them exactly, just make sure you don't walk by a scat." No pressure. . . .

An adult lynx weighs between eighteen and twenty-four pounds and is very similar in appearance to the bobcat. The lynx has gray-white fur, long black tassels on its ears, and a very short, black-tipped tail. It has longer legs and bigger feet than a bobcat does. Dan Ryan says the best way to tell lynx and bobcat apart when spotting one in the wild is that the bobcat will run from you while the lynx won't seem perturbed. But really it's the feet. The only lynx I have encountered is at the Minnesota Zoo, where three sisters can be seen springing up fake-rock cliff faces and leaping across a trickling recirculating stream. Those feet are big.

Also unlike the bobcat, which can be found in most forest types, lynx are boreal forest specialists. The core population of the Canada lynx is therefore in Canada, where it is found nearly coast to coast across large swaths of almost every province. Lynx territory also crosses into Alaska,

A Canada lynx at the Minnesota Zoo, 2015

but the populations in the contiguous United States and in Alaska are considered completely separate from a management standpoint.

The listing of the lynx in 2000 was the climax of more than ten years of legal and administrative wrangling. The contiguous US population was first considered a candidate species in 1982. In 1991 the US Fish and Wildlife Service determined that listing for the Cascades population, at least, wasn't warranted. The agency was promptly sued, re-evaluated its findings, and again decided not to list the species. But in a 1993 settlement, the USFWS agreed to look at the entire contiguous US population for possible listing. A year later the agency again decided not to list the lynx anywhere, mainly because there was not sufficient evidence that the lynx was resident in any of the four areas where it was occasionally found. Another lawsuit was lodged in 1996.

Here's where it gets a little complicated. The court ruled in that 1996 case that the USFWS basically had to go back to the drawing board—had to reanalyze its finding within sixty days. So the USFWS reversed its opinion, but said there were other priorities that needed more immediate attention. Essentially, the agency said: Fine, we'll consider listing, but only after we do a whole bunch of other species. This of course did not satisfy the original plaintiffs, Defenders of Wildlife and fifteen other environmental groups, so they sued again for immediate consideration of listing.

The USFWS settled that suit in 1998 and agreed to a very tight timeline for listing. In fact, the Federal Register listing from January 2000 all but apologizes for its out-of-date science. The USFWS relied mostly on the data gathered from the original 1993–94 examination (upon which data, remember, the agency declined to list the animal), rather than the most current research. That 2000 listing, as a result, says that there is no evidence of permanent lynx residency in Minnesota or elsewhere. And that's why wildlife biologists in Minnesota and elsewhere set out to study the animal and find out whether it was resident and breeding in the contiguous United States. They have found that it certainly is.

But the 2000 listing isn't the end of the story. The USFWS listed the lynx as threatened, and was immediately sued again on the grounds that it should have listed the animal as endangered, meaning "in danger of extinction throughout a significant portion of its range," and also should have designated critical habitat for lynx. The court sided with the plaintiff and sent the USFWS back to the drawing board again with the task of re-evaluating its findings. In 2002 the agency again listed the lynx as threatened, not endangered, and again demurred on the critical habitat designation, specifically citing low funding and staffing levels to accomplish the task.

But the USFWS got to work on designating critical habitat. For the next ten years, different habitat options were proposed, criticized, remanded, and redrawn. Finally, in 2014 the agency published a final critical habitat rule. In Minnesota, everything east of Highway 53 from Duluth to International Falls is critical lynx habitat, except for the core of the Iron Range itself and the Grand Portage and Bois Forte Reservations. The total area included is just more than eight thousand square miles. Critical habitat was also designated in Maine, Montana, Wyoming, and Washington.

On the heels of the lynx's listing on the endangered species list, and at about the same time Dan Ryan began collecting scat in the Superior National Forest, Ron Moen started catching lynx and fitting them with radio collars, with significant assistance from former graduate student Christopher Burdett. Ron is a wildlife biologist and professor of biology with the University of Minnesota Duluth's Natural Resources Research Institute. In 2003 Ron began putting collars on lynx in Minnesota and tracking them from small airplanes. Between 2003 and 2009 he collared thirty-five lynx in all. He was trying to answer some general questions about how lynx move and how much time they spend in Minnesota. He was also curious about how the different laws in Canada and the United States would affect lynx populations. "The Endangered Species Act stops at the border," he says. In Ontario, the lynx is a furbearer that can be legally caught during the trapping season. In Minnesota, federal law disallows any deliberate taking of the animal.

Ron is a large, soft-spoken man with strong hands weathered from decades of working with scientific equipment in the Minnesota cold. He has studied moose, lynx, and the recently listed northern long-eared bat. For his lynx study, Ron and a team put box traps about the size of coffee tables out in the woods and baited them with legs from roadkilled deer. The traps had to be checked daily because, says Ron, "You have to be cognizant of the animal relying on you to survive" once it is in a trap. The cat is anaesthetized with a syringe on a long pole and then fitted with a collar. When the study began, GPS was not widely available and affordable, so pilots in small planes (most often Mike Nelson, a biologist with the US Geological Survey) would fly back and forth across the landscape to find the animals' locations. The study continued until 2009, with the most significant report coming out in 2008. Ron found that lynx definitely were living in Minnesota, but that few kittens born in the state were entering the breeding population. One-third of the collared lynx went to Ontario, some as far east as the northern bend of Lake Superior.

Ron stresses throughout our conversation in his Duluth office that the Minnesota lynx population is an extension of the Canadian one. Minnesota lynx are and will continue to be periodically supplemented from Canada. Looking just at Minnesota lynx is like looking just at the outskirts of a city and making assumptions about population density.

"Northeastern Minnesota is the southern tip of the boreal forest," says Ron. "We've got several species that are either on the southern edge of their [historic] range or because of human action—that's the wolf—are at the southern edge of their range. We would never expect to have a large population of lynx in northeastern Minnesota." Ron's own 2008 report suggests that the maximum number of cats in the state would be about 250. There are probably between a hundred and 150 now. "It's not like we'd expect them to necessarily thrive. The snowshoe hare population is patchy."

Along with the radio collar study, Ron's team also did counts of hare pellets (poop) within different cover types and arrived at a predicted density of hares. And where the hares were or should be more dense, that's where the lynx stayed. The lynx *is* the hare. "Lynx require disturbance," Ron says, "not because the lynx need it, but because snowshoe hare does. We don't manage for large patches of eastern Minnesota to be disturbed like that."

About five minutes after leaving Dan Ryan's truck, I am physically exhausted and mentally drained. I have to keep asking Dan to help me keep the path. I feel like a liability, but he is patient and obviously having fun. He's been out here in twenty below zero and worse. He's been out here in even deeper snow. I'm breathing hard and Dan is happy to have it so easy. But he's getting entangled, too. "Big open area right over there and they have to walk us through this thicket," he says with fond exasperation.

The lynx tracks are obviously following the hare tracks. Sometimes the cats have traipsed alongside the hare, sometimes they walk in exactly the same line. Follow the leader. The hare is seeking the thick, brambly areas where it feels safe and also can reach the tips of spruce and birch

weighted down by snow. It is moving across the landscape from copse
to copse, perhaps unaware of the silent cat following it. The lynx is following food, too, but its food is mobile and leaves a telltale pathway
to its whereabouts. The track of a hare is like spooling thread. The
hare unspools it outward, while the lynx spools it back in from behind.
If the two spools meet, a battle ensues that usually leads to death for the
hare and nourishment for the lynx. If the lynx can move more quickly
than the hare across the same landscape, it will eventually come to the
end of the tracks—the spot where the hare is browsing. But if there's
too much thread—if the track is too old and the hare too far away—the
lynx will fail.

The relationship between the hare and the lynx illustrates ecological
principles at their most basic. The relationship boils down all the com-
plexities of nature into a simple equation. The more hares in the woods,
the more likely the lynx to catch one. And the inverse: fewer hares equals
hungry lynx. Let's imagine a particular moment in time with few hares.
The lynx won't eat well, won't reproduce well, and will die off. Fewer
lynx will survive to adulthood, and fewer will hunt hares. This gives the
hares a breather. Bunnies are good breeders, so they quickly produce
lots more bunnies. The forest is full of bunnies. Now, the remaining lynx
will eat very well indeed. There is less competition among lynx, and the
hares are easy to catch because the woods is crawling with them. The
lynx have more kittens; the kittens have plenty to eat and grow up to
be hare-hunting adults. Now the pressure is on the hare: they are being
hunted without pause to feed the booming lynx population. Their population crashes. The cycle returns to the beginning, with the lynx now
struggling to find food.

Of course, even in this relatively simple equation wherein 95 percent of one species' food is another species that has few other predators,
it's not as simple as my explanation. But this idea of cyclical scarcity
and abundance and the interrelationships between animals and plants
is foundational. Dan and other scientists see an approximately ten-year
cycle of boom and bust for hares and lynx. Current thinking is that the
hares are governing the cycle. Hare populations may crash for reasons in

addition to lynx, but the variety of factors contributing to these crashes are largely unknown.

The knowledge of that ten-year boom-bust cycle comes mostly from trapping records. Minnesota has the most robust historic trapping records of any state, with annual data for forty years. Lynx were regularly trapped in the state, along with beaver, coyotes, bobcats, wolverines, and foxes. The lynx harvest in the state ranged from zero to four hundred animals per year, with peaks in 1940, 1952, 1962, and 1973.

Hunting and trapping are protected in the Minnesota state constitution, because of a 1998 amendment passed by referendum. Trapping is certainly a far less popular activity than hunting, but the fur trade brought Europeans into the state and gave them a foothold in the north woods. Though beaver was the big draw for the fur companies, other animals were both sought and incidentally captured.

In the 1970s, the state's trappers experienced several seasons with no lynx, and the state instituted a quota of five total animals starting in 1977. The quota was regularly exceeded, so in 1983 it was further reduced to two cats. Nine were taken, again exceeding the quota. Wildlife managers became even more concerned with the low numbers combined with excessive take, so the season was closed in 1984 and remains closed today. This prohibition on trapping lynx of course coincides with the broader national discussion about the species' status.

Today, the Minnesota Trappers Association is active with chapters across the state. The organization provides classroom and practical training to budding trappers. It publishes a readily available pamphlet called "How to Avoid Incidental Take of Lynx While Trapping or Hunting Bobcats and Other Furbearers." Though I could not find a trapper willing to speak with me about endangered species, it seems the association is doing its part to reduce take. And all the scientists I spoke with (consistent with the Federal Register listing) didn't feel trapping is now or ever likely was responsible for low lynx numbers in the United States. The fact is the boreal forest is patchy here, and it can't support that many hares—and therefore can't support that many lynx.

★ ★ ★

I come to a T intersection of tracks, quite confusing in the forest. Dan helps me out again: "Yeah, this is one walking *this* way; yours keeps going back that way. Keep backtrailing." We have been following the lynx in the opposite direction it is walking (that's backtrailing), so I find and follow the tracks coming into the junction rather than walking away from it. Then what I thought was a single track suddenly develops a spur trail that heads toward the tracks Dan is following over behind the next thicket. I alert him.

"Okay." He pauses to look around. "It might be this one coming toward you. Is it going this way or that way?" I try to discern the direction of travel, but I can't tell. The paw prints aren't as perfect as those first ones I saw. Dan starts to walk over to me. I wonder aloud if there are tracks in both directions right on top of each other.

"Yup," he confirms. "They like to confuse things. See, they're kind of stepping on each other. Keeping in their tracks. Easier to stay up on the snow. Let's just walk this and see." It's all a big puzzle. Lynx tend to circle around seemingly aimlessly, though I am sure they have a purpose in their ambling. They use other lynx's tracks, even tracks that might be days old. It's possible to be following what seems like a single track, only to have different sets edge off to one side or the other, plunge through thickets, stop, return through the thicket, and rejoin the original tracks heading in the opposite direction. Especially when there's been a kill or the cat is close to finding a hare, following the tracks can feel like following a strand of spaghetti through a bowl of pasta primavera. Though my eyes are tuning to the shape and the subtle difference in light and color of lynx tracks in the snow, I still can't read the story. I do notice some nuance: a long, straight line of tracks that seem too close together and might be two lynx walking in line; a mess of prints in a thicket that I don't follow in detail because there's one clear entry and exit.

"It's fun to follow them and just get a feel for what they do," Dan says with a smile, as we pause a moment to catch our breath. "Especially families. A lot of times, the families are just in line, they're not hunting, the kittens are probably tired. You'll find a bed soon after that. And other times, like here, where they're doing this kind of stuff." Dan gestures at the circular paths of overlapping prints at our feet. "They're hunting; the kittens have a lot of energy. The kittens are the ones that will jump and climb on top of stuff. When they're young, the kittens have these long legs and huge feet. They really look out of proportion." I see tracks on top of bent-over tree limbs in lines that follow the bending arc all the way along; single tracks on the ground, on top of low branches, and on the ground on the other side, as if a kitten leapt up, then down. We're in a rather open thicket following a bunch of tracks that Dan thinks is a family. He's no longer following the tracks exactly, as I am, but getting the general impression of movement. "I like to think by now I can think like a lynx," he chuckles.

We're not moving like lynx, though, and my muscles are aching. I expect I must be slowing Dan down, but I keep up as best I can. Then, forty minutes after I plunged hip-deep for the first time, Dan finds what he's looking for. "Look over here," he calls to me from his set of tracks. "Scat in the bucket. See, the tracks came here, he stepped right here, squatted right here." We have a good laugh about this dainty lynx, who took a moment to deposit its business not on the cold ground but in an old rusty bucket wedged between a couple of logs. This placement looks entirely deliberate. "It's in a national forest," says Dan. "It knows to use the latrine."

Dan puts the scat in a brown paper bag and labels it LS41, with the date and location. The number means this is the forty-first scat Dan has collected this year. Last year he got a hundred. At the end of this season he'll be up to seventy-three scats and eight hair samples. He sends all the collected samples to the National Genomics Center for Wildlife and Fish Conservation in Missoula, Montana. Genetic analysis can identify individual lynx, so Dan can essentially map those cats for whom he has collected scat and determine the interrelationships between males, females, and kittens.

The scat in the bucket was from a female lynx called GLNR-S-551. Dan was right about following a family: S-551 had a new kitten (likely born the previous May), whose scat was picked up in another location. S-551 has a lineage that proves lynx are resident in Minnesota—exactly the kind of information Dan hopes for. She was originally found in the winter of 2013–14 as a kitten, two years prior to my visit with Dan, but in the same general location. She is the daughter of a cat called Loch132, which is one of the oldest cats in the database, having been first identified in 2010. That cat's identifier comes from Steve Loch, a retired Department of Natural Resources biologist who is a mentor to Dan. Steve left his job at the DNR to fully focus on lynx, researching the animal and collecting scat on his own time. Almost half the samples in the overall scat-finders' database are attributed to Steve.

The lynx Loch132 has produced many kittens in the area, mostly with a male called GLNR-S-270, who was dominant for many years but seems to have been replaced in part by another male. Loch132 had another litter the year after giving birth to S-551 and was found again in 2015–16 but appears not to have had a litter. Nevertheless, the bucket-scat lynx's mother would be six years old and has been found nearly every year in the Isabella area.

Having collected what he came for, Dan leads the way back to the truck. We have come quite a ways into the woods and circled around, so I'm glad for Dan's sense of direction. At the truck, he logs the find in a notebook, including the date, location, and his name. This scat-finder's database grows each year and includes a few different names (though mostly Dan's), just as the number of known lynx also grows as families change, newcomers enter the territory, and kittens are born. The truck grumbles to life and we are off again to find the next set of tracks.

Several times through the afternoon we plunk through deep snow to follow tracks Dan spots from the road. As the day continues, I become able to see the roadside tracks and distinguish between deer, hare, and lynx at a distance. At one stop we see an odd set of tracks: four tiny paw prints in a row, then a big gap, and then four more, on and on. Dan thinks it might be a pine marten run-jumping through the snow, desperate for cover. Later, we follow clear lynx tracks that Dan thinks might be a big male lynx—maybe the new main breeder in the area. He's eager to get a scat sample to test that hypothesis. We follow prints that stay at the fringe of the forest, then return to the road and disappear. The animal has been peeing regularly, trying to indicate his presence and/or dominance. Dan swears this is the last tracking of the day, but I can tell he doesn't want to stop until he gets some scat from this one. We walk up and down the road from the truck trying to find where the tracks might re-enter the snow.

"He must be using the road," says Dan, peering off into the distance in both directions. We get in the truck and drive slowly. After a while, Dan feels like the cat should have left the road by then, so he turns around and drives slowly in the opposite direction, passing our previous foray. At last we find another set of big tracks likely to be the same cat. As we follow them toward the woods' edge, Dan says, considering how much it seems to be using the road, "People must be seeing him. He's a big breeder."

Near where the lynx tracks leave the road is a culvert under the highway. Otter tracks lead to the culvert, descending the slope from the woods. The track is a continuous line in the snow, broken by deeper clusters of messy paw prints. I can almost see the otter belly-whopping down the slope, pushing off with all four feet to keep the slide going. We follow the lynx tracks as they loop in and out of the forest, coming into the open for long stretches and then plunging through the thicket.

"Some of these guys have their own personality," says Dan, as we seem to cover the same ground over and over again. "Sometimes I'll be following what I think is a family until I walk it all and find it's just one looping around. Something about that area he must really like."

The looping ends in another plunge deeper into the woods. In a small clearing within the thicket, with a few bent-over trees piled up with snow, we encounter a maelstrom of tracks. The snow is packed down with them. Loops of disturbed snow extend into the woods, like flares reaching out from the sun's surface. It's chaos. And in the middle of it all the snow is spattered with blood. Three small bits of white-gray fur are the only evidence of what died and was eaten here. It appears to have been quite a chase. The hare had the advantage of its small size to duck under branches and fly quickly through the thicker parts of the thicket. The lynx had the advantage of reach and length. The hare clearly attempted to dart across the surrounding openings, then thought better of it and returned to the thicket, pursued by the cat. In the end, the lynx was fed.

Dan was excited for me to see a kill site, but even more so because it looked like the lynx ate the hare right there—and that means it might have relieved itself nearby. We follow the tracks heading away from the kill. Dan lets me lead. I pay close attention to the tracks themselves, not wanting to lose the trail.

Behind me, Dan says, "Hey, why don't you retrack this section here." I turn around and within two steps see a scat, perched atop a little hummock of snow, prominently displayed for me. How did I miss it? As before, Dan packages up the cat pie and we head back to the truck. "See, I told you," he says. "Last one of the day. This was the one."

Scat number forty-two for the year was, as Dan thought, a male. So-called GLNR-S-729 had been identified the previous year about five miles from where we tracked it. In all, Dan found this cat six times in 2015–16, with a fairly wide range of ten to fifteen miles. He was not the father of either of the two litters of kittens in the area, but Dan thinks he was setting up a home range in hopes of breeding in the coming year. Thus all the urination and constant roaming, even along roads.

When Dan enters the data in his log for number forty-two, he puts my name as the finder. I try to demur, especially because I had, after all, walked right past that prominently placed poop. Dan chuckles at me: "I didn't see it. I just told you to rewalk it."

I must admit I find it oddly satisfying that my name appears in the official Minnesota scat-finders' database.

The rain has come. The forecast was correct. We are getting a dousing shower that will clear away the last dregs of snow, raise the creeks, and wash our winter-weary cars. Up north, the hares may start to turn brown for summer. This spring rain will certainly refresh the denizens of this northern city, Minneapolis, and bring us out of our semi-hibernation into sunny days of frolic and short sleeves. But this year, rain feels like a coming death. It is mid-February. That is far too early for April showers to be bringing, well, *March* flowers. The Minnesota Public Radio meteorologist who made today's forecast said last week that "the Arctic is broken." Rather than lifting my spirits toward summertime, this gloomy cloudbank has me unsettled, nervous, on edge. It's not right, this early warming. I lament the loss of winter.

The warmest year on record globally was 2016. It beat the previous record holder, which was 2015. Up through April 2017, Minnesota had experienced twenty months in a row of above-average temperatures, a streak not matched in 143 years of recorded weather. These are the true facts—to which there is no alternative "theory." Time itself is becoming strange. The earth has warmed and cooled throughout its history, a slow, million-year oscillation like one's breath while asleep. But this current warming is a hyperventilation. Winter is shortening at a rate unseen in the historical and geological record.

The anecdotal evidence is perhaps even more powerful. Any Minnesotan over the age of about twenty has stories of massive snowfalls in December, snow days in April, unfettered skiing in the woods on glorious depths of natural snow, and sledding anywhere and everywhere. The winter of 2016–17 in the Twin Cities was an utter disappointment. Nordic skiers had only the few loops in the metro that have snowmaking capabilities. All winter, my youngest son asked to sled—and I was looking forward to seeking out the best spots in the city to swoosh downhill with him—and we didn't go even once. Snowman building, snow fort excavation, and snowball fights have all been limited pastimes. The ice skating was good, but even that got started well late of normal (after the first of the year) and then closed in February for about two weeks due to high temperatures. No one I know can remember a Minnesota winter with only a month of ice skating.

But so what? Weather doesn't need to oblige my or anyone else's need for recreation and beauty. The preceding paragraph is an easy one to write. It is easy to document all the things we can't do, all the pastimes missed. What has me most unsettled is that winter, up north here, was always a hopeful reassurance that the climate wasn't too far gone. While

Al Gore was traveling with his inconvenient road show, we had feet of snow on the ground and were teaching the kids to downhill ski. While the IPCC (Intergovernmental Panel on Climate Change) was forecasting doom and gloom in the Arctic, we got caught in a "polar vortex," which spun out two weeks of below-zero temps. When the Larsen C Antarctic ice sheet was calving off an iceberg as big as Delaware, I was getting up in the subzero dark and clearing ice from fishing holes augured into two feet of ice on a northern lake. As long as I had winter, climate change felt reversible. As long as I had winter, it felt like we could still fix the world before it was too late.

Now it feels too late. It feels like all the things climate scientists have been predicting for decades will actually happen, and there's nothing anybody can do about it. And the wake-up call is made even harsher on the heels of the 2016 election. We can expect at least four years now of (at best) inaction and (more likely) outright denial on climate and environmental issues. Maybe four years wouldn't have mattered anyway, but the gradual positive creep in fuel efficiency requirements, renewable energy percentages, and building energy consumption will certainly halt. Yet, the unexpected bombastic president, the big oil companies, and Wall Street financiers are easy marks. I have helped kill winter just as surely as they have. I am an oil consumer.

So this coming rain fills me with sadness and guilt. In January, the day after Inauguration Day, I marched on the state capitol with a hundred thousand other Minnesotans. My wife and two boys were with me, and another family of four. It was a pleasant 40 degrees. I had never taken part in a march or protest of any kind before. Strictly speaking, this was the Women's March, but liberals of all kinds were there: gender rights advocates, immigration advocates, and environment/climate advocates. I had a conversation with my friend, the dad/husband of the other family, about climate change. We talked about the weather, of course, but mostly about our own actions. I noted—perhaps to assuage my guilt—that I felt like I could have done more, but also wonder what a few fewer car miles by me and my one family would have really done. And my friend said, true, but imagine if we all had done that. Driven a few fewer miles. Kept the lights turned off. Turned down the heat. Diligently bought local produce year-round. Created less demand for oil.

In the short term, it's not mainly humans that will bear the brunt. "With climate change, [the lynx] will probably be pushed north," Dan Ryan told me in the truck that day in 2015 between tromps through the snow. The Endangered Species Act petition to list the moose specifically references climate change. Ron Moen thinks the US Fish and Wildlife Service, as it manages endangered species, will have to address range shifts driven by a warming climate. If the boreal forest in northeastern Minnesota is replaced by the red and white pines and aspen of the mixed Laurentian forest just to the south, all the animals will move north with the forest. Already, there are more bobcats seen than is typical, and Dan's genetic analysis shows increased hybridization between lynx and bobcat. Bobcats eat a variety of animals, are less dependent on the snowshoe hare, and do better in low-snow years.

"A lot of this is going to depend on habitat," said Dan. "On what the boreal forest looks like in the future. If the forest starts retreating north, the lynx are going to go with it."

So I feel the winter-shaped hole in my soul. I also remember why winter has a place there to begin with. Last November I got caught in an early-season snowstorm at Mille Lacs Kathio State Park on the southwestern shore of Lake Mille Lacs in central Minnesota. As I worked and read in a camper cabin four miles from the park entrance, the woods (to borrow from Frost) gradually filled up with snow. The snow was heavy and the branches of pines and alder became laden with what looked like gloopy frosting. The alder tops bent to the ground in great arcs of white—arc upon arc, creating a pillowy Seussian landscape. A DNR employee checked on me in the morning, left a snow shovel, and made sure I had enough water, food, and fuel. He said he wouldn't be able to plow me out until the next day. The feeling of being caught in place by weather was comforting and thrilling. The snow came sideways at the cabin, and the gas fireplace glowed. The next day, the woods were silent in the way only a blanket of snow can bring. I snowshoed in the buttercream wonderland, threading through branches weighed low to the trail. An owl left its perch and flew down the trail in front of me, silent as the winter woods.

Once the ice rinks opened in Minneapolis, after a pleasant two-week stretch of cold, the boys and I went to Lake Hiawatha Park and glided on borrowed skates. My ankles tired before theirs did, so I put my boots back on and sat on a snowdrift looking west across the lake. It was close to the winter solstice and around 4:15, so the sun was nearly down. The frozen lake appeared liquid, with drifts of snow seemingly ready to crash on the shore like waves. Ethan came and sat by me in the amber glow. He had been writing haiku poems at school, inspired by photographs of winter distributed by his teacher. The poems and images adorn each child's locker, and I have been surprised by these third graders' word craft. So there at Lake Hiawatha, with the weather a windless and comfortable eight degrees, Ethan was inspired and spoke the first line of a haiku: five simple syllables with a lovely resonance. We finished it together, there on the snowbank:

Winter lake looks like
A picture of a windy
Summer day—frozen.

For all the times I have been to Nerstrand Big Woods State Park, I had never gone in winter until this year. The boys and I went after dropping Kerri at the airport for a short work trip. We were on the trail at 9:00 AM and had the woods to ourselves. Enough snow blanketed the slopes to make the whole landscape sparkle every time the sun found a break in the overcast sky. We snow-tromped and slip-slid right down to Hidden Falls. The creek was running on one side, exploding from under a thin, transparent dome, revealing itself, and then dropping into a hole to course downstream under thick ice. At the other side of the falls, a stable cascade of ice curtained over the lip and merged with the frozen floor. Behind the curtain and under the rock overhang, a low ice cave beckoned with fantastical formations and a floor so slippery we found it impossible to stay put. The three of us crawled in on our bellies. We rolled over on our backs and gasped at crystalline stalactites, thick floes of perfectly smooth and transparent ice that revealed the rock underneath as if in a snow globe, and fragile frost-stars clinging to the stone ceiling. The curtain of ice separating us from the outside world glowed in various shades of white and gray, depending on the thickness of the ice. Our breath rose to the top of the cave in clouds, and we could almost see it adding to the delicate formations. We were at once in awe and feeling playful, scooting about on the super-slick floor, taking pictures, and pointing out new discoveries with shouts of excitement.

Around Valentine's Day, Kerri and I took a few days away by ourselves. We went to the National Forest Lodge, a cross-country skiers' haven near Isabella, in the Superior National Forest. We had a one-room cabin with a bed and a chair, and access to a bathroom and shower building, outdoor hot tub, wood-fired sauna, polar plunge hole cut into the ice of Lake Gegoka, and around thirty kilometers of ski trails in the national forest. We parked our car in front of the cabin and didn't move it for three days, taking our meals with all the other lodge-goers in the communal dining hall. The place was like a summer camp for adults—in winter. On Saturday we skied through frozen tamarack/black spruce bogs and up over red and white pine ridges and around Flathorn Lake—one of the most beautiful winter trails I have ever experienced. We saw otter tracks, the pawed slide disappearing into the Little Isabella River at the outlet of the lake. We heard a bird call like a struck crystal but never learned what it was. In the silence of the woods, ravens would startle us with their *bronkling*. We returned to the lodge for hot soup and grilled sandwiches, then descended to the lake in swimsuits, wool socks, and boots and entered the dry warmth of the sauna. The little wooden room was full of National Forest Lodge veterans, old friends who have been coming north in winter since the 1990s. Stories were shared and laughter reverberated. Once in a while, someone would sprinkle water on the hot rocks and we would feel that flush of heat on the back of our neck for which there is no word (we tried to invent one—some Germano-Finnish compound noun—but nothing stuck). Then, in pairs and small groups, people would dash from the sauna to the lake, plunge in the icy tea-colored water, and re-enter the sauna.

Kerri and I had never done this before. But we ran in swimsuits and water shoes to the hole. A moment's hesitation can turn into a *No*, so we blanked our minds and jumped. Emerging, I found it hard not to cry out ecstatically, to howl, almost, there on the snow in the cold. I experienced a moment of discomfort, my body reacting latently to the vice of icy water after I had already climbed the ladder. Then peace settled in. The air breathed not a wisp. My skin throbbed gently: skin—taken for granted as a living organ, unlike the heart, which always beats. My skin became an active life-form. Lines of heat cashed about in it. Hairs stood up, evidence of thin muscles all over my body I never understood so fully. I had no urgency to return to the sauna. The vista across the lake captured me: white expanse; black, jagged forest; gray-white sky. An essence of landscape, a simplification of forms, and, as always in winter, silence—an active silence that drowns the usual bodily beatings and ringings and leaves not the silence of self but of the world.

The next day, I skied alone in the morning, taking a different loop than what Kerri and I had done the day before. Striding along in the classic tracks, climbing slight hills and poling back down the other sides, I was suddenly struck by a sense of another presence. It came over me like a chill wind. Animal-like, my neck hairs stood up. I stopped, and the silence settled in. I peered deep into the woods, trying to distinguish something furred from among the living weave of aspen and fir. I felt fear and exhilaration. The Isabella area, Dan Ryan told me the winter before, is the heart of lynx habitat in the United States. He had told me the best way to distinguish a lynx from a bobcat is that the former isn't scared of you. A lynx will lackadaisically hang out and watch you with those contemptful feline eyes. It will go when it wants, not when you get too close. Wolves are here, too.

I paused for some time on the trail, my senses on alert. Nothing. Another hundred yards down the trail, I felt that presence again and again stopped and scanned the landscape. Those who study wolves and lynx and other forest mammals will tell you these animals are rarely surprised. They see you first, and if they prefer not to be seen they won't be. I saw nothing. I heard nothing—not a cracking branch, not a rustle of leaves, not the slightest break in that winter quiet. Yet still my skin told me something was there. I will never know for sure.

The shape of winter in my soul is those experiences and many more. It is the fun and the contemplation, the discomfort and the warmth, the visual contrast in daylight and the variability of night—sometimes complete and utter darkness, sometimes, with just a little moonlight, a brightness as if we were owls. It is crow calls and otter tracks and the songs of unknown birds and footprints undecipherable. It is the hiss of skis and the crunch of snowshoes. It is becoming aware of my own skin and the desire to enter my lover's as outside the wind howls and inside the fire glows. It is the chance of seeing the aurora borealis tint the sky and snow unnatural colors. It is the ability to enter a bog and wind amongst black spruces as strange as Truffula trees. It is the danger of exposure. It is admiration for adaptability. It is the possibility of lynx in the woods.

Western prairie fringed orchid

8

Orchid

What is it about orchids?

The 2017 Minnesota Orchid Show at the Como Zoo and Conservatory, is, actually, a zoo. Ten minutes after the show opens its two-day run, the line to get in snakes out the building entry and down the sidewalk. The sales area—the first thing I encounter after paying my entry fee—is a gauntlet to run: narrow aisles crowded with gawkers, salespeople like hawkers watching for any glimmer of interest, showy bursts of color leaning out into the crowd to say "take me home, love." Inside the conservatory proper, people jostle for space in front of the carefully arranged displays of flowers scattered throughout the indoor gardens. Each display of maybe a dozen or so plants attracts a shuffling line of aficionados craning their necks to get a glimpse. Photographers with serious equipment wait patiently for a gap in the throng, then click, click again, and saunter away with self-satisfied grins. Orchid-ese is spoken everywhere. "That's a beautiful Paph." "Yes, ah yessss, the yellow bird." "The best Sophronitis display I've seen all year."

As a tribe, the orchids entrance in a way few of us—even the orchid lovers—can fully articulate. Statements like "They're beautiful" or "They're so interesting" or even "They're a fantastic challenge to grow," though all true, don't quite explain it. Orchids, behind ivory, rhino horn, and tropical hardwood trees, are the most illegally harvested and traded natural resource. Of the world's roughly thirty thousand endangered plant species on the CITES list (CITES is the Convention on International Trade in Endangered Species—it's an international treaty governing rare species), about twenty-four thousand are orchids. Border police regularly bust people for transporting orchids illegally, either individuals who feel just one taken plant won't make a difference or highly sophisticated smuggling rings. A 2015 report by TRAFFIC, a wildlife trade monitoring group, and the Center for International Forestry Research exposed widespread illegal trade in Southeast Asia. A survey of markets in Thailand found that more than 16 percent of all the orchids offered for sale were endangered and listed as such. The study even turned up in the markets species that were new to science.

The best-known analysis of the obsession with this plant is Susan Orlean's 1998 book *The Orchid Thief.* "Orchids are the sexiest flowers on Earth," says the book. So also says the book's unusual movie adaptation, called *Adaptation.* Orlean becomes a character in the movie, entangled in a world of sex and (orchid-derived) drugs and murder in the Florida swamps. The screenwriter Charlie Kaufman (who also appears in the movie as a character played by Nicolas Cage) says he wants to make a movie about flowers, but can't, because the flowers and the ensuing obsession are really about us. Says Orlean's character in the movie: "I wanted to see this thing people were drawn to in such a singular and powerful way."

Orchids are the most abundant and varied plant family on earth, with twenty-eight thousand species (as of 2016—the list keeps growing). They are everywhere, from the Arctic tundra to the drippiest rainforests, though most are tropical. They are, of course, known for their flowers, which can range from the bulbous pouches of the lady's slippers to rice-grain-sized blips of color barely noticeable against the leaves to ones that look like monkey faces, or wasps, or trumpets. When I visited the orchid show I saw shapes I didn't think possible in nature.

A couple of key things make an orchid an orchid. The flowers, for all their variety, are always symmetrical down their vertical midline. There are always three sepals and three petals, one of which is modified into some kind of showy lip, which acts a bit like a runway or landing pad (more on that later). The defining characteristic, not always noticeable, is the fact that the male and female sexual organs—stamens and pistils—are fused. This so-called column keeps the pollen and the ovaries rather close together at all times. The sexiest flower on Earth. . . .

But, despite this proximity, orchids don't self-pollinate. Almost all orchids rely on others for reproduction, and this is the reason for the variety in their flowers. Orchids have evolved to attract bees, wasps, bats, butterflies, and moths. These variations are not all that unusual in the plant world, but the lengths to which orchids go is often extraordinary. Many have transformed themselves into likenesses of animals, and may even smell like females ready to mate. It's the most diabolical trick: a wasp lands to mate with a lovely lady wasp and gets instead a packet of pollen stuck to its head—and no satisfaction (though, really, how can we know for sure?).

Orchids are needy in reproduction, and also in early life. They produce huge quantities of seed, in some species small as specks of dust, but the seed has no food stores, no endosperm to get it through those first key days before the green leaves can start to pull energy from the sun. Instead, the seeds require fungus to give them a kick-start. The fungus may be in the soil, on the bark of a tree, floating in the air—wherever a particular orchid is evolved to grow and develop. And just as most orchids require a certain species of pollinator, they also require a certain fungal profile to succeed. This, scientists think, is why there are so many different species and why most are extremely limited in their habitat. As the soil profile and the fungal composition change, from valley to valley, elevation to elevation, wetland to upland to forest, so must the orchid change, differentiate, become unique.

Minnesota is home to forty-three species of orchids, including the state flower, the showy lady's slipper (*Cypripedium reginae*). Ten appear on the state's rare and endangered list, and one is listed as threatened on the federal list. That species is the western prairie fringed orchid (*Platanthera praeclara*).

Nancy Sather has studied the western prairie fringed orchid for decades. Unable to join me on my trip during the summer of 2016 to look for orchids in northwestern Minnesota, she does the next best thing.

The western prairie fringed orchid in bloom (courtesy Peter Dziuk, www
.minnesotawildflowers.info)

During a phone call while I camp at Buffalo River State Park, she gives me detailed instructions for finding western prairie fringed orchids. She gives me a verbal treasure map that involves distances in meters, certain gravel roads, conspicuous rocks, and other landmarks. This is on Saturday night. I had tromped (carefully) in prairies all that day, in places she had told me about during a meeting earlier that spring, and had found nothing. I had been hot and exhausted, surprised at how tallgrass prairie, especially damp prairie, can wear the knees and scratch the face and hands and fill the clothes with ticks. I hang up from our call reinvigorated for Sunday's exploration. She thinks I might be a bit early to see the western prairie fringed orchid in bloom, but asks that I report back on what I find, and send pictures. Northwestern Minnesota is a long drive from St. Paul, and she and her colleague Derek Anderson want to be sure there are blooms before making the trek.

Let me pause from the story a moment to explain what comes next. Throughout this book, I have been specific about the places I have traveled. I believe place is important to the story, and I have the faint hope that you, the reader, if intrigued enough, might venture out and make your own discoveries. In the case of every other species in this book, there's little harm in being specific. The animals are mobile, and the other plants are either very hard to reach (Leedy's roseroot) or already pretty well marked (dwarf trout lily). Minnesota populations of the western prairie fringed orchid, however, are few. They have a tenuous hold on survival, and fanatics will harvest them illegally. Therefore, I will not share the treasure map. I will say only that I was on public lands (these are the only places the orchid is regularly surveyed and protected). You may glean from other facts in this chapter the general area I explored and the type of habitat where orchids are found, but place names will be conspicuously absent here.

This is a more difficult decision for me than it might seem. I tend to believe that awareness breeds affinity and affinity breeds concern. I want to lead you, reader, right to that glorious prairie sentinel, and trust that you will be careful with your steps and take only pictures—not even a single flower, nor a seedpod. But there's something about orchids that makes me just a little bit skeptical of everyone's intentions.

On Sunday morning I break camp at Buffalo River and drive north. I come up empty at the first of two sites. After hiking for two hours, I sit down on a pair of glacial erratic boulders and eat lunch, then drive on. At the second site, I begin hiking at one of the landmarks described to me on the phone, counting paces as I swish through a windy prairie, roiling dark clouds overhead. Yellow lady's slippers and showy lady's slippers—both slightly past prime bloom but still bright and obvious—color the linear low areas where the soil is wettest. Western prairie fringed orchids require moisture, too, but their needs are more subtle on the surface. The landscapes in which they grow tend to look dry, but have a shallow hydrology pulsing just under the surface. I walk and walk until the ground rises up ever so slightly and the composition of the prairie changes. It is getting drier. I have gone too far. I search the prairie even more carefully on the way back, but still find nothing.

After two hours, reluctantly (ever so reluctantly) I pull out my phone to call Nancy. No service. It is getting late and a storm threatens, so I give up for the day, intending to try again tomorrow. Driving off, I notice, a little farther along, a landmark strikingly similar to the first. A trick in the treasure map! A duplication to throw off the searcher. I walk again, counting paces, and this time, within a step of the distance I was told, I come into a loose circle of about a dozen orchids. They are unmistakable in the prairie: bright spring green contrasting with the dun olive of the grassland, taller by far than all other plants, and stout-stemmed in a way grasses never are.

Western prairie fringed orchids have stems that rise abruptly from the soil, with pointed clasping leaves from root to crown. A gentle curve in the upper stem gives the plant a certain grace and confidence, like a willowy beauty slouched to the side with a hitch in her hips and a cant to her shoulders. Each plant is crowned with a dense cluster of bright green bulbs, about the size and shape of garbanzo beans. Nancy was right: I am early (about eight days early, she would tell me later when I sent pictures to her and Derek). But she is pleased, because she expected this would be a poor year for orchids.

The buds of a western prairie fringed orchid in northwestern Minnesota, 2016

In 2016 the first orchid leaves emerged on March 26, when temperatures rose enough to tempt them up from dormancy. On May 12 several orchid sites were deliberately burned, which is done every four or five years to manage the prairie overall. Fire seems to affect orchids depending on its timing. Circumstantial evidence from a study performed in southwestern Minnesota by the Department of Natural Resources and a long-term volunteer suggests that late-summer burns can halt next year's blooming. A spring fire is likely survivable, as the orchids are still small. But the day after the 2016 burn, on May 13, a late frost visited northwestern Minnesota. A similar situation—early emergence and late frost—had occurred in 2012, and that year Derek found no flowering plants during his surveys. Add the fact that the area is in the midst of a multiyear drought, and Nancy doubted I'd see any buds at all. If it's possible to gauge the tone of an email, Derek and Nancy, upon receipt of my pictures, seem thrilled and eager to perform a rich survey, which they had thought would be an exercise in frustration.

The fact that early emergence and late frost has happened twice in four years, in the midst of a region-wide drought, is not lost on Nancy. It's actually the first thing she mentions to me about the orchid. Moments after we sit down in the cafeteria of the Minnesota DNR, I ask her what I should focus on with the orchid. "Climate change," she says. "That's the problem." This was a few months before my trip to northwestern Minnesota. She references a landscape transect that DNR botanist Welby Smith created in southwestern Minnesota. Basically, a transect is a documented line in the landscape that can be revisited year after year for comparisons. Smith's transect included "climate buttons" that gauge temperature and other factors over time. Western prairie fringed orchids bloom along the transect, but those at the higher elevation end have disappeared. And the higher end has gotten warmer. In addition, warming temperatures may be leading to earlier emergence, which can make orchids vulnerable to those occasional "late" frosts in May.

None of the federal documentation of the orchid, however, mentions climate change. The western prairie fringed orchid was listed as threatened under the Endangered Species Act in 1989, along with its close cousin, the eastern prairie fringed orchid (*Platanthera leucophaea*). The distinction between the species only dates to the 1970s and is based both on range (the Mississippi River seems to be a general dividing line) and subtle differences in physiology. Both species have showy white flowers around two inches in size. The name comes from the bottom edges of the flowers, which look like the tassels or fringe on some western clothing.

The 1989 listing is pretty early for a plant, and consideration of both of these orchids dates all the way back to the original Endangered Species Act of 1973. Section 12 of the ESA directed the Smithsonian Institution to develop a list of vascular plants considered rare, endangered, or extinct. At the time of the ESA, several high-impact animals (like the wolf) were well known and studied, but plants weren't on the national radar, and certainly not in the public eye. The Smithsonian did as it was told and in 1975 presented a whopping list of seventeen hundred plant species for possible listing, including the prairie fringed orchid (at the time considered to be one species). The US Fish and Wildlife Service endorsed the Smithsonian's work and proposed all seventeen hundred as endangered.

But several amendments to the ESA between 1978 and 1982 kept many of those plants—including the prairie fringed orchid—in limbo. By the time it was eventually listed in 1989, the main reasons cited were loss of habitat due to the conversion of prairie to crop- and pastureland and "Overutilization for Commercial, Recreational, Scientific, or Educational Purposes." The former reason shows up in almost every endangered species listing. Essentially, species are most often rare because we humans have converted their habitat to something else. That second reason is less common, and in this case the listing specifically calls out private collectors. In the case of the western prairie fringed orchid, the listing says, "overcollecting may become a serious problem for this species. At least one instance of removal of a . . . plant for commercial purposes has taken place in Minnesota." The USFWS also opted not to designate critical habitat for the plant. It was felt in 1989 (and remains the opinion today) that habitat designation could actually be a detriment to the orchid. "No benefit to the species can be identified," says the listing, "that would outweigh the potential threat of vandalism or collection, which might be exacerbated by the publication of a detailed critical habitat description." So say the feds: collectors might love a series of maps showing exactly where these orchids are—let's keep that a secret.

The prairie fringed orchids, incidentally, have been on the CITES list since 1975. They're in Appendix II, so not under a total import/export ban, but transport is strictly regulated and cannot be done for commercial purposes.

In 1996 the USFWS published a recovery plan for the western prairie fringed orchid, and a five-year review came out in 2009. Though it identified some additional threats, including herbicides, pesticides, impacts to drainage from off-site activities, and invasive species, it recommended keeping the orchid at threatened status rather than increasing protection to endangered. This was in large part because the vast majority of known populations are on protected lands, where government and nonprofit agencies are working to create management plans to sustain the orchid.

The western prairie fringed orchid is found in two different areas with somewhat similar geology and hydrology. The main recipe for orchid success seems to be soil that stays moist (though not wet) due to the presence of coarser soils than those strewn across the landscape as a whole. Put very simplistically, if you dig a hole in the black dirt or clay of your yard (assuming your yard is black dirt or clay) and fill it with sand, and if your groundwater is high enough that the sand stays wet, that's where to grow your western prairie fringed orchids.

These conditions exist in two places on the tallgrass prairie that once covered the United States between roughly the Mississippi and the middle of the Dakotas. One is a small pocket in southwestern Minnesota, centered on Pipestone National Monument, where the bedrock rises up to break the surface of the prairie. Here, the orchid grows on the broad flats between the cliffs of quartzite. The geology here is one of the most unusual in the world, because under that quartzite are thin layers of Catlinite or pipestone, out of which native people have carved ceremonial figurines and pipes for thousands of years. The stone was traded across the continent. The quarry in southwestern Minnesota was considered neutral ground, and people from many tribes came there to dig the stone. Nancy thinks that at Pipestone, the bedrock is having a "bathtub effect." Over the years, depressions have filled with coarse soil—soil kept moist by the inability of water to drain through the bedrock. The more widespread populations of orchids, however, live in a narrow north-south band stretching from just south and east of Moorhead up into Canada near Winnipeg. These are the Glacial Lake Agassiz beach ridges.

Louis Agassiz was a Swiss scientist who dabbled in quite a few different disciplines in the mid-1800s. He was the foremost authority of the day on the classification of fish (especially fossil ones). He classified classification—cleaning up the morass of taxonomy that had become unruly in the age of discovery. But most importantly, he studied ice. In 1840 he published *Études sur les glaciers* (*Studies of Glaciers*), an examination of the formation, movement, and historical extents of Alpine glaciers. He is remembered today (there are animals, creeks, peaks, peninsulas, and even a crater on Mars named for him) because he went way beyond the Alps to posit that the northern hemisphere had once been under a great ice sheet.

Of course, now this is accepted science, with modern-day geologists debating the exact timing and direction of various ice sheets but never questioning the basic premise. But in 1840, it caused a sensation. The glaciation theory was rather quickly embraced Agassiz became a scientific celebrity in his own time. (Unfortunately, no man seems to remain untarnished, and Agassiz's legacy ends with his lifelong denial of evolution and his "scientific" inquiry into the differences between "races" of humans.)

So Agassiz was likely top of mind for the Minnesota Geological Survey's Warren Upham. Upham was born in 1850 and moved to Minnesota in 1879 specifically to study the geology of what others were starting to notice might be a massive lake bed in the northwestern corner of the state. (Upham, like Agassiz, was a polymath: in 1920 the Minnesota Historical Society published his seven-hundred-plus-page volume on the history of Minnesota place names.) In 1895 the US Geological Survey published Upham's simply titled *The Glacial Lake Agassiz*, in essence officially affixing the Swiss geologist to the Minnesota and Manitoba landscape.

Glacial Lake Agassiz is believed to be the largest lake ever to exist in North America. Its lake bed covers the northwest corner of Minnesota starting around Browns Valley (the little lump on the state's western border) and heading north and east all the way to Rainy Lake. The fat

pan of the Red River Valley in Minnesota and North Dakota is Agassiz
lake plain. But that's only a small portion of this behemoth. The lake at
times covered most of Manitoba, lunged east halfway across Ontario, and
stretched a long bay northwest over almost the entire width of Saskatch-
ewan. Upper and Lower Red Lakes, Lake of the Woods, and the massive
Lakes Winnipeg and Winnipegosis are all remnants of Agassiz. Though
its shorelines ebbed and flowed over the minimum twenty-three hundred
years of its existence, at its maximum possible extent it was 170,000 square
miles. That's nearly twice as large as the five Great Lakes combined.

Agassiz formed as a result of the presence and weight of glaciers extending southward from the north polar regions. Several glacial advances
had plunged into Minnesota prior to about twelve thousand years ago,
building up a series of high, hilly moraines that cross what is now roughly
the center of the state. A continental divide (the Laurentian) was well
established by this time, dividing water flowing north to the Arctic
Ocean from that flowing east into Lake Superior and the Mississippi
River. The last glacial advance was the Des Moines lobe, and as it melted
back toward the pole it exposed a swath of land that was lower than both
the ice and the Laurentian Divide. That depression filled with water. Incidentally, the land sloped generally northward because the polar glaciers
were so heavy they weighed down the land (it is still rising today, like a
squeezed sponge returning to plumpness). In essence, all the drains
were plugged by the ice and the bathtub just kept filling with meltwater.

The gradual change in the lake over two thousand years is complicated though pretty well understood. Reading the lake in the present-
day landscape is possible because no subsequent glaciers came along to
rearrange things. I won't go into the stage-by-stage details here, except
to say that as various different drains unplugged or as the lake got so
high it overtopped the moraine to the south, Agassiz changed size and
shape—and changed other landscapes nearby. The most catastrophic
and lasting change wrought by the greatest lake is the broad valley of
the Minnesota River. Ice dams at the northern lake outlets caused the
water level to rise to a low spot in the continental divide near Browns
Valley. The water began to slice easily through the soft glacial till and run

exuberantly southeast as the Glacial River Warren. The Minnesota River still runs in this channel, where in places 3.5 billion-year-old bedrock is exposed, but it's a shadow of its former self. The Warren cut a valley five miles wide and 150 feet deep and plunged over a waterfall near downtown St. Paul that would have outshone Niagara in volume and spectacle. The Mississippi River gorge, Minnehaha Falls, and St. Anthony Falls are all vestiges of River Warren. The ancient river is named for General G. K. Warren of the US Army Corps of Engineers. Warren, while surveying the area in the 1860s, correctly suggested—decades before Upham studied and named Lake Agassiz—a massive river must have flowed out of a massive lake to the north. (Upham has a glacial lake named for him, too, an area now occupied by the extensive tamarack bogs in St. Louis County between Duluth and the Iron Range.)

Glacial Lake Agassiz, being absolutely huge, possessed an entire lacustrine ecology, including currents, variations in lake-bottom texture, fish and frogs and birds, and beaches. Whenever the lake water elevation was stable for a long enough period of time (hundreds of years, perhaps), wave action driven by winds from the west piled up sandy, gravelly strands on the Minnesota side. These beach ridges are apparent in the landscape today. They mark the eastern edge of the Red River basin as the flat, silty, rich farmland begins to rise up into the hilly, forested lake country to the east.

The most prominent beaches are named for a string of towns along Minnesota Highway 9 southeast of Breckenridge (just across from the North Dakota–South Dakota border). To come the right way forward in time, you have to travel west. The highest and oldest beach, dating from the earliest days of Lake Agassiz around twelve thousand years ago, is the Herman. Younger and about thirty feet lower is the Norcross. Another twenty feet down is the Tintah. The lowest and newest, dating from the most recent incarnation of the lake about ten thousand years ago—and about forty feet below the Tintah—is the Campbell. This youngest beach, not surprisingly, is the most obvious and continuous. It forms the eastern ridge at Buffalo River State Park and runs nearly due north all the way to Canada.

On my 2016 orchid hunt in northwestern Minnesota, I spend some time driving and walking in the Glacial Ridge National Wildlife Refuge, a mosaic of federal, state, and private lands just east of Crookston in Polk County. The beaches are easier to see traveling eastward. They're not mountains, but coming up from the absolute flatness of the Red River basin, a thirty-foot rise is something indeed. On US Highway 2 east out of Crookston, the Campbell rises up between County 46 and the Gentilly River. The beach is signaled by the sudden strain of the engine and by the S&G gravel pit. Another six miles on, another rise, and another group of gravel pits: Strata Corporation and two unnamed ones. That's the Tintah beach. That one feels smaller, but it's still visible. This corner of Polk County is the spot where the shoreline of Lake Agassiz turned hard to the east (Red Lake is directly east of here), so the ridges are starting to diverge a bit. Farther south on Highway 10 just east of Buffalo River, you get all four in rapid succession before you reach Hawley. They're so close together they kind of blend.

Up in the national wildlife refuge, the ridges are bending east. The Herman is a barely noticeable hump right at the little town of Mentor. I take a right here on Minnesota 45 and head back west to find the Norcross at County 32. That road through the refuge runs on top of the ridge and, though there is only about ten to fifteen feet of elevation change from the road to the surrounding prairies, it feels like a viaduct.

Perhaps the most interesting and obvious way to enjoy the ridges is to drive the Pembina Trail. It's a little tricky to find in the field but easy on a road map. It's the one road in Pennington and Marshall Counties, between Dorothy and Carpenters Corner, that wiggles all over the place instead of being grid-locked north-south-east-west. There are two reasons for that. The more recent reason is that today's road follows an old oxcart trail laid down in the mid-1800s. And, of course, the other reason is that the trail follows—what else?—the Campbell beach ridge. Between the Pennington and Red Lake County line and Old Mill State Park in Marshall County, no fewer than fifteen gravel operations dig into the old lake edge. To the east, the land is lower than the road, but rolls a little—maybe there are other beach ridges in the distance giving the landscape some relief. To the west the land is lower still, and flat. And mostly treeless. That's the lake bed itself—the agricultural land of the Red River Valley.

So what does all this geologic and landscape history have to do with orchids? Well, remember the kind of environment orchids like: sandy/ gravelly soil with reliable moisture? The beach ridges make this happen. Western prairie fringed orchids are most often found between ridges, especially right beside the feet of them, where the gravelly rise tapers into flatter, loamier prairie. The ridges create a seepage zone just below them. They seem to take in and hold water, then discharge it gradually into the prairie just to the west. Depending on the minerals and nutrients in the soils, this can create wet prairies, calcareous fens, or shrub swamps growing up out of nothing more than cobbles in standing water. These orchids have never been found below the Campbell ridge—never on the lake plain proper. They seem to be most common between the Campbell and Tintah. That raises some questions about how to best conserve this finicky species.

Having spoken with Nancy more than once already by the time we meet to discuss the orchid at DNR headquarters, I knew it was just a matter of time before she started writing in my notebook. She waits only about fifteen minutes before seizing my pen, turning my book around, and sketching a diagram of conservation. (A little while later she also drew a fairly detailed map of northwestern Minnesota, for which I would be very thankful in my travels.)

"One approach—the present and prevailing approach to conservation," she explains, "says to buy the very largest landscape that you can protect. Protect huge landscapes and they will be the most resilient and will carry nature forward into the future through environmental change." The other end of the spectrum is to find the truly rare entities and preserve them, even if only a small land purchase is possible. She notes this is the way the Nature Conservancy operated when it began in the 1970s. "There has been a big paradigm shift since I came [to the DNR] in 1979," she remembers, "from protecting the little rare places to protecting the big places. My personal take on this is that we need both. This is because in part the dwarf trout lily, and certainly the orchid, and *definitely* [she taps my pen hard for emphasis] the Leedy's roseroot exhibit an affinity for microhabitats."

She knows I have been studying endangered species, so she uses them—and the Minnesota landscape—to illustrate the point. Minnesota has lost 98 percent of its prairie, and has therefore lost 98 percent of its prairie habitat. For a more generalist species like big bluestem, presumably, 98 percent has been lost. But the big bluestem is not endangered because it grows pretty much everywhere on the land that has been preserved. In contrast, if 98 percent of the southeastern Minnesota Driftless Area habitat were lost, we would not lose 98 percent of the Leedy's roseroot habitat. It lives on a cliffside. It would be possible to lose the whole rest of the landscape and still have Leedy's roseroots because the cliffs are not arable. That's the optimistic version. The sad version is that we could preserve most of a landscape and still lose species—if we miss preserving certain microhabitats.

"There are a number of people that think if we save these big prairie ecosystems, we will of course save these rare plants," says Nancy, "but in point of fact, even the prairie bush clover—which is probably the most ubiquitous [endangered plant]—they never were over 98 percent [of the prairie]." If, she says, we focus on the biggest tracts of land we can get, we might miss the microhabitats necessary for certain species. In the case of the western prairie fringed orchid, what if the decision were made to buy up all the land between the beach ridges, but allow extensive gravel mining of the ridges themselves? Hundreds of thousands of acres could be protected, restored, and managed and the orchid might still disappear. Landscape happens at the macro and micro scales simultaneously, and must also be protected at both scales simultaneously.

Nancy then notes a third conservation paradigm: to conserve off-site. She references the butterfly conservation efforts at the Minnesota Zoo and then brings up David Remucal's work with her beloved orchid.

"Some of what we do here could potentially be seen as controversial," says David Remucal. To be honest, it doesn't look all that controversial.

I am sitting with David in his office at the Minnesota Landscape Arbc-
retum, a University of Minnesota–run facility amidst the specialty crop
fields and burgeoning suburbs of the western Twin Cities metro area.
David is the arboretum's curator of endangered plants. His office has the
scientific clutter—specialized books crammed onto rickety shelves, field
gear strewn in the corner, old conference speaker nametags here and
there—I have come to expect in my scientific interviews. The controversy to which David is referring is the creation of an alternative to landscape preservation—also known as "in-situ" conservation.

"Preserving the landscape preserves all the unknowns," he says. "Is
there something in the soil that is important? Is there something in the
air? Is there something in the hydrology of the site?" Clearly, the western
prairie fringed orchid, with its reliance on a particular water regime,
fungus, and pollinator, is the perfect example of this.

David states, however, that it is an undeniable fact that humans are
dramatically changing the landscape. Climate change for starters, but
even for those deniers out there, there is still the conversion of prairie
to cropland, the drainage tiling of that cropland (which affects hydrology far beyond the land tiled), and many other activities that are funda-
mentally altering that complicated web of ecosystem interconnections.
"There needs to be a backup to the landscape preservation model,"
David says.

So David is growing western prairie fringed orchids. And he is creating a species seed bank. David is tall and wiry, rather young-looking, his
hair buzzed close to his scalp. He has been at the arboretum for three
years, previously having spent most of his career in the west. He was a
noxious weeds expert in Colorado and worked at the Denver Botanic
Gardens. He was a vegetation ecologist for the Navajo Nation's Natural
Heritage Program. Over the next couple of hours, David and I wind
through mazes of hallways into rooms that don't at first glance appear
particularly, well, sciencey. We enter a brightly lit office with little plastic cups scattered around on tables and shelves. At the bottom of each
cup is a layer of translucent yellowish gelatin. In some, green fronds
reach toward the lid; in others, white tendrils that look conspicuously

like bean sprouts snarl against the sides of the cup. These are grass pink orchids and small white lady's slippers. Fringed orchids aren't the only ones David is working with.

Behind a door is a device called a laminar flow hood. It's a square box with one end open to the room. The back is a surface of silver metal pores—it's like looking at a tall stack of corrugated cardboard, end-on. Air issues from that screen, creating negative pressure within the box. A scientist can sit in front, as if sitting at a desk, and work with tiny particles, and no germs can accidentally drop into the hood.

This is important because orchid seeds are tiny. David shows me a test tube filled with the same gel I saw before—a nutrient-rich goop called *agar*—and a sprinkling of what looks like black pepper. These are western prairie fringed orchid seeds, collected from the wild at the very location I saw these plants about to bloom. But David is not sure about these: they have been in those tubes for more than a year and there is

Western prairie fringed orchid seeds at the Minnesota Landscape Arboretum, 2016

no indication they are germinating. This may be because the necessary fungus is not present.

We walk down another hallway and through two locked doors to a back office with stacks of bankers boxes—those sturdy cardboard cubes you see in the back rooms of accountants' or lawyers' offices David starts opening boxes. Inside are rows of glass jars with plastic cling wrap over their tops. The jars have various shades of gel in the bottom, like the ones I saw in the lab. Some are cream colored and opaque, some are jet black.

"In a lot of cases we don't really know the best way to grow these plants," David admits, "so we have to experiment with different types of [growing] medium." Two years prior to my visit, in David's first year working with orchids, not many of them germinated. But last year was better. "I feel very lucky to have been as successful as we have, especially because people don't study the terrestrial orchids as much." Here David is referring to the fact that, though the commercial orchid propagation industry is huge, most of the focus is on epiphytic species—those that grow not so much in the soil but in the air. If you've ever owned an orchid, you'll remember that it was probably "planted" in a very loose medium of dry and airy stuff, and that its roots would just as soon creep up over the edge of the pot and explore the living room as dig down into the soil. Most of those orchids would be content sitting on a counter, occasionally spritzed with water. At the orchid show at the conservatory, a significant percentage of the plants on display were just affixed to pieces of bark or branch, or sat in an open-slatted basket. Minnesota's orchids, on the other hand, do grow in soil. But these haven't been commercially cultivated because, David says, they're just not showy enough (or, presumably, federal and state law prevents collection of seeds or plants). There seems to be a growing market for the lady's slipper types, but they are much more difficult to grow than the epiphytic types.

David lifts out a jar with an inch of black gel at the bottom and hands it to me. "So . . . if you look right on the edge here you see that white ball of tissue," he says, "you will be able to see some kind-of hairs—it makes it look like *Sputnik*. That is a very young western prairie fringed orchid."

This is a growing protocorm, the first stage of orchid development after the seed. All orchids have protocorms, but terrestrial ones develop in the dark, under the soil surface. It looks like a tiny larva of some kind, rounded at one end and pointed at the other. In the next jar is an even larger protocorm. David seems pleased and a bit relieved. He hasn't checked on his crop in a while and didn't know how they were faring. "So we *do* have some growing." He smiles. "Phew." These are the first successful propagations of the western prairie fringed orchid in his lab.

Our next stop is the freezer. It's nothing at all special, just a deep freeze like you might have in your basement. It occupies the corner of a room seemingly used for just about everything: there are files and tools and lab equipment. Inside the freezer are glass jars with machine-printed labels, plastic bags in metal baskets, and cardboard envelopes in cardboard boxes in metal baskets. Inside these vessels are seeds of rare plants. This is the ultimate backup to the landscape preservation model: a seed bank. An ark.

Seed banks are unseen repositories of the world's vegetable matter. The most prominent, the Svalbard Global Seed Vault on the icy island of Spitsbergen, Norway, has 880,000 seed samples in cold storage. Seed banks are an insurance policy against catastrophe. They are the stuff of apocalyptic science fiction, where the world as we know it has been wiped out and, after a time, we (hopefully) surviving humans must re-grow the crops and forests and grasslands that sustain us. The seed banks (hopefully) will be there. Or maybe a blight of some kind wipes out all the world's wheat. Once we discover how to beat the blight, we can pull some wheat seed out of the cold storage and start anew. More recently, seed bank thinking has turned to conserving species for their own sake.

The Center for Plant Conservation was founded in 1984 with a mission to conserve—regardless of what happens with the conservation of landscapes—the most imperiled plants in the United States. Forty of the top botanical gardens in the nation have signed on, each taking responsibility for a handful of the one thousand plants CPC chose from state rare and endangered lists and the federal endangered species list. The idea is for these gardens to learn how to propagate and grow these species in controlled environments and to develop both a seed bank and a collection of living plants. In addition to the western prairie fringed orchid, the Minnesota Landscape Arboretum, under David's leadership, is working on two other federally listed species in Minnesota, the Leedy's roseroot and the dwarf trout lily; the federally threatened Fasset's locoweed, found only in a few Wisconsin counties; and three others on state lists: the western Jacob's ladder, Iowa golden saxifrage, and kittentails. (The other federally listed plant in Minnesota, the prairie bush clover, is being managed by the Chicago Botanic Garden.) These seven plant species are in essence David's wards.

In a greenhouse behind his lab/office building, David shows me the Jacob's ladder, a tall, spindly plant with lavender flowers. He's had great success with this plant, and the Leedy's roseroot. David's roseroot specimens are strong and full of flowers, despite not hanging from a cliff face. (I resist the temptation to start counting inflorescences.)

Outside, where rare plants are growing in blue plastic kiddie pools under plastic hoop houses, David goes back to the controversy over conservation methods. "What exactly is the best way to manage the loss of species?" He poses a few rhetorical questions: "If you lose a species from an area, do you try to replace it? And if you do, is it okay to move seed from another population into that area? Or are you then falsely preserving that species?" Key in this discussion is the fact of climate change. Some current predictions suggest that southern Minnesota will become more like Nebraska, and northern Minnesota will have climate like today's Iowa. That means some part of Canada will end up looking like northern Minnesota. Nancy Sather brought up this point when I talked with her. She raised the profound concern, with regard to the western prairie fringed orchid specifically, that northern Canadian geology is entirely different. The new Minnesota—climate-wise—may not look at all like Minnesota physiologically.

But as a thought experiment, what if there were landscape corollaries farther north? Helping the plants move there is an established theory called assisted migration. And that's a tough discussion. "A lot of very smart biologists are very against the idea of assisted migration," says David. "It's not a done deal that biology has agreed we should do that. On the flip side, some believe we should be doing that already, that we should be expanding ranges now before we lose species. My stance is that either way, we need to have that knowledge." He says we at least need to have the genetic resources and the know-how to put the plants back on sites where they are lost, but we also need to know how to move plants to new areas if it comes to that. "If we don't have that knowledge," he says, "and we decide in fifty years that maybe we should [reintroduce or move plants], it'll be too late." Seeds in a seed bank will not live forever, so we need to know *how* to use them before we get into a situation (like extinction) where we *need* to use them. "In a lot of ways, I write all that controversy off, and I put my head down and do my work," he says.

But, David admits, part of that study is figuring out how to get rare plants to survive on new sites—and that's something he can't do in a lab. So, in the near future (and here's where he's going to be beyond just "putting his head down" and will instead end up at the center of controversy), David plans to work with private and public landowners to reintroduce his arboretum-grown rare species on their land. There is a whole raft of philosophical questions around that, and a complicated permitting process to make everything legal if he experiments with listed species, but he believes circumstances may become dire enough to warrant it. "I'm not necessarily deciding what the right way of doing things is," he says, at once sidestepping the discussion but contributing to its underlying science. "I'm making sure we have all the right tools to do species conservation, once people finally decide what's the right way to go."

In the meantime, David wants to increase awareness. He loves his work at botanical gardens because they bring the public in contact with rare and interesting orchids and other plants. "All the sexy stuff is animals," he says. "There are charismatic megafauna, but not charismatic megaflora—except people actually know orchids." David would like to have western prairie fringed orchids on display at the arboretum, "to get something showy and pretty. People have to appreciate plants, they just have to, or we're screwed!"

Yes, orchids are pretty, showy, sexy. But orchids are what they are because of where they live. When are orchids most alluring? In a pot in a climate-controlled greenhouse? Or in the landscape that gives them life?

I park at the Pembina Trail Scientific and Natural Area to experience the (very sexy) beach ridge seepage zone firsthand (this is not, by the way, where I saw orchids). The parking area here is right up on the Tintah ridge, and the land descends rather quickly to the west. It is a dewy morning, and I am soaked to the knees after twenty paces into the upland prairie. Despite that wetness, I can tell the ground is dry: it is hard underfoot, with little give.

As the land descends, the vegetation changes, with different types lining up in rows parallel with the ridge. Willow, alder, dogwood and green ash offer perfect edge habitat to excitable songbirds. Between rows of trees and shrubs are grassy clearings where the soil is soppy. More than once I plunge ankle-deep in the mud. At the last line of trees, the soil seems to go away entirely, with just cobbles left behind, and a thicket of dogwood and alder. This, too, gradually gives way to a grassier expanse, becoming drier the farther I travel west. The whole transect is perhaps a quarter-mile walk. I climb back up the ridge by a different route, noticing more closely the subtle changes from sedge to grass to shrub.

Walks like this are the quintessence of the midwestern landscape for me: a subtle beauty that must be examined, peered at, appreciated at a minute scale. It's like intimacy, this kind of appreciation—like knowing the locations of birthmarks and scars on a lover's body, and knowing the stories behind the scars. The almost imperceptible interweave of slow hydrology, soil texture, delicate grasses, and little brown birds with perfect beaks and bright eyes is like a living, breathing body. And nowhere is the body more interesting than at the points where one thing becomes another: the corner of the mouth, the edge of the iris, the curve at the nape of the neck, the slope of a beach ridge, the twist and blush of an orchid's complicated petal.

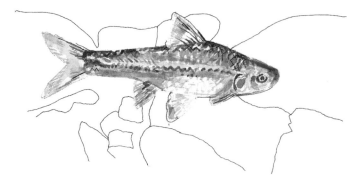

Topeka shiner

9

Shiner

The survey group steps from the bankside vegetation onto a mud-spit. Aaron Besaw and Pat Ceas unfurl the seine. It's a simple contraption: a big mesh square tied to long poles on its short sides and strung with metal weights on one long side and foam floats on the other. Pat and Aaron drag it through the water, making a big arc against the shoreline. The weighted edge of the net drops to the bottom and drags on the muck. They circle toward each other, Pat calling out instructions, and they finally drive the seine up into the shallows where the rest of us are standing. We're in the Rock River just north of Luverne, Minnesota. The Rock flows through Pipestone and Rock Counties in Minnesota, then continues into Iowa, where it eventually joins the Big Sioux River, which in turn hits the Missouri River at Sioux City. The Rock is lazy and brown, and it moseys between steep banks, conveying cottonwood fluff downstream.

A teeming mass of silver rises from the brown water. "That's a lot of minnows," says Margaret Edwards. There are hundreds: creek chubs, Johnny darters, sand shiners, sticklebacks, fathead minnows. To me, they all look the same. To me, it's a pile of two-inch silver and black fish, but there can be more than fifty different species in these prairie rivers.

Pat is a professor of fisheries science at St. Olaf College in Northfield, Minnesota. He has brought three students, Aaron, Marisa Stachowski, and Bryan Giordano, from his summer fisheries course to help him look

Pat Ceas and Aaron Besaw working a seine in the Rock River, 2010

for minnows. All three have history with fish. Marisa grew up with a basement full of tropical tanks she lovingly tended with her dad. Bryan wants to do his graduate work in Montana, so he can study trout by fly rod and reel. Aaron lives on an island in Menominee Lake on the Menominee Indian Reservation in Wisconsin and has caught monster walleye through winter ice by spear.

Margaret works for the Minnesota Department of Natural Resources, the agency that officially commissioned this study, so she is the state's eyes in the field.

Pat can identify every fish we might find here. He and Margaret and the students, though, are really just interested in one kind of fish.

"So," says Pat, as the group starts combing by hand through the wet ball of life in the net, "red fins, that's what to look for." He is jovial and casual: field ecologist, not classroom lecturer.

"First one to find one gets Marisa's second Reese's cup," says Bryan with a grin. His hat has a trout fly hooked through the fabric, and his face has a close-cropped goatee of a color not unlike the dun of his waders. He is thin, energetic, and often smiling. Marisa, who had previously offered that treat to the first one to fall in the river, smirks. She is tall, with long, straight brown hair cinched into a ponytail under a bright Pepto-pink baseball hat—the only flash of color in the whole scene.

"I'll buy that person a beer," Pat says, upping the ante on the search for the Topeka shiner.

The Topeka shiner (*Notropis topeka*) is the only Minnesota fish on the federal endangered species list. The mention of it certainly doesn't stir the heart like the walleye or the brook trout, but, in its own way, it is an interesting little fish, especially in springtime. It's a small minnow, between two and three inches long at maturity, with a blunt snout and a small mouth that is forward-facing rather than downward-facing (like a catfish or sucker). Its body is yellowy-green above and silvery-white below. Overall, it's a lot like its cousins and neighbors, various other types of minnows, like chubs and fatheads. It does have a distinct black band that runs all the way from the snout to the peduncle (the narrow part of the body just in front of the tail), where it ends in a little flourish: a chevron that elegantly parallels the shape of the tail fin. The Topeka is a silver-green race car with a nice sleek pinstripe, a big-tailed midcentury Chevy with a paint job to accentuate the fins.

Topeka shiner larvae emerge from eggs from spring to midsummer at a micro-bite-sized two millimeters. After a month or so, they are just under an inch long and can finally be called fish. They have scales and color. They feast on tiny crustaceans, bits of algae, and whatever else they can find. They spend the winter hunkered down in the deepest reaches of streams and ponds.

In spring, the male Topeka shiner looks for a nest. He doesn't build his own. Instead he seeks out the nest of an orange-spotted or green sunfish. Those nests look like little craters in the creek bottom, and the male

Topeka shiners (courtesy Konrad Schmidt, Minnesota Department of Natural Resources)

Topeka positions himself right near the outer ridge. The panfish don't seem to care.

When the water temperature rises to 70 degrees, the Topeka shiner puts on his makeup. He turns his fins and head bright red, perhaps to make himself stand out from the murky water and creek bottom, perhaps simply to prove his masculinity. Perhaps at the prospect of sex his blood boils, rising to his extremities in a flush of rose. He defends his territory from other males, chasing them away with bursts of speed. Sometimes, when he leaves his post to chase off an interloper, another male Topeka circles around from behind and occupies his spot. He returns and rams the trespasser in the head or side. He is like a bull elk, head-butting for dominance. He even grows small pimples on his head, like the horns of a deer.

Soon a female approaches. She hangs back a bit, and the two fish eye each other. She is blushing, too, but not as vividly as he. She approaches

him, but when she comes within his territory he chases her away, too.
He is testing her. Is she fit enough to bear strong offspring? She returns,
and he chases her away again. The two fish zip away from the nest in
an underwater version of playground puppy love, then return slowly, he
first, then she following sheepishly behind.

She returns again. He is wary but less aggressive. They pause together
on the ridge of gravel. They face each other, heads close together, then
look skyward, their bodies vertical in the water, their bellies millimeters
apart but never touching. He releases his sperm into the water and she
her eggs. The invisible particles of reproduction drift downward, past
his and her red tails, combining in the water and settling on the floor of
the creek. The shiners slip back to the horizontal and rest a moment,
then rise up again. They rest and rise once more perhaps twice, then the
lovers leave the nest, never to connect again

She will find another male, insinuate her way into his nest, and mate
again. He may entertain another female, if she is persistent enough. If
he isn't well nourished, or if this is his third spring, he will die; the same
goes for her. A small percentage of her four hundred or so eggs will
hatch in about five days, and the microscopic larvae will begin the fight
to become a blushing, sky-gazing parent the following spring.

It is soon apparent that Topeka shiners won't be jumping into our hands.
They are rare, after all, but we only need to find one. Pat is leading
what's called a "presence/absence survey." It is one of the activities
the state takes on to fulfill the requirements of the federal Endangered
Species Act. This kind of survey is basic science. It asks whether there
are shiners present in the state and how widespread they are in their
historic range. Each year since 2005, Pat has randomly selected twenty
one-mile stream segments from the 605 miles of Topeka shiner critical
habitat that were designated in Minnesota by the federal government in
2004. He only needs to find one fish in a segment to confirm "presence."

To find a Topeka shiner as quickly as possible, Pat uses his expertise and
starts seining in the most likely areas: slack-water oxbows, off-channel
pools, or little bays in the riverbank. If he doesn't find the Topeka at the

first site within the mile-long segment, he moves on to a second. He will seine ten separate sites before giving up on a segment. That confirms "absence."

This stretch of the Rock River just upstream from Luverne is called segment 133, and the big haul we're sifting through is considered site number 133–1. If we find a Topeka here, we'll march back through the bean field and the baseball diamond to the van and head for Mound Creek. For the next three days, Pat's crew will seek the Topeka in Kanaranzi Creek, Elk Creek, Champepadan Creek, Beaver Creek, Chanarambie Creek, Flandreau Creek, and several unnamed tributaries. They'll try to find it in channelized ditches between fields of corn and beans, in slow meandering pastureland watercourses, and even in ponds dug for watering cattle.

Right now, though, the Topeka fishing isn't good at 133–1, so the students test their fish identification skills.

"Is this a bigmouth shiner?" asks Marisa, holding a minnow toward Pat.

"No, that's a creek chub," he says after a quick glance, then returns to his own sorting.

Marisa tries again: "What's this? Creek chub?"

"Sand shiner."

And once more: "Is this a common shiner?"

"That's a carp," suggests Margaret, with authority. She is the polar opposite of Marisa: spiky blonde hair and tattooed arms. She seems like she might be more at home on a motorcycle than seining for fish.

"That's a sand shiner," says Pat, with a grin. He kneels like a bear at a honeycomb, his bottom on his heels, water to his hips, the seine up in his lap. He lifts great handfuls of fish and scrutinizes them, letting them flop about, looking for something indiscernible to me, before returning them to the river.

A month or so after seining for shiners with Pat, I meet Jay Hatch. Jay is thin and active, and seems trapped in his office like a minnow in an aquarium. For more than a few years, he's been working to create a digital database and online natural histories of all the fish in Minnesota.

Pat Ceas examines fish netted in the Rock River, 2010

Jay is a regional expert on Topeka shiners, and his studies on the breeding, gestation, and growth of this fish are the basis for much of the state and federal legislation in effect today.

When Jay first started looking for Topeka shiners in southwestern Minnesota, he crawled through a lot of river-edge muck. At the time, everyone looked for Topekas within streams and creeks, because that's where they were first found way back in 1844 in Topeka, Kansas, and where scientists from the lower Midwest had found them through the years. Jay saw his first Topeka in 1995 and first collected them for study in 1997 from Mound Creek. He relives those early survey days for me.

"I literally had to lie down and do the military crawl," he says, "to prevent myself from sinking so far into the sediment that I wouldn't be able to get out. For a while, I thought this fish had no class at all."

Jay teaches in the University of Minnesota's General College, not its biology or zoology departments, which is unusual for a scientist of his

stature. His position in the General College is the result of some frustration with academic science.

Prior to moving to Minnesota in 1976, Jay was doing research for his
master's degree in Terre Haute, Indiana. He was studying the impacts of
power plants on large river fish. The mid-seventies was a big time for
environmental concerns, but the science wasn't quite keeping up with
the regulations, so students like Jay were in the rivers finding out what
effect human consumption was having on the natural environment.
Also in the seventies, the Environmental Protection Agency began requiring potential polluters to file "life cycle forms" for fish found nearby.
Essentially, they had to document the species present, when and where
they spawned, how fertile they were, and how quickly they grew and
came to maturity to spawn again. Mostly, people were considering the
big fish, like catfish, northern pike, and bass.

But Jay was finding a lot more of something else, something much
smaller. "We would get all kinds of neat minnows and darters and mad-
toms," he tells me, a glint in his eye. "No one knew what the hell any of
these things were."

Then he moved to Minnesota to pursue a PhD, a degree for which
students in the biology disciplines typically devise some ultra-specific,
groundbreaking research project. Jay just wanted some basic knowledge.
"I was getting tired of having to say 'we don't know' on those [EPA-
required life cycle] forms," he explains, tapping on the table. "It was time
we started studying nongame species." By nongame, he means the ones
people don't eat—like minnows.

I ask Jay what makes a minnow a minnow. He says that a minnow is
a freshwater fish that in Asia is generally large (carp and koi are minnows) and that in North America is generally very small. Here in the
states, people tend to call every small fish a minnow, but that's not the
case (scientifically speaking). Shiners, chubs, and dace are minnows. The
equally small freshwater-dwelling darters, topminnows, and killifish are
in different families entirely. When scientists classify a fish as a minnow,
it means that the fish has teeth on its pharyngeal arch but none on its
palette (the roof of the mouth) or tongue (yes, some fish have teeth on

their tongues) or jaw (where ours are). The pharyngeal arch is, essentially, the throat. Minnows have a pad on the base of their skulls that feels a little like a fingernail. They catch, hold, and swallow their food by pushing their throat teeth against the base of their skull. To sort of feel what that's like, swallow hard, but stop in the middle, when your larynx is highest. You're nowhere near the base of your skull, but this is the general idea.

Minnows also have excellent hearing. Almost all bony fish have something ominously called the Weberian Apparatus. Pieces of the first four vertebrae reach back from the head and touch the fish's swim bladder. The swim bladder is an air sac inside the body that allows a fish to control its buoyancy in the water. It is particularly sensitive to vibration. The Weberian Apparatus efficiently transfers those vibrations to the head. Jay calls it a "guitar in reverse," whereby instead of a string causing vibration (sound) in the belly of the instrument, the air-filled instrument vibrates first and in turn makes the strings wiggle. Minnows are fine-tuned for vibration, which is why every kid can marvel at how all the little fish scatter at just a single hand clap.

The Topeka shiner was first described (scientists say "described" instead of "discovered" when they classify a new species) in 1844. It was found in the Shunganunga Creek, which today flows through the heart of Topeka Kansas. In 1844, though, Topeka sat amidst the territory of the Kaw (Kansas) people. The only bit of European settlement out there on the prairies was a ferry service to bring wagon trains across the Kansas River. Kansas, of which Topeka is the capital, spent much of the 1800s and early 1900s conflicted over slavery and equal rights. It was admitted to the Union in 1861 as a free state, but narrowly. In 1954 the landmark civil rights case *Brown v. Board of Education*, which ended the segregation of public schools, was decided. The board named in that suit is the board of education of Topeka.

Between the days of the Kansas River ferry and *Brown v. Board*, the prairie was rather quickly replaced by millions of acres of family farms, parceled out in 160-acre quarter sections. Throughout the twentieth century, as demand for grain rose, farmers worked hard to make their land more productive. They dug trenches into their fields, laid down segments of clay pipe, and filled the trenches. Rain and snow that used to seep deep into the soil now dripped into these subterranean pipes and ran quickly to the nearest creek. Much of this so-called drain-tile still exists and is still being installed today, and it allows farmers to use land that was once marginal and to get into the fields earlier in the spring.

The government got involved, too. Those twisty prairie streams started backing up because there was a lot more water getting into them than they were used to. Everyone knows the most efficient way to move water is in a straight line downhill, so the counties, the states, and the federal government started transforming the prairie creeks into ditches. They also built brand-new ditches between fields, to whisk more drain-tile water directly to the nearest river. As farms became industrialized, the pace of tiling and ditching increased. Uniformity makes money, and that goes for farm fields, too.

In the 1980s, university and US Fish and Wildlife Service scientists started wondering about how the minnows were coping, and they discovered that they could hardly find the Topeka shiner and several other prairie creek species. In 1990 the USFWS initiated an official review of the Topeka shiner and in 1991 recommended it be listed as an endangered species, which it finally was in 1998.

In 2001 the Biodiversity Legal Foundation sued the USFWS for failing to adequately protect the shiner. The foundation does this a lot: sue in defense of plants and animals. The USFWS settled the case by agreeing to designate critical habitat throughout the Topeka shiner's range. Some species, those with limited and controllable ranges, benefit from the outright preservation of their habitat. Such action is especially helpful if this habitat is already government owned, since the provisions of the ESA don't forbid alteration of habitat unless government money or resources are being used. For instance, a rancher can dam up a stream on his property as long as he spends his own money, even if there are Topeka shiners in the stream and even if the stream is designated habitat. However, if that stream runs through a national wildlife refuge or a national park it may not be dammed, since the critical habitat provision would apply.

Because the Topeka shiner's habitat was largely private, the USFWS felt that critical habitat designation would be a waste of time and money—and redundant, since the species was already protected by the ESA itself. In the final critical habitat designation, published in the Federal Register on July 27, 2004, the very first statement after the executive summary has a chip on its shoulder strangely uncharacteristic for an official federal publication: "In 30 years of implementing the [ESA], the [USFWS] has found that the designation of statutory critical habitat provides little additional protection to most listed species, while consuming significant amounts of conservation resources. . . . We have been inundated with lawsuits for our failure to designate critical habitat, and we face a growing number of lawsuits challenging critical habitat designation determinations once they are made. . . . This leaves the [USFWS] with little ability to . . . direct scarce listing resources to the . . . actions with the most biologically urgent species conservation needs."

Translation: Stop bugging us with lawsuits so we can get on with actually helping the Topeka shiner recover. For instance, the USFWS must perform a review every five years of every species on the list. The agency finally completed one for the Topeka in 2009 (eleven years after listing) and still does not have a federal species recovery plan. This, says the USFWS, is because between 2001 and 2004 the agency devoted staff time and program cash to several lawsuits and the subsequent designation of critical habitat.

But the ESA specifically requires the USFWS to designate critical habitat for every species—within a year of listing the species. Environmental groups have used this language to regularly force the agency to, in their view, follow the law. In 2004 the USFWS designated critical habitat along 836 miles of streams in three states: Minnesota, Iowa, and Nebraska. There are only six miles in Nebraska because the fish has been almost completely eliminated from that state. The bulk of the designation is in Minnesota (605 miles), but there are likely more Topekas in South Dakota. Local pressure ultimately forced the USFWS to leave

Topeka shiner management in South Dakota, Kansas, and Missouri up to those states.

The overall picture for Topeka shiners today, after more than a dozen years on the endangered species list and a half dozen with critical habitat designation, is mixed. In Missouri, where three populations were known at the time of listing, one is gone, one is declining, and one is stable. In Nebraska, access to one of two known Topeka shiner sites is now prohibited by its landowner. In Iowa and Kansas, numbers are low and seemingly declining. In Kansas, the westernmost outpost of the shiner is gone. In Minnesota, the number of known Topeka locations has increased from fifteen to seventy-five since 1998. In South Dakota, a similar increase from eleven to fifty-nine specific sites has been documented, including some of the largest catches ever recorded—more than nine hundred individual fish were once caught in a single seine.

This, of course, sets up a dichotomy in the range. The Topeka is doing well in the north but continues to decline in the south. According to Jay Hatch, this is because the streams have been channelized and made uniform, eliminating the little bays and oxbows that occur naturally along prairie streams. These areas away from the main channel constitute the best environment for Topekas. Jay explains it pretty simply: "In the southern part of the range, the off-channel habitat is gone—long gone."

After twenty-five minutes at site 133–1, the seine has been completely sifted, the fish inside are getting stressed, and Pat says it is time to move on. Bryan and Pat drag the seine into open water and shake out the remaining fish, then we all wade upstream. Pat searches for the yet-to-be-determined site 133–2. We cross the river on shallow gravel, the water almost breaking into exuberant riffles and seeming somehow less midwestern muddy and more mountain trout stream. We climb up over a hump of sand being colonized by cottonwoods, their hand-sized leaves out of scale with their wire-thin stems. The steep banks have parted company, opening a wide, flat floodplain. Margaret finds a leopard frog, then a baby painted turtle. The breeze agitates the water and the thick cottonwoods on the banks, turning both silver, like the sides of minnows.

The Topeka shiner is a fish of the prairies—the great tallgrass prairies that used to cover central North America from Manitoba south to Texas and from Indiana west to Kansas. The big prairie rivers—the Mississippi, the Missouri, the Kansas, the Des Moines—twist crazily across the plains and function more like small streams than like the world's other big rivers, like the Nile, which runs straight-arrow through the desert to the sea, or the Amazon, which is more accurately a fluctuating channel in a vast continent-spanning floodplain, or the Danube, which carves its way through multiple mountain ranges and charts a course of necessity through Europe. In contrast, the Missouri and the Mississippi wander whimsically, in no hurry to reach the ocean, content to explore the prairies, to turn back on themselves again and again, to take the slow road.

The smaller and smaller streams that feed these rivers move the same way. The drainage system of the prairies is what's called a dendritic system. It looks like veins and capillaries, or the branching of a tree. In fact, this is about as dendritic as it gets. There is a greater density of small streams in the midwestern United States than anywhere else in the world. There is also a pleasing randomness and unpredictability to the movement of these waters. In some places, two creeks run nearly parallel for miles, then diverge to find different receiving streams that then head off in completely different directions. In southwestern Minnesota, Pipestone Creek rises just a stone's throw from the Rock River, but it heads north, then west, into South Dakota, makes a big arc, and empties into the very Rock River it could have joined more than twenty river miles upstream. In western Iowa, the Little Sioux River runs parallel to the Missouri for about five miles, in the same floodplain, collecting a half dozen other streams, before finally plunging into the big river.

The key to all this is the fact that a very small percentage of the water that falls on a prairie actually runs overland. These small creeks are mostly fed by groundwater. A prominent Chicago-area landscape architect once told me this: "The historic hydrologic regime of the Midwest involved rainwater and snowmelt soaking into the ground very near to where it fell." In a nutshell, there wasn't much runoff. The rain took its lazy time seeping through the soil to the creeks.

These twisty rivers run fastest along the outer edges of bends, and they carve at the land, washing away the earth, exposing roots and toppling trees. In effect, the river lengthens as it cuts sideward into the slope. A twisting river has more length between headwaters and confluence than a straight river would, and it therefore has less overall slope. Less slope means slower-flowing water. Prairie streams like the Rock or the Elk or the Pipestone have had about ten thousand years since the retreat of the last glaciers to cut their wildly meandering courses into the soluble and accommodating prairie soil. In contrast, think of mountain rivers, hemmed in by rock and forced to run in straight lines. These are the renowned fast-water streams prized by kayakers, white-water rafters, and hydroelectric engineers.

As a river bend cuts outward, it leaves behind a sandbar on the inside of the turn. Sometimes, the river cuts a turn that doubles back on itself so severely that the water manages to eat through the sandbar at the neck of the turn and take a shortcut. For an illustration, look at a map of the state of Mississippi and notice how that state's border with Louisiana doesn't exactly follow the river. It did once, but now there are old channels and oxbow lakes where once there was fast-moving, outside-of-the-turn water.

In front of us as we descend the low cottonwood hump, the Rock River makes a sweeping left-hand turn, which explains the wide floodplain. Just downstream of this bend a thumb of water reaches around behind a gravel bar. It looks like a river without current, and I can picture how the Rock once flowed through here and then, by the whim of a tallgrass prairie creek, decided to take another route. Pat grins and gets the seine ready. It's almost as if he can see the Topekas down in there.

Aaron and Pat work the net around the edges of this backwater, struggling in the mucky bottom, then flop the net up on the grassy shoreline. The group gathers around. The fish are bigger than before. There are black bullheads, catfish-like bottom-feeders with stinging barbs on their fins; orangespotted sunfish; a crawfish as long as my hand, which Margaret induces to pinch her, just for the experience of it, and which manages to draw blood; and white suckers nearly eight inches long. Sorting through these fish doesn't take as long as at the site downstream: they're bigger, and bigger fish usually are incompatible with Topeka shiners. Pat dumps the seine, and the group moves farther up the side channel. A small, grassy knoll pushes in from the side, creating a second, even more isolated bay right up against the edge of the floodplain slope. Pat is already even more optimistic, because the substrate isn't as mucky.

The seine comes up. "Okay," says Pat, "this is better."

"Better?" says Margaret, trying to break off a little of Pat's expertise for herself. "Talk to me about better."

"No big fish," explains Pat, meaning that those bigger fish are Topeka predators. The group sifts through the mass, which has the look of the haul at 133–1 but not quite the volume. The fish are about the same, though: mixed shiners, minnows, and darters.

Without a word, Margaret hands Pat a fish. He raises it to his face and peers at it, then dips it in the water, holding it gently between palm and thumb, and studies it again. "Well," he announces, "it looks like I owe Margaret a beer."

Margaret, standing hip-deep in the water, celebrates her find. "Hey, he's red," she says, smiling like a kid on Christmas morning. "Look at his fins. A Topeka shiner on his way to looking like a stud."

Marisa leans over the net to see, and her, Pat's, Aaron's, and Bryan's heads make a tight circle over the fish. "He looks pretty red," she exclaims.

"Nope," Pat contradicts. "He gets even better." Pat fills a bucket with water and drops in the minnow. Later, Marisa crouches down in the grasses on the shoreline with an open palm. Pat lays the shiner on her hand and takes a few pictures. Then she closes her fist, dips her hand into the water, and lets the fish go free.

"Let's get out of here," says Pat. Aaron and Bryan stow the net, and we all wade back downstream toward the van. Pat tells me that though it's nice to find a Topeka that quickly, he wishes there were more of them. He tells me of times when he's brought up a seine almost entirely filled with Topeka shiners—up to three hundred of them. "Sooner or later we'll hit on a hotspot," Pat assures us.

* * *

When Jay Hatch finished his PhD, there weren't many job openings, so he took the position in the General College, an entry point to the University of Minnesota. Jay teaches basic science, but he also teaches students how to be students—how to take notes, complete a research paper, succeed on tests. He spends his out-of-class time doing what he calls nineteenth-century research.

"I figured out how this fish makes its living," he announces with justifiable pride. "The kind of stuff we figured out for all of our game species—that's what I've been doing for several decades for our nongame species." In 1997, in the midst of this research, he begged his wife to accompany him on a trip to southwestern Minnesota. She of course wouldn't have to crawl through the muck with him, but he thought it would be a nice getaway. They could spend their evenings together, and she could have some time away on her own. She reluctantly agreed, as long as Jay would spend at least a day visiting antique shops in Luverne with her.

In one of the shops, Jay got to talking with the owners about why he was in town. The owner's twelve-year-old grandson bounded up and said that he caught plenty of minnows in the little pond behind the shop. He even got some of those red-finned ones in his traps, plenty of them. The pond was near a creek but not directly connected to it. It was essentially a hole in the ground that had filled with water. Jay humored the kid and sent him off to catch some minnows, envisioning a teaching moment, wherein Jay would explain the differences between minnows and how the particular rare fish he was seeking lived in the creeks.

The boy came back with eight Topeka blushing males and about a dozen females full of eggs. Jay was shocked. "That was more Topeka shiners than I had seen in my entire lifetime," he tells me, laughing at the memory and slapping his hand on the office table. He initiated a scientific study of the pond and in 1998 began seining for fish. He found thirteen different species. The first time he dragged the seine through, he raised 370 Topeka shiners—which was more than existed in all the collections of all the universities and museums in the world at the time. (The boy would later earn an undergraduate degree in biology.)

"I began to think about that," Jay says. "Maybe they thrive in slack water." Previously, Topekas had always been caught in the creek channels themselves, but Jay wondered if those small numbers being caught were just moving between the off-channel oxbows and bays where they bred and congregated. And maybe these off-channel pools would connect to nearby streams during floods, allowing the shiners to migrate in.

Over the next decade, Jay would lead stress studies on the fish, confirming their exceedingly high tolerance for both heat and low oxygen—good adaptations for residents of isolated ponds without regular freshwater input. He would lead a habitat study finding Topekas were about twice as abundant off channel as in channel, with better growth rates. These discoveries changed the places surveyors looked for shiners, which would ultimately reveal the huge, previously unknown populations in South Dakota, and are the basis for where Pat Cees looks for them during his surveys.

The antique store pond study revealed something else, too. In 1998 Jay caught exactly zero bass in the pond. Bass are not native to prairie streams and ponds, so he didn't really notice their absence. In 1999 he caught a few little bass. No one had stocked the pond, so they likely entered at flood stage the same way the shiners did. In the third year, the bass were much bigger, on their way to being full-fledged game fish. In 2001 Jay caught exactly zero Topeka shiners. Other fish eat Topeka shiners, but bass seem to clean them out entirely.

After leaving the Rock River, the survey crew moves on to segment 131: one mile of Mound Creek just downstream from Blue Mounds State Park. Mound Creek rises in northern Rock County and flows south for about fifteen creek-miles to its confluence with the Rock River in Vienna Township. Pat parks the van along County Road 8, where the creek slips under a bridge and heads due east through bean fields. He is immediately frustrated: "This is definitely not the best spot that we have that's for sure."

The surface of the water sits about ten feet below the elevation of the surrounding farmland, and the banks are nearly vertical. The whole creek channel, top of bank to top of bank, is about twenty feet wide. It's a canyon. In a lot of places, bare soil is exposed near the top of the bank and clumps of grass sit down at water level. The beans run to within five feet of the top of the bank, where they give way to a strip of low grasses. Standing in that strip, I can see the roots of the grasses on the other side penetrating down maybe a foot and a half into the soil.

"Look at how shallow these roots are," says Pat, pointing, his voice notably more agitated than during our time on the Rock River. "They're nothing. Prairie grasses would go ten to twelve feet down and really stabilize these banks here. The stream undercuts and the banks just slough right off, and all that silt goes right in the water." He takes a few steps east, apparently not wanting to show his frustration, his biased mind—a chink in the scientific purpose of these three days in southwestern Minnesota. But, year after year, he has seen more and more farmers install drain tile, which whisks water into the creeks faster than it ever would have flowed naturally. He has five years of data that tell him what works for Topeka shiners and what doesn't. So he can't resist the rant. He believes that replanting these agricultural buffer strips with prairie species, like big and little bluestem, Indian grass, junegrass, sunflowers, blazing stars, coneflowers, and leadplant, would have a significant positive impact on water quality.

"It sure would cost some money right now, but it would put a lot of people to work," he says, then gestures out across the bean fields, "and it would save this guy's topsoil if he backed up. That's the other problem, too: they're always trying to maximize profits every year, while if he backed up from the creek just a little bit, he'd get a better return, because he'd maintain more soil on his land and the soil would be in better shape."

Pat turns and walks along the creek, his shoulders slightly slumped. Then he stops and announces we are at the beginning of the segment. The group gingerly descends the bank and soon stands knee-deep in the water at the bottom of the trench.

I have to admit it is an interesting experience to be down here in channelized Mound Creek. The expansive vistas above give way to a narrow view that ends abruptly just ahead, where the creek makes a right-angle turn to the south. Water moves by at pace but silently.

Pat and Margaret and the students start seining. The first haul brings up a few creek chubs, green sunfish, and stone rollers, but no Topeka shiners. The quantity is far less than we've been seeing. As we sort through each haul, Aaron takes a GPS reading and I keep track of the sites and location coordinates for Margaret, who will input that data along with Pat's presence/absence assessments. The sites tick away: 131-3, a promising little bay between two collapsed banks, offers up almost nothing at all. 131-5, a slow, deep pocket where everyone surrounds the net and kicks the water to scare fish into the seine, prompts Margaret to lament, "I expected more out of that; I'm not going to lie." 131-7, 131-8, and 131-9, clustered together where Mound Creek jogs back west, then south again at a confluence of property lines, bring up barbed bullheads, an even more barbed tadpole madtom, some perch, and pumpkinseed sunfish. At 131-10, nearly two hours after leaving the van, Pat reminds the group that all we need is one and tells us to get in there and kick. Again we bring up the usual, no Topekas.

"Well, it happens," says Pat, standing in the creek with one hand on the seine pole and a hangdog expression on his face. "You get shitty ditches like this, and you get skunked." He turns to me: "There's a quote for your book."

This shitty ditch in fact reminds me quite a lot of Buck Run, which flows through my father's farmland in northern Illinois. My great-grandfather amassed five contiguous quarter sections during the Great Depression. I grew up going to the "red farm" and the "white farm," the former of which had pigs, a hayloft with a rope swing, and Buck Run. The corn came right up to the edge of the creek, and there wasn't that much to see there. At the time, my grandparents lived on a lake nearby, so we stayed at their place and rode water skis and kneeboards behind the motorboat.

Going to the farm was a treat, though I have to say I never really noticed the little creek until my father moved down to the farm from the Chicago suburbs in the late 1990s. My grandparents had died, my parents were divorced, my dad was out of work, and he took the red farm as inheritance and moved there to live rent free and collect ag-land rental fees from our cousin John. My dad began to notice the creek, and to ask me about it. Back then, I was a fledgling landscape architect and thought I knew a lot about land management, so I probably ranted about agricultural pesticides and the lack of no-till farming that was silting up the creek. My dad, the mechanical engineer, who knew a little something about the velocities of liquids, heard something in my comments about runoff. He saw how the creek backed up at the culvert under Governor Beveridge Highway just south of his property line. He noticed the stand of willows at the low spot of his 160 acres where a century-old clay drain tile had broken. He watched the creek spread out over the three acres by the red barn every spring.

He told cousin John to pull the corn and beans back one combine-width from the creek. Then the next year he told him to step back another width. John didn't like these mandates at all. Not only was he getting less crop from the land, those buffers, he felt, would spread weeds into his corn and beans. My dad took his rent as a percentage of John's crop income, to make the financial point moot.

Willows began to spread north along the creek edge from the area of broken tile. Compassplants, smooth nettles, three kinds of goldenrod, and prairie sunflowers sprang from the fallow land. Then the low three acres flooded three times in one year, wiping out two plantings of beans. John said he'd had it with that piece of land, and my dad put it in the Conservation Reserve Program, a federal initiative that pays farmers to take marginal land out of production—marginal land like prairie creek floodways. The Illinois Department of Conservation seeded a wet prairie there.

For eleven or so years, my dad has hosted a fall folk festival at the red farm. The music, which is produced by friends and friends of friends, is of sporadic quality and runs from noon to dark. Attendees, also friends and friends of friends, gorge on brats and burgers and potluck casseroles laid out on folding tables under a tent close up against the bean fields. Everyone takes a walk or drives the little John Deere runabout down the

Buck Run Nature Trail, all the way to the end, where there's a little clear pool overhung with willow and mulberry. The creek channel is a woodsy vein through the crops, protected on both sides by wide swaths of volunteer grasses and scattered prairie flowers.

When I told my dad I had been to southwestern Minnesota to search for the Topeka shiner minnow, he first asked how the heck I got involved in that kind of expedition. Then he told me that recently, after a dozen years of living at the red farm, he saw minnows in Buck Run. These would not be Topeka shiners; Illinois was never home to that Great Plains red-fin. But I immediately wanted to see that red farm creek, to see what I could find.

The survey group heads back to the road across the beans, the students and Margaret up ahead, Pat and I bringing up the tail end of our strange line of wader-clad field walkers. I venture whether there might be some degree of vindication or relief that there aren't any Topekas in that segment. I ask if this "absence" finding might bolster Pat's argument.

"Well, yes, it does," Pat admits, his scientific mind obviously at pains to do so. "It does, but these are tough little fish, actually. They just need pool habitat to survive. You can get a site like this that's horrible, but then just get one nice developed backwater or a pond that gets flooded every couple of years and they can be doing just fine there. They really don't need a lot. In fact, I love it when we get places like this except they do have one or two nice pools and we do get them, then we make the argument that if there were a couple more pools they'd be doing much better. And it doesn't take much to make a pool." In fact, the local water company, in consultation with Pat, took a backhoe to a stream bank in 2008. In 2009 Pat found Topekas in that new off-channel pool.

"Just like most species," he continues, "if you give them half a chance, they'll be just fine. What we're doing is kicking them when they're down."

Three months after mucking about in the creeks with Pat and his crew, I return to Minnesota's Topeka shiner country on my own. I want to apply my knowledge to the landscape in general; and I want to talk to a few farmers.

Driving west on I-90, somewhere between Worthington and Adrian, I notice a slight rise prickled with wind turbines—the Buffalo Ridge—which signals my change in watershed. This move from the Mississippi watershed into the Missouri is my entrance into the land of the blushing fish. The first place to see critical habitat is three miles before Adrian, where an unnamed tributary of the East Branch of the Kanaranzi Creek races under the freeway in a straight-line ditch. Just north of Adrian, the main stem of the Kanaranzi swoops past the Highway 91 interchange as a mud-banked pool studded with about twenty-five head of cattle.

Pessimistic, I leave the freeway and cruise the gravel back roads of Nobles and Rock Counties. This is corn, bean, and cattle country, and the land is neatly divided between animal and vegetable. I become accustomed to the rhythm as I drive due north or due west on this gridded landscape: rise up above the creeks amidst the corn and beans, drop down into the valleys for wide swaths of cattle pasture. Over and over again, I ride this gentle roller coaster. It makes sense, of course—farm the high dry ground, put the cattle down where they can drink. These low beef lands are usually in pretty sorry shape: muddy, trampled, devoid of the pasture grasses you might expect would have to be there in order to graze cattle on them. The streams, however, still twist their way across the landscape like crazed snakes. I see very little channelization.

The land of one rancher (let's call him Carl) is a prime example. It's a bit of a mess. Carl, a thirty-something younger-generation farmer, owns three-quarters of a section in Magnolia Township. That's 480 acres. His home is a brown, vinyl-sided one-story with an attached garage and a rickety wood porch at the main entry. It fronts a massive gravel access road where he parks the semitrucks that haul his 250 head to market or to the two other pastures he owns just a little way farther south. It has a view of Elk Creek, which meanders across the section generally from the northeast corner to the southwest. Elk Creek runs in a wide diagonal swath of pastureland, with wire fences cordoning it off from the corn and beans Carl grows on the rest of the section. Within that swath, the water is left to its own devices.

I don't find the view from Carl's porch particularly Edenic, though. The creekway just below us is a mud pit. The cattle have hoofed it into submission, trampled the banks, and left very little living. Carl tells me he used to have his feedlot down there, right on the creek, until the Minnesota Pollution Control Agency made him move it away from the water and better contain the animal waste. He sees that as a hassle. He tells me with that pensive squint so typical of people who spend their days in the sun examining long views that he's not trying to harm anything. "No farmer's going to purposefully hurt that fish or anything out there," he says. "That's our livelihood."

Carl has a wife and three kids to feed. And out of a little pond in the cattle pasture, Pat Ceas pulled more Topeka shiners than anywhere else that year. I can see another similar watering hole while I stand with Carl on his porch. There's not a blade of grass on its banks. The water is exactly the color of the rich prairie mud surrounding it. Pat and Jay would call this an off-channel pool: fed by groundwater, connected to the main creek from time to time by flooding, and prime Topeka shiner habitat. Carl tells me that the whole pasture floods most springs. That connects his watering holes to the creek and allows the shiners to disperse.

I tell Carl about the haul from his pond: around fifty shiners, compared to the two the crew found the entire day I was with them. He smirks. Carl already has a healthy skepticism of government. He mentions again how the MPCA and the county land conservation office have been bothering him about the condition of his property. "If I'm doing such a bad job," he says, gesturing at the pasture. "how come they say there's minnows all in here? How come they found so many?"

Across the street and just upstream, an older couple (let's call them the Newmans) doesn't farm. They pour concrete for agricultural building foundations all over the region. They keep horses. Their home is full of horse memorabilia. The horses aren't allowed down by Elk Creek, says Gladys Newman. The floodplain is fenced off and lushly vegetated. A few years ago, the Newmans put the land into the Conservation Reserve Program. With help from conservation agencies in the state, the Newmans have planted five thousand willows and other fast-growing, easily resprouting trees along the creek. They have let whatever grasses want to grow grow.

As I stand on the road that separates the two neighbors, the difference between the landscapes is stark: the Newmans' side is lush and flowering; Carl's side is close-clipped and muddy. I want there to be Topekas on the Newman land. I want there to be more of them, bigger ones, healthier ones. I want this side-by-side comparison to prove to farmer/ranchers like Carl that even though they have the fish on their land they could still do much better. I want to bring Carl over to talk to Gladys, to experience her concern for the environment and endangered species.

Gladys doesn't know anything about Topeka shiners, though. She tells me she seems to remember something about them a few years ago—likely the critical habitat designation public hearings—but she doesn't know that they are probably in her creek. I also get no satisfaction on whether they are actually thriving on the Newmans' side of the road. Pat's survey segment number 135 begins at about the middle of Carl's land and ends before the Newmans'.

More recently, the version of this duality from one side of the street to the other has become the law of the land. In 2015 the Minnesota legislature passed Governor Mark Dayton's "buffer law," which requires landowners to install vegetative buffers along public waters, ditches, and tributaries. A statewide mapping project led by the DNR shows where and how wide these buffers must be (but a fifty-foot average is the goal). Private owners needed to be compliant by November 1, 2017. The main reason for the law is to protect water quality, but it may have associated benefits to stream and river fish, like the Topeka shiner. Since the law was passed, there has been plenty of pushback and several attempts to change the law through exemptions and delayed implementation, but Governor Dayton has been forthright that he will veto any watering down of the buffer requirement. As these new requirements roll out, hopefully a lot less land will look like that narrow ditch I seined with Pat and his team and a lot more will look like the Newman land.

I drive into Blue Mounds State Park, set up my tent, and head down into Luverne for dinner. No one at the Magnolia Lounge, where tonight's special is local prime rib, can tell me much about the Topeka shiner. "Topeka?" asks one gentleman, recoiling from his Miller Lite, "like Topeka, Kansas?" With his facial expression, he seems to wonder what some Kansas fish is doing up here.

In the morning I hike the park trails down below the lower of the two dams that impound Mound Creek. This dam is far less elegant than the quartzite outcrop upper one, but the creek below it immediately returns to its prairie character.

(In June of 2014, a few years after this visit to Blue Mounds, severe rains washed out a portion of the lower dam and drained Lower Mound Lake. In 2016 the DNR decided, based on public input, not to rebuild the dam and instead to restore the former Lower Mound Lake to a naturalized stream channel. It specifically cited the Topeka shiner as a factor in its decision-making, and expects to increase habitat for the fish through the restoration of the channel.)

I swish through the grasses to the bank and sit on my haunches. A few blackbirds flit overhead. Hawks soar on the updrafts above the quartzite cliffs in the distance on the other side of the river. A frog leaps from cover into the creek and lankily swims away. To my left, upstream, there's a perfect little back bay. The current is coming around against the far bank and leaving a grass-enclosed pool barely connected to the main channel. I am sure there are Topeka shiners in there.

A flit of motion catches my eye, and I gaze into the water about three feet from the shoreline where I rest. A minnow is peeking back at me, flipping back and forth with barely perceptible movements of its tail. It's about two or three inches long, with a nice dark stripe on its side, and the end of its tail has a red-pink blush.

Topeka shiner? I have no idea, but I let myself think so.

It keeps watching me, moving back and forth near the surface. I begin to think I might be bothering the little fish. Maybe I am being perceived as a threat. Maybe I am causing it to expend energy it should save for mating or hunting or evading predators. Maybe I am, quite unintentionally, harassing it. So, in order to not be in violation of the federal Endangered Species Act of 1973, I stand up and walk away from the water.

Gray wolf

10

Wolf

Five wolves are alert and restless. They trot under the young spruce trees in that focused, unflagging way wolves move. Wolves don't ever seem to either walk or sprint—they are still or they jog like marathoners. These five wolves circle their enclosure in intertwining loops, never running together, never running all at once, each wolf alternating between that intense, wide-eyed jog and a stock-still stand that is almost as disconcerting. They are agitated, interested. The coyotes in the pen next door are being fed. The Minnesota Zoo handler is directing the coyotes' feeding, beckoning them with outstretched hands and fingers to different quadrants and then tossing raw meat to them. Keeping them separated during feeding ensures they all eat enough. The wolves, separated from the coyotes by a black chain link fence, perhaps wonder if they will be fed next. They associate the handler with food, for this is their captive life. But even here, ensconced, they seem wild.

The Minnesota Zoo is inside-out from most zoos: the animal enclosures are large and naturalized, while the viewing areas are mere protrusions into the animal's space. At times, it seems as if the wolves, particularly that smaller black one, are coming to see the humans in their cage. That smaller black one, it stares me down. It trots right up to the fence (which is set back about ten feet from the wooden walkway and railing that defines my human space) and cocks its head and shoulders to the side, not tilting them, but sort of reaching sideways with its

Gray wolf (courtesy David Mech, University of Minnesota)

neck, as if trying to look at something behind me without moving its torso. Its eyes are bright yellow-gray, its face is relaxed, and its feet are enormous. I stare back, something I know I would never be able to bring myself to do were this not a controlled encounter. The wolf both meets my eyes and doesn't. It's looking right at me—I can tell because sometimes it glances away for a moment and then returns its gaze to my face—but I don't feel "there" to it. I find myself glancing behind myself to see what the wolf is really looking at.

Beside me, leaning casually on the wooden rail, are two girls, maybe sixteen, brightly dressed, hair in ponytails, sparkly things festooned about them. They are watching the black wolf, too.

"It's so scary," says one, "like a creepy werewolf."

Responds the other: "It's so cute, I want to just cuddle with it."

The wolf (*Canis lupus*) is not a complicated animal. It is an apex predator, and in order to fill that role it has had to become smart, strong, social, and fit. But it is not complicated. We humans have made it complicated.

We have sought and sustained an often fraught and sometimes venerating relationship with the wolf. We have loaded it up with lore: the werewolves, the wolf children, the man-eating wolf, the wolf brother, the lone romantic inspiring wolf, the depraved destroyer of livestock. We hunted it almost to extinction, and then we loved it as a prime symbol of the wilderness ideal. There is no other animal on earth like it.

Strip away that human baggage and a wolf is an average-sized, rather bland-looking predator that is as flexible in its habitat needs as a squirrel. It has no unusual body physiology like the giraffe or rhino. It is not jaw-droppingly huge for a mammal, like the tiger or the elephant. It affects no strange metamorphosis like a butterfly or frog. It cannot fly It is neither the biggest, smallest, fastest, most narrowly distributed, oldest most social, nor most powerful of animals. When we say a wolf is regal or majestic, that's about us, not the wolf. When we say the wolf is cunning, diabolical, and evil, that's about us, not the wolf.

Barry Lopez covers this ground in his seminal 1978 book *Of Wolves and Men*. That book, which he began researching well before passage of the Endangered Species Act, examines the wolf as a pure animal and as a cultural touchstone. "Wolves are wolves, not men," writes Lopez.

Because of our complicated relationship with the wolf, no animal or plant has a more complicated relationship with the Endangered Species Act. And Minnesota is integral to the wolf's story as a species and its story as a sometime political volleyball.

The gray wolf was one of seventy-eight species (all vertebrate animals) included in the Endangered Species Preservation Act of 1966. It was then one of the first species to be listed under the new protections of the ESA, making it onto the list less than a year after the act's passage in 1973. At the time of the ESA, in the United States the wolf was present only in Alaska, in northeastern Minnesota and on Isle Royale in Lake Superior. The Minnesota population was considered the last bastion of the wolf in the lower forty-eight states.

Nevertheless, almost immediately after the wolf was added to the fledgling endangered species list, the Minnesota Department of Natural

Resources issued a letter to the US Fish and Wildlife Service, on October 4, 1974, requesting that Minnesota be excluded from wolf protections under the act. The DNR cited depredation of livestock and the wolf's impact on the deer herd as its main reasons—neither of which, it should be noted, have anything to do with population stability of the animal to be protected. In response, the USFWS later that same year decided it would reconsider the listing. According to Federal Register documentation, extensive public comment was received, especially from those opposed to delisting or downgrading the wolf. Conversely, Minnesota governor Wendell Anderson issued a letter requesting complete delisting. The Minnesota state legislature passed a resolution in the same vein, noting that the wolf was doing well in northeastern Minnesota and was now expanding into areas "not heretofore inhabited." The legislature claimed the state could manage its wolves just fine on its own, thank you. It also cited depredations as a reason for delisting the wolf. The USFWS rightly called the legislature out on the inaccuracy of the wolf's range. Prior to widespread sanctioned hunting and poisoning, the wolf had been everywhere in Minnesota (and the entire United States). The wolf, more accurately, had "heretofore inhabited" the entire state a mere 150 years ago.

These comments in the mid-1970s are a precursor to the state of Minnesota's controversial role in wolf management all the way up to the present day. In 1978 the US Fish and Wildlife Service did change the wolf's status in Minnesota from endangered to threatened, in order to allow for legal killing of wolves that preyed on livestock. The service, in the first of a long list of Federal Register narratives that read a bit like "Fine! You win" statements, says that it will allow legal take because that is the only way to minimize conflicts between humans and wolves. "Such conflict would hinder conservation efforts," says the 1978 ruling, "and thus work against the long-term welfare of the wolf. A legal take is considered the only practical means by which depredations can be handled and current problems relieved."

The 1978 ruling also established five management zones in Minnesota. Zone 1 includes, basically, the range where the wolf was never extirpated:

the northeastern arrowhead of the state. Zone 2 runs south from Ely
almost to the North Shore of Lake Superior, where wolves do interact
with human settlement. Zone 3 is farther west, mainly in the peatlands
south of the Canadian border. These three zones were designated as
critical habitat for the wolf. Zone 4 includes the entire remainder of
what might be considered the Laurentian mixed forest province, while
Zone 5 was the deciduous and prairie portion of the state. Legal take by
government personnel of deprecating wolves was permitted in Zones 2
through 5, but not in Zone 1. This effected a compromise that would last
nearly twenty years.

Since the very beginning of the growing appreciation for the wolf in the
United States in the 1960s, David Mech's name has been synonymous
with the increasing body of knowledge. Barry Lopez relies on Mech
for the Minnesota part of the story in *Of Wolves and Men.* Almost all
of the USFWS's proposed delistings reference his work. In 2000, as the
service was preparing to change the status of the wolf for the first time,
he edited *The Wolves of Minnesota: Howl in the Heartland,* still the best
resource on the history, study, and likely future of this wild canine in
the state. He founded the International Wolf Center in Ely, Minnesota,
and was chief consultant on its landmark exhibit about the wolf in
human culture.

Despite his profound impact on the wolf discussion in the Midwest (it
really is all but impossible to read anything on midwestern wolves without seeing his name), David is generous with his time and easy to talk
to. I sit on a rickety chair in his requisitely cluttered office on the University of Minnesota's St. Paul campus. I think I expected a more rugged
person to sit down in front of me. David, after all, has spent twenty-five
summers living with and radio-collaring wolves on Ellesmere Island in
the Arctic, and twenty-five winters on the ground and in the air in the
vast wilderness of northern Minnesota. He has made his career studying
a powerful, maligned carnivore. But—perhaps a bit like the animal he
studies—he's not what you might expect. David has soft features and a
boyish face. He is unsentimental about the wolf, slow to trust absolutes,

and able to change with the times (as I would soon discover when he opened his computer).

In many ways he reminds me of Barry Lopez, whom I met a few years ago, more than thirty years after he published his seminal wolf book. These two men spent time together in the 1970s, journalist and researcher, learning about wolves. David remembers the writer, though only vaguely, and cites *Of Wolves and Men* as an important pillar in the new, less persecutory thinking about the wolf.

David started out as a fur trapper in upstate New York. He tells me he was always fascinated by carnivores, and therefore jumped at the chance to be part of a major predator-prey study after receiving his undergraduate degree. In 1958 he came to the Midwest to be a researcher in the groundbreaking Isle Royale wolf-moose study, which examined the close relationships between animals sharing the same ecosystem. At the time, the very idea of landscape-wide ecology was still in its infancy, having been posited by Aldo Leopold just a decade or so earlier. Leopold's *Sand County Almanac* summarizes the idea, but Leopold also wrote and taught the concept right up to his death in 1948, a year before the publication of *Almanac*.

Leopold began life as a paid government wolf hunter in the West. It was just a job that let him be outdoors. But as he removed wolves from the landscape, he began to notice other changes. Deer became more plentiful and ate too much vegetation, which caused erosion that silted the streams. Smaller mammals and birds were affected as their food and shelter-building materials were removed by deer. The idea of the keystone species—those animals or plants without which an ecosystem cannot function the same way—comes from Leopold. He saw the interconnectedness of the landscape and is considered the father of ecology and wildlife management.

David followed this legacy, livetrapping and studying bears as an undergraduate in summer and then tracking moose and wolves as a graduate student in the winter. He says that when he started working for the wolf-moose study in the late 1950s, he cannot remember anyone who was pro-wolf.

But that began to change in 1966, when the wolf was listed under the Endangered Species Preservation Act in the forty-eight contiguous states. Though that early law had no functional protections for the animals it listed, it began to create awareness that species were being lost. It forced people to rethink how habitats were being changed and how certain animals (especially the wolf) were being treated. David is blunt about the culture in the 1950s and before. "It was downright persecution by the federal government and the states," he says. "[The wolf] is the only species I can think of that had an actual war waged against it." (If you're thinking about the bison or the passenger pigeon here, remember that those two species were hunted for meat and sport, not for the purpose of eradication—which is truly what the intent was with the wolf.)

The mid- to late 1960s were a time of environmental awakening for the United States. Spurred in part by authors like Peter Matthiessen (*Wildlife in America*, 1959), Rachel Carson (*Silent Spring*, 1962), Edward Abbey (*Desert Solitaire*, 1968), and John Hay (*In Defense of Nature*, 1969), the federal government acted decisively and often. The Wilderness Act of 1964. The Wild and Scenic Rivers Act of 1968. The National Environmental Policy Act of 1970. The Clean Air Act of 1970. The Clean Water Act of 1972. And of course the Endangered Species Acts of 1966 and 1973. This era envisioned a change from earlier times of setting aside big landscapes—the national parks and forests—and instead focused on the landscape as a whole. The purpose of the NEPA, for example, was to "encourage productive and enjoyable harmony between man and his environment."

So by the early 1970s, the stage was perfectly set for the wolf to become the cause célèbre for wilderness. It was the perfect symbol: the tireless marathons through the woods, its habitation of the inaccessible Boundary Waters Canoe Area Wilderness, the redemption and reconciliation its protection would mean for us, that mournful yet uplifting howl.

"Its whole image shifted in the public eye," David remembers, "and pro-wolf people began to outnumber anti-wolf people. It was the poster child for endangered species—literally it was on the poster." The wolf was one of the first species to receive protection, and its protection was a profound leap. In the case of many species of plants and animals, the protection afforded by the ESA is from incidental take (like prairie plants plowed up for farm fields), or from some environmental factor not having directly to do with that species (like the effect of DDT on eagles), or from loss of species with extreme habitat limitations (like the endemic Minnesota dwarf trout lily or the specialized Leedy's roseroot). But in the case of the wolf, the ESA put an end to targeted, widespread, and deliberate killing of wolves wherever they were found. It ended the leaving out of poisoned carcasses, the destruction of pups in dens, the shooting of entire packs from small airplanes, and the government bounties paid to individuals who did all these things. The distance between status quo and protection for the wolf was huge—bigger than for any other species.

And the wolf rebounded. There is absolutely no question about that. In about thirty-five years, wolves in Minnesota have almost tripled in number, have recolonized north woods territory in Wisconsin and Michigan, have raised pups as far south as Isanti, Minnesota, and have been seen in Hugo, in the northern suburbs of the Twin Cities. The overarching intent of the ESA is to recognize and protect species in danger of extinction, require a management framework to improve their lot based on sound scientific evidence, and then remove them from the list once recovery has been successful. This has been true of the bald eagle (delisted in 2007), the Florida manatee (down-listed from endangered to threatened in 2017), and the humpback whale (nine of fourteen populations delisted in 2016). One could argue it should be true for the wolf.

But there was a distinction. While most of the American population was coming around to the value (in large part spiritual and symbolic) of the wolf, those who lived in or near wolf country held the old fear and frustration. "They're beautiful animals . . . when your ox is not being gored by them," David smirks.

During the years of the wolf's recovery in the Upper Midwest, that conflict of perspective simmered below the surface. Then, in 2000, the USFWS did something that, under certain conditions, it is called to do

under the ESA: it proposed a reduction of protection for wolf populations. A recovery plan drafted in 1978 and revised in 1992 called for
the western Great Lakes population of wolves in Minnesota, Wisconsin,
Michigan, and the Dakotas to consist of 1,250 animals in Minnesota
along with one other established viable population of at least one hundred animals anywhere else in the Midwest besides Isle Royale. In 1998
there were nearly 2,500 wolves in Minnesota and another nearly 250 in
Wisconsin and in Michigan's Upper Peninsula. So the service proposed
listing the entire Great Lakes population of wolves as threatened,
thereby also allowing some legal take of depredating wolves in states
other than Minnesota. Essentially, all upper midwestern wolves would
drop down to the same protection levels Minnesota wolves had had
since 1978.

Then, just a year later, the USFWS went even further and delisted the
Great Lakes and all eastern wolves, from the Dakotas eastward to New
England. The reasoning was that some information was offered too late
to be included in the 2003 rule, namely Minnesota's wolf management
plan, completed in 2001 (Michigan and Wisconsin had completed theirs
earlier). With these state management plans in place and population
numbers up, the service now said the animal had met all its thresholds
for recovery.

This 2004 action was the first of several attempts by the service to delist or downgrade the wolf, each of which has successfully been blocked
by the courts. After the 2003 rule, nineteen conservation organizations
led by Defenders of Wildlife sued in the Oregon District Court, where
US judge Robert E. Jones vacated the rule. The basis for his determination was these words from the ESA itself: "a significant portion of
its range." A species must be recovered across a significant portion of its
range—taken to mean its historic range. The judge felt it was not enough
that the wolf had recovered and expanded somewhat from its *current*
range. That current range was a tiny proportion of where wolves used
to live. Though the court case centered on the downgrading from the
2003 rule, because the 2004 total delisting of eastern wolves was based
on the 2003 rule, it was also vacated through a similar court case. Wolf

management returned to where it had been in 1978: endangered everywhere but threatened in Minnesota.

In response to the court-ordered relisting, Wisconsin and Michigan
applied for special permits to kill wolves depredating livestock. Minnesota had long benefited from the special rule that allowed such activities.
When a species is "threatened," special rules can be written that allow for
taking of animals or plants under certain circumstances. According to
DNR endangered species coordinator Rich Baker, this is an important
tool to ensure the public can embrace the species and its listing. The original 1978 listing acknowledges this, in essence saying that unless we allow
for some take (in this case for depredating wolves), the public backlash
would be so great that no wolf would be safe. Poaching on principle
would be rampant and no dialogue about the animal would be possible.

In May of 2006, the USFWS granted to Michigan and Wisconsin permits generally following the Minnesota rules. But in August of the same
year, a district court judge vacated the permits, handing a legal victory
to the Animal Humane Society.

Undaunted, in 2007 the USFWS again proposed to delist the wolf.
Here's the reasoning in the service's own words: "We propose these
actions because available data indicate that [the population of wolves
in the western Great Lakes] no longer meets the definitions of threatened or endangered under the Act. The threats have been reduced or
eliminated as evidenced by a population that is stable or increasing in
Minnesota, Wisconsin, and Michigan, and greatly exceeds the numerical
recovery criteria established in its recovery plan."

Wolf census data from the winter of 2002–03 showed more than three
thousand wolves in Minnesota and more than seven hundred in the
other Great Lakes states. Those numbers were up from the 2003 downgrade attempt, and to scientists (including David Mech, whose data were
used in the annual winter counts) it meant a stable and increasing population. But again the service was sued and again the conservation groups
won. The wolf was relisted in 2008.

And we're not done yet. In April 2009 the service again delisted the wolf, then was forced to relist it just five months later because of a suit and settlement that called out the service for failing to provide adequate opportunity for public comment.

In April 2010, in response to that relisting, Gerald M. Tyler and Dale K. Lueck filed suit in federal court to force the USFWS to remove the wolf from the ESA. Their arguments: Tyler could not safely use his property near Ely because his dog might be killed by a wolf, he was experiencing harm because wolves were reducing the deer herd and hindering his hunting, and he could not safely exist in town because wolves were visiting Ely dumpsters and alleys. Lueck raised cattle in Aitkin County and was being harmed by wolf depredation and was also a deer hunter harmed by wolves reducing the herd. The National Rifle Association and two sportsmen's groups also joined the plaintiffs in the suit; the Minnesota DNR signed on as a friend of the plaintiffs, which is more than a little complicated. The DNR has the dual—and in this case conflicting—roles of managing game animals for public hunting and also implementing the Endangered Species Act within the state. Minnesota's legislature and DNR have waded into the wolf controversy in the past, but to take a side here essentially endorsed the claims of several individuals concerned with cattle depredation (an issue which the state was already allowed to manage under the act) and reduction in the deer herd by wolves (which has no scientific basis).

In December of 2011, even while the Tyler/Lueck suit moved through the courts, the service again delisted the wolf relying on the numerical data of wolves in the Great Lakes states. The Tyler/Lueck case was dismissed in February 2012, made moot by the delisting. Also in 2011 the US Congress passed a rider on a general government budget bill that stripped all protections from western wolves—the first instance of a species being added to or removed from the endangered species list by legislative action rather than by due process.

It took longer this time, but again conservation groups got the delisting decision (but not the congressional action on western wolves) overturned in court, and the Great Lakes wolf went back on the list in December 2014.

What caught the federal and state agencies short in all this, says David, was the level of pro-wolf advocacy that had developed since the wolf was listed in the 1970s. It had risen to equal the level of emotion of the anti-wolf perspective. And these two emotionally charged viewpoints clashed—in the courts, in the state legislature, and in public hearings about delisting.

The rift is stark: those who live at the so-called "wildland interface," especially those with economic interests in the land—the ranchers and deer hunters—want numbers controlled aggressively. That can't be done while the wolf is on the list. Those who live in cities and towns, those who go into the wilderness for recreation, and those who hold some romantic ideal of the wild (but don't rely on land for their livelihood) fear the continued persecution that could be wrought by the first group. The live-off-the-landers feel the love-the-landers want to swipe their income out from under them without understanding their actual situation. The love-the-landers believe the live-off-the-landers want to destroy a critical piece of nature for their own narrow self-interest.

Not only is the wolf a tortured symbol of America's relationship with the land, it is emblematic of the issues on which America is currently divided. Rural versus urban, economically depressed versus economically successful, natural resource extraction versus natural resource conservation. The country is divided politically, economically, racially, and also over the fate of the wolf.

And it all goes back to landscape. The conflict centers on those areas, usually at the fringes of wilderness, whether in the Rockies or in the Upper Midwest, where humans are making a living on land into which the wolves are trying to expand. It's like two warring armies trying to claim territory. There's a lot of talk about how if the wolves stayed in "their landscape" (the wilderness), everything would be fine.

David is skeptical of that argument. "The wolf is landscape neutral," he says, almost matter-of-factly, considering the gravity of the statement.

Unlike the Topeka shiner or piping plover, the wolf doesn't much care where it lives, as long as there are prey animals to eat. "We tend to think of the wolf as a wilderness animal," David continues, "but that's because we have restricted it to the wilderness. It's a leftover view of wolves." He notes that in 2014 a wolf produced a litter of seven pups within a forty-five-minute drive of the Twin Cities. That wolf mother was happy about the deer, foxes, squirrels, and denning opportunities there. But humans weren't happy about the wolves being there. David is cagey about exactly where those pups were born, and about exactly what happened to them. He says only that they were wiped out because "the landscape was such that they conflicted with people." Presumably that conflict was twofold: the people were there nearby, and the people had a certain perspective on wolves that prevented these two species from living together.

In the intervening time between the 2011 delisting and the 2014 relisting, Minnesota held a wolf hunt. The Minnesota state legislature approved the first hunt for the winter of 2012–13. It happened quickly, though with significant controversy, and despite the state's own management plan, which called for waiting five years after delisting before holding a hunt. In that first winter, hunters took 413 wolves. The next season (the fall and winter of 2013), they took 237.

Significant concerns about these hunts came from Minnesota's Indian tribes. In 2010, the Red Lake Reservation had declared itself a wolf sanctuary, and in 2012 Minnesota Public Radio interviewed members of that and other tribes about wolves. Individuals were quoted as seeing wolves as brothers and sisters, and easily drew parallels between the historic wolf extermination policies and the forced removal of Indians from their ancestral lands.

During the legislative deliberations about the hunt, I have a conversation with an elite big-game hunter who lives in north-central Minnesota. This is a man who spends fully one-third of his days every year on some kind of hunt somewhere in the world. In his home is a taxidermy menagerie of bears, rams, antelope, even a lynx. Of the proposed hunt, he says he feels hunters would definitely take or exceed their quota in the first year (which they did each year a hunt was held), but that numbers would drop year after year—not because there would be fewer wolves, but because the wolves would get wise. This man was hunting before there was an Endangered Species Act, and he has tracked and interacted with wolves. He says they no longer fear humans, that they have come to learn we are not a threat. They have come to realize we don't shoot at them, for whatever reason. But they would learn. A season or two, says this hunter, and the wolves would get wise. Wolves are smart— smarter than deer—and they would adapt to life with hunters. They might even, the hunter suggests, learn the seasons and alter their behavior month to month.

We will never know if this man was right, because the Minnesota wolf hunts stopped after three seasons when the wolf went back on the list.

The fact that the wolf is again on the list (as of this writing—who knows what will happen immediately after this book is published?) has to do with range. The argument most of the conservation groups take up when filing suit is the act's requirement that species be restored across a significant portion of their range. Conservation groups argue that because the wolf was formerly pretty much everywhere in the lower forty-eight states, the isolated populations in the Upper Midwest and the Rockies do not warrant delisting. They argue that when the scientists cite increasing numbers and stable populations in a few areas, that's nice, but it's a mere shadow of the historical range of the wolf. If there were perhaps millions of wolves across the United States prior to widespread human persecution (and official government tallies of killed wolves prior to the 1960s indicate there were easily millions of wolves), then a few thousand hemmed in across the north woods of the Great Lakes is paltry. The numbers aren't anywhere near where they once were, and neither is the range. Aren't they still therefore endangered?

David is forthright when I ask him about his perspective on delisting the wolf. He believes that according to the terms of the law it should be delisted. Decisions under the ESA are based on published recovery plans, which call out numbers, ranges, distinct populations, and targets. When the plans are met, the federal government is supposed to step out and let the states manage the species. David is firm—and he can be because he is the one who did the studies and has calculated the numbers firsthand— that the wolf recovery plan goals were met in 1999, a little more than twenty years after listing. The wolf still needs management, and a continued public relations campaign, and some strategy for ensuring domesticated livestock and wolves can live together as the wolf expands its range. But it's not threatened or endangered with extinction in the western Great Lakes any longer.

Noah Greenwald would disagree. He is the endangered species program director for the Center for Biological Diversity, one of the groups that advocates for the protection of endangered species and for the Endangered Species Act itself This nonprofit has a whole legal arm devoted to petitioning the federal government to list species and filing lawsuits to protect them. CBD tracks congressional activity related to the act and conservation in general. The wolf, as a poster child of charismatic megafauna, has been one of the CBD's primary nationwide focus areas.

"One of the basic problems we have with removing protection [for the wolf]," says Noah, "is that though there's been great recovery, it represents less than ten percent of their historic range." He is quick to admit that it's not possible to recover them everywhere they historically occurred, but he believes there are plenty of places they could live today, without too much issue with humans.

Chief among Noah's concerns with the wolf specifically is the fact that people actively want to kill wolves—and will do so when permitted by law. Evidence: the Minnesota wolf hunt, Wisconsin's plan to manage wolves by reducing their population by half, and Idaho's "wolf control board," which is charged with reduction of wolf numbers through sometimes violent means like cyanide grenades and the destruction of dens. His fear is that if the wolf is delisted, management will be left to the states, and the states may manage the wolf down to unsustainable numbers.

I ask him about David Mech's opinion (an opinion grounded in the most extensive wolf research nearly any individual has performed) in support of delisting the wolf. "Mech has been problematic for us," Noah says. "Years of great work, but on policy stuff he has come down in favor of delisting wolves." Noah seems disappointed, above all. A voice like Mech's could tip (and may be tipping) the balance, and his advocacy for delisting feels to Noah like a betrayal. The two men haven't met, but Noah grew up in Minneapolis—he left in 1988—so he is well aware of the landscape, both physical and political. I can't help but notice they both have the same aim: to ensure that wolves survive as a species for generations to come. Their methods and the nuance of the science put them at odds.

For Noah, the big mistake is the segregation of wolves into "distinct population segments" rather than seeing gray wolves as a single population with a currently fragmented range—a fragmentation caused by humans. The segmented view, according to Noah, allows managers to give a thumbs-up to recovery in a few upper midwestern states while wolves still struggle in the Northeast, the Cascades, the Rockies, and everywhere in between. True, the wolf has achieved recovery criteria in the Great Lakes, but overall, nationwide, little progress has been made. Noah essentially believes the recovery criteria themselves are wrong and therefore basing delisting on them is inappropriate. "The job of recovery is just not done," he says.

But is reestablishing even a significant portion of the wolf's historical range even possible today? American history is ugly. Europeans came over and plowed the prairie, killed millions of the native human inhabitants, sequestered the remaining ones on poor reservations, and then went after the animals, too: bison, passenger pigeons, wolves. We Americans have a shameful legacy often glossed over by the doctrines of "Manifest Destiny" and frontiersmanship and self-made-manliness and productivity. That legacy has left deep scars that we don't always see, scars that especially European Americans don't see. One of those scars is that the wolf may never reoccupy its historical range. Nor will the bison. And the passenger pigeon is gone entirely—a casualty of the days before the ESA.

The questions, therefore are these: Should we be content with the wolf's current range(s)—the Upper Midwest, the northern Rockies— and assess its recovery on whether it is thriving there (in places not largely inhabited by humans)? Or should we recognize that the wolf was everywhere across North America and only delist when it is once again that widespread? A "yes" on the first question is what is driving the USFWS to continually attempt to delist the wolf. A "yes" on the second would essentially require us to forever keep the wolf on the list as a testament to our ruination of the American landscape. Noah Greenwald actually is advocating for a middle ground: identify those areas that can still support wolves, such as the Adirondacks of New York, the southern Rockies, the Cascade Range, and others, and delist the wolf after it recovers in those areas. He reiterates in this context, though, that several states, including Wisconsin, Idaho, and Wyoming, have active policies to reduce wolf populations. That would have to change before delisting, he says.

And that raises a third line of questioning. Do we need to forever keep the wolf on the list to protect it from that deep and strange animosity we humans have for this animal? If we rush in for the kill the moment the leash is off, should we keep the leash on?

I made a playlist on my phone of wolf songs. The first one is "The Wolf" by Eddie Vedder, of Pearl Jam fame. It's from the soundtrack to *Into the Wild*, the movie based on Jonathan Krakauer's book about Christopher McCandless, who so sought an escape from society that he ventured alone deep into the Alaskan wilderness. The legend of the wild, untameable soul unfit for civilization is as old as time. McCandless is just one of the more recent installments. But whenever that kind of character appears, allusions to the wolf invariably appear with it.

Vedder was a fitting choice to soundtrack this movie. He's a wolfy guy: rough around the edges, with a slack moaning voice and countercultural lyrics. "The Wolf" is a tiny, minute-and-a-half song that features merely an organ playing minor-key chords beneath Vedder's voice. When the song appears in the movie, McCandless, played by Emile

Hirsch, stands atop a lonely mountain, arms wide and face to the sky. Vedder utters no words, just a few open syllables that rise in intensity as the seconds tick away. On the high notes, Vedder is clearly at his vocal limit. His earlier crystalline tones become breathy, gravelly, labored. The notes waver. They slip into bitonality, a sudden lower register harmonizing with the high notes. The camera spins around McCandless, the silver-gray mountains scrolling behind him. Then the voice ceases, leaving the organ to hum on alone. That howl coupled with the grandeur and freedom of the scene sets the idea of the wolf in a powerful, positive light. But the one time actual wolves appear in the film, they are sinister. They skulk into camp and eat the rotting moose carrion that McCandless has failed to properly preserve. McCandless glares at them in hate. The wolves are inelegant scavengers.

Vedder's howl and the 2007 film are examples of a vast repertoire of songs, books, movies, legends, fables, fairy tales, stories, paintings, sculptures, and performance art about the wolf. No other species on earth has attracted such tribute. Barry Lopez mines this phenomenon very deeply in *Of Wolves and Men*, so I will provide only surface treatment here. Historically, in lore, the wolf was at times caregiver (the wolf children Romulus and Remus founding the great city of Rome), deceiver/murderer (Little Red Riding Hood, wolf in sheep's clothing), sexual aggressor and symbol of base emotions (werewolves), and noble savage or isolated individual who steps away from society for reasons of freedom or banishment (the lone wolf).

We humans drew wolves on the walls of European caves as part of our first artworks, and we haven't stopped drawing them and singing about them and writing about them since. Wolves are the most powerful symbol we have of either fear, freedom, depravity, or nobility, depending on our need at the moment or our own personal perspectives. Writes Lopez: "The wolves of the plains were, of course, whatever one wanted to make of them. Thus the howling wolf was the Pawnee's spirit talker, the missionary's banshee, Maximilian's music, and the lone traveler's sleepless nightmare." Today, the wolves of our imagination are no less frightening and beautiful, beloved and threatened.

* * *

David Mech and Noah Greenwald are not particularly interested in the wolves of our imagination. They are interested in the wolves in our landscape. Over his more than sixty-year career David has captured and released more than 1,225 wolves. He used to fit them with radio collars, as Ron Moen did with lynx, and track them in winter from small airplanes. But as technology has evolved, so has David's work. He now uses GPS tracking devices. David logs on to the PC on his desk, which features a background picture of wolf cubs on a tundra landscape. He activates a Google Earth–based mapping system focused on the Superior National Forest. Lines like masses of yellow and white spaghetti cover the landscape. David is actively tracking five wolves in the forest, and the GPS tags signal satellites every four hours. A few clicks and David isolates the movements of "7246," which over the past week has prowled almost exclusively around Lake Four. Then we look at "Road Wolf," who tends to follow the forest and lake cabin access roads.

He brings up another window and we are above the tundra of far northern Canada, Ellesmere Island, where he is tracking four wolves. Here, the satellite picture is of a rocky, icy land with no trees at all. The lines run along the ocean shore and circle inland and frequently visit a weather station at the water's edge. The image is so clear and the time points on those lines so recent I half expect to see a wolf, its image captured by a satellite whirling beyond the stratosphere.

Tracking wolf movements in the remote tundra and in the "wildland interface" is helping David answer the biggest question of the day. He learns something when they venture into human settlement areas; he learns something when they die. The question—which is one I think Noah might also be asking, with a slightly different emphasis: "Why can't we have wolves everywhere?"

The eighteen-foot Alumacraft grates on the gravel as I push off into Lake One in July 2016. Drizzle threatens, then meets me and my family as we paddle into one of the first designated wilderness areas in the United States. Prior to the Endangered Species Act, the Wilderness Act of 1964 set aside large tracts of land for the preservation of nature. Though not intended to protect wolves specifically, the Boundary Waters Canoe Area Wilderness in northeastern Minnesota created a bastion for the animal. This million-plus acres is a maze of more than a thousand lakes scraped, gouged, and cracked into the granite of the Canadian Shield, all of it laid over with a carpet of boreal forest. Many picture this particular landscape as wolf country, but the wolf is not of this landscape the way the lynx is.

We coast south down Lake One, our cozy canoe packed with gear and food for four people for three days. Kerri paddles in the front and I pilot. Mason and Ethan, between us amongst the gear, paddle, too, on opposite sides from the adult nearest them. We look like a little Viking ship, with multiple oars dipping the water on both sides, bags rising above the gunwales. This is our first time together in the BWCAW as a family—in fact, the first time doing any backcountry camping as a family. It will be a short trip without portages, to test our mettle gently. I had been in here twice before, once far to the east with Kerri and two other couples, once here at Lakes One, Two, Three, and Four with my mother on her sixtieth birthday.

Near the outlet of the Kawishiwi River at the western edge of the lake we find a lovely site, which we name "Yoda's Hand Camp" for the three moss-covered granite peninsulas protruding into the bay like fingers. For the next three days and two nights we do what people do in the wilderness: hike, pick ripe berries, paddle around the lake, fish, make evening fires, eat food that somehow tastes so much better than at home, battle mosquitoes, and swim. The boys, ages five and eight, paddle the canoe by themselves (making their parents feel like royalty), snag their fishing lines regularly on trees, and become scared at night. We watch birds new to us, like common goldeneyes, and those we already love, like bald eagles and spotted sandpipers. Mink visit one of Yoda's fingers, an adult and two little ones who peek out at us from behind rocks as we paddle away.

At Bear Head Lake State Park a few days later, we brave more rain in our family-size tent (car campers now) and spend a windy day on the beach finding kaleidoscopes of rocks underwater. Then we move

Mason at the shore of Lake One in the Boundary Waters, 2016

again, drive farther north, and board the *Edie Marie* for four days of
motoring the great lakes of Voyageurs National Park. Established in 1974
as one of the very few "water-based" national parks, Voyageurs hugs the
Canadian border and offers up grand rocky cliffs, an impossible number
of islands (most without formal names), and sandy coves on which to
beach the houseboat, build a little fire, and listen for loons. And maybe
wolves. We cruise during the day and pull down the kayak from the boat
roof for evening paddles into small coves quiet as caves.

The houseboat fleets in Voyageurs are like a single roving hotel—
complete with room service. Radio contact is ever present, and home
base even hosts million-acre trivia night on Fridays. Every day a fast
motorboat makes the rounds of Crane, Sand Point, and Namakan Lake
to resupply boats that make requests. No request is denied. Over the
radio in the morning, we get glimpses into the lives of others floating
on these northern waters. "Two dozen leeches, Marlboro lights, and
lemonade." "Frozen pizza. *What kind?* One cheese, one pepperoni and
sausage." "Two walleye fillets, a bottle of Merlot, and a divorce lawyer."

On our third day on the water, we beach the *Edie Marie* on Kabe-
togama Lake and drive the outboard to the Ash River Visitor Center. We
get our national parks passport stamped, pick up junior ranger activity
books, and watch the movie about Voyageurs. We touch a stuffed loon,
handle the skulls of various small mammals, and pet wolf fur. Entering behind us is another family of four who drove to the center from
International Falls, where they are staying at a resort. The husband and
kids are dressed casually and appropriately for a hike—khakis and jeans,
sweatshirts, closed-toed shoes—while the wife appears ready for dining
at a fancy restaurant. By comparison to all of them, we look a bit worse
for wear: unshowered for days, clothing beginning to reek of the week
of sweat and dirt and mosquito repellant. On the way up to Ash River,
they had seen a wolf on the road.

"Just walked into the road up ahead of us," says the husband to the
ranger. "Just stood there. We stopped and waited for it to go on. Then it
crossed the road and went back into the woods."

"Smaller than I thought it would be," says the wife.

"Yeah, they're around here for sure," replies the ranger. "We see them sometimes on the interpretive trail." He gestures out to the woods, referencing the half-mile loop just beside the visitor center building.

Another man chimes in that the day before he had been cruising down Namakan Lake in his fishing boat and saw three wolves on a rock ledge near the water. He almost didn't notice them at first, he says, because the gray of their coats blended in with the granite. They stood there a few moments and then trotted uphill into the woods.

The family and the angler aren't overawed by these sightings, but neither are they matter-of-fact. I am hoping for a bit more recognition of how amazing it is that they saw these wolves. I am, frankly, jealous. I want to be able to write that experience as the climax to this chapter. I want to know what it feels like to encounter the apex predator of the north woods on its own terms.

I have only ever seen wolves behind fences: at the Minnesota Zoo and the International Wolf Center. So the real wolf the wolf that has hopped on and off the endangered species list for more than a decade, has been elusive to me, though I have traveled often in wolf country.

But the story here is that people do see wolves in the wild. Not me, not my kids or my wife, and not even some people I know who go deep into the BWCAW every year for far longer periods than I just did. But people see wolves. Maybe you have seen a wolf. In the 1970s we humans did something that makes that possible today—makes possible these occasional chance encounters, makes possible the tangled snarl of lines on David Mech's computer screen, makes possible the fact that next year or some other year we might hear or see a wolf with no chain link barrier between us.

Epilogue

Bat

Sometime between 9:15 and 9:30 PM a female big brown bat (*Eptesicus fuscus*) flies into a net at Elm Creek Park Reserve at the western edge of the Twin Cities metro area. She chatters constantly and flails her wings and feet, which only serves to entangle her even more. She is lactating, which probably means she has a brood of baby bats stashed in a dead tree somewhere around here, in these forty-nine hundred acres of deciduous forest. Just as the sun set, she launched herself from her nest and began picking bugs out of midair, locating them by sound, not sight. Like all mammal mothers, she will turn that food into milk for her young. At 9:31 PM Peter Kienzler approaches the net and scans it with a headlamp. He sees the big brown and carefully disentangles her and drops her into a cloth bag. He wears thick work gloves covered by rubber surgical gloves, the former to protect himself from bites, the latter to protect the bat from diseases. He carries the bat back to a large mesh tent (like the ones you see in campgrounds erected over picnic tables), and the examination begins.

Peter is one of nine scientists, technicians, and hangers-on (including me and Rich Baker, the Department of Natural Resources' endangered species head, who organized tonight's tagalong for me) who are spending the evening catching bats as part of a state-funded study of the federally threatened northern long-eared bat (*Myotis septentrionalis*). In the tent are some portable card tables piled with boxes of rubber gloves, clipboards with data sheets, cleaning supplies, more cloth bags (for, hopefully, more bats), and various medical instruments. The interior is lit by headlamps and hanging battery-powered lights. It's a glowing oasis in the dark forest—a strangely lit operating room in the wild.

Peter and Morgan Swingen, who works for the University of Minnesota Duluth's Natural Resources Research Institute and is the team leader, pull the big brown from the bag and Morgan holds it tightly in her gloved hand. The bat opens its mouth wide and repeatedly sinks its tiny, pointed teeth into Morgan's glove. It makes a constant chipping sound, as if it were saying *uh-uh, uh-uh* over and over. I have never seen a bat this close before.

Bats are intricate creatures. Their ears are festooned on the inside with ribs; their faces are so tightly packed on their heads that eyes, nose, and mouth seem to jostle for space with every bite and chatter. The mouth, in particular, is a scary little opening, with pointy teeth and a deep throat.

I am not sharing these details to creep you out, and certainly not to reinforce unwarranted stereotypes about bats (they won't drink your blood; they won't get tangled in your hair—their sonar is too good for that). In truth, I was amazed. Here is a mammal that flies, a tiny being that weighs (in the case of our lactating big brown) twenty-two grams and can grab insects on the wing without actually seeing them. There are more species of bats than of any other mammal. They live everywhere, from the tropical rainforests to the cold and snowy north woods.

And they are very much in danger. Bats have been hard-hit nationwide by a rather newly discovered fungus called white-nose syndrome. Since it was first seen in 2006 and 2007 in caves in New York, WNS has been moving gradually westward. This fungus collects on bats' noses and wings during the winter, when they are hibernating. It can cause them to wake up and leave their cave, where they starve or freeze. It can weaken them through the winter so they can't hunt effectively the following spring. And because bats tend to winter in large groups, WNS can rage through a population while it sleeps and destroy most of a colony. WNS is not entirely understood, but it could be spread by people entering infected caves and then subsequently entering other caves. However it has managed its rapid cross-country leap, WNS made its way to Minnesota in 2016, when it was discovered in Soudan Underground Mine State Park. That site has seen a 73 percent decline in overall bat population.

Thus, among other data, Morgan and her team are collecting information about WNS. The fungus can damage the thin membrane of a bat's wing, so Morgan stretches the mama big brown's wing wide (which is actually like uncurling a finger, because the whole wing is really the equivalent of an elongated webbed hand). "Wing score zero," she says, which means no WNS damage. That's the hope tonight: lots of bats and lots of "wing score zeros." And, in fact, that is what happens. The team catches at least thirteen bats in three and a half hours, and only two have WNS damage.

The northern long-eared bat winters in caves (including Soudan Mine) and moves into the woods in summer to bear young. It's about three and a half inches long with a wingspan of up to ten inches. It is also one of the state's more recent federally listed species—as of January 2015—and one on which Rich Baker has had quite a bit of influence. In October 2014 Rich convened a working group of scientists from twenty-eight states to discuss what the US Fish and Wildlife Service should do about this wide-ranging but declining mammal. A main point of discussion was how the bat should be listed. An endangered listing would disallow any killing of the animal. That, according to Rich, would have created a huge conflict with the powerful timber industry in the Northeast and Upper Midwest. A threatened listing would allow for a 4(d) permit that timber interests could live with, while still calling for protection, study, and management. Rich advocated for threatened status and wrote a key comment letter to the USFWS that led to the bat's listing as threatened.

"The [Fish and Wildlife Service] can figure out ways to allow certain kinds of take," explains Rich, "that also allow for conservation of species." Rich was concerned that the entire consideration of the long-eared would be scuttled if the law got too aggressive.

The 4(d) rule for the northern long-eared bat says that if roost trees are known, they can't be cut in June or July, when the bats have young there. There is no requirement for agencies or land managers to look for roost trees, which sits well with the timber industry. Essentially, bats can be incidentally killed in the normal course of logging activities, but they must be protected if found. It's a compromise, for sure, but one Rich feels protects the species overall. He believes that if conservationists had to fight timber, they would lose, and there would be no listing at all—and no money for study, no mandate to monitor, no protection on federal land, no environmental review, and, quite possibly, no more northern long-eared bats.

The Center for Biological Diversity, the Sierra Club, and two other environmental organizations have together filed a lawsuit over the 4(d) rule, calling it "a clear case of logging and energy interests taking precedent over wildlife." The organizations take exception to the threatened listing (it was originally proposed as endangered in 2013) and the "loophole" that would allow potentially widespread incidental take. This illustrates again how people and organizations with the same ultimate goal can view the function of the Endangered Species Act differently.

For Rich, the listing and 4(d) rule was just the first step. Next he went out and got money to look for roost trees. The more that are found, the more bats can be protected. This strategy is another big reason the survey crew is out in the woods battling bugs and untangling bats from nets.

The nets the crew is using are called mist nets, and they have webbing so fine the bats can't "see" them with their sonar. Each net is strung up between a pair of poles rigged with rope pulleys that raise and lower it. It's a bit like working a flagpole. Two of the team's nets are strung across trails and a third crosses a small creek. The trails and the creek form good open flyways for bats in pursuit of bugs. The crew arrived at 7:15 to set up the poles and attach the nets, but left the nets down until sunset: 9:15. The excitement is palpable as the forest dims and small groups leave the tent to raise the nets. Each net is then checked every fifteen minutes, religiously. Bats, you might expect, don't like to be tangled for very long.

The 9:45 net check comes up empty, but Morgan finds one at 10:00. She spends nearly ten minutes untangling it, all the while trying to suppress her excitement at what she has. She doesn't want to say anything to anyone as she speeds back through the dark woods to the tent, but her grin gives her away, so I mumble-ask her why she's so happy. It's a *Myotis,* she tells me, the genus name shared by little brown and northern long-eared bats. We both practically skip along the trail, hoping for the latter. The *Myotis* gets a thorough examination at the tent, with several crew members peering at it and rendering their opinions. In the end, the consensus is little brown bat (*Myotis lucifugus*), but it's a female, so they decide to put a transmitter on it.

The only way to find a roost tree is to follow a bat to it. So some bats caught during the night get transmitters and are set free to feed through the dark hours and then return to their trees. A different survey group comes out during the daylight with radio locators. They wander the forest triangulating the transmitter's location, then flag the roost trees with tape. They return to the trees at dusk and count how many bats emerge. This "emergence survey" is another way of counting bat populations. And if the group catches and tags any northern long-eareds, they can identify roost trees to protect under the 4(d) rule. Though there is less threat in public parks like Elm Creek, roost tree identification is very important farther north within the state and national forest areas. That's why there are multiple crews out across the entire state.

Morgan holds the little brown from the 10:00 check facedown on her lap while another crew member shaves a small patch of hair off the center of its back. Meanwhile, a third crew member tests a transmitter and enters its call signature on the data sheet for the bat. The bat barber then puts a bit of glue on the little brown's back and sticks on the transmitter—which looks kind of like a Tootsie Roll with a long wire coming out one end. The wire extends straight backward over the bat's tail and between its wings so as to not restrict its movement

Once that procedure is complete, Morgan takes the bat outside. She holds up her hand and opens it. The bat pauses as if to get its bearings, then explodes silently from her hand and is gone from the light.

During the transmitter work, the 10:15 net check arrives. Three bats in the creek net: big brown, little brown, and a silver-haired bat—which does sport a little mane of silver-grey hair. It takes twenty-five minutes to untangle the silver-haired (that's a long time, as untanglings go). The little brown has some WNS damage. It gets an identification band like all the rest and also a wing punch tissue sample. Another little brown hits a net at 10:45, then two big browns at 11:00. At this point, there's a backup. Bats in cloth bags hang from a clothesline, waiting their turn for examination. Rich sits in a camp chair in the tent recording data; four or five crew members examine bats and clean down the whole works between procedures (so as to not possibly spread WNS). When net checks are needed, some crew members go untangle bats, and I step in to take pictures of splotchy wings when they occur. A pregnant little brown gets a transmitter.

Things seem to be winding down around 11:30, but then the 11:45 check turns up four bats in the creek net: another silver-haired, two big browns, and a bat with a transmitter that had already been caught once earlier in the evening (that one is untangled and let go immediately). Soon after, Rich and I leave the woods.

"I believe the Endangered Species Act is the best and most powerful law we have [for conservation]," says Rich Baker. He cites several facts to support that assertion. The law calls for the evaluation of species for listing and delisting based on science alone. There is no political element, no let's-get-a-lot-of-signatures, no economic evaluation. The law sets forth processes for both listing and delisting. It allows for a recognition of success. The Topeka shiner expert Pat Ceas would add that he might like to have seen something more along the lines of an endangered *landscapes* act, but that listed species stand in for entire landscapes.

As you might suspect by now, I have studied the act closely, traveled extensively on my own and with scientists into the field, and followed the news on species conservation. I know that species are being continually listed and delisted, that public perception of the act itself and certain plants and animals on the list is ever changing. I know that by the time you read these words there may have already been new successes to report, new species to examine, new extinctions to mourn. But a discussion about the act will still be a discussion about our relationship with the earth and the species with which we share our home.

Having spent years now trying to understand that relationship, I tend to agree with Rich about the importance of the act. I would posit that the list itself brings recognition and awareness necessary for conservation to succeed. Southern Minnesota landowners who have dwarf trout lilies or Leedy's roseroots on their properties have undertaken conservation measures that also protect water quality, reduce erosion, and benefit other species of plants and animals. Would they have done so without the knowledge that they had special resources on their land?

The act was passed in the 1970s as part of a multiyear package of conservation measures (Clean Air and Water Acts, National Environmental Policy Act, Wilderness Act) meant to give voice to the voiceless landscape. It was signed by a Republican president who believed the nation's natural heritage was its greatest asset. Today the act is increasingly seen as a barrier to progress. It kills jobs, say its detractors, by limiting resource extraction and requiring extensive environmental review. It stops transportation projects and pipelines, they say, making America vulnerable. Recently, attacks on the act have approached a fever pitch. The 114th Congress was intent on undermining the act, and the 115th has reintroduced many of the previous session's failed bills. The Gray Wolf State Management Act of 2017 (H.R. 424 and S. 164) would legislatively reissue the 2011 and 2012 delistings of wolves nationwide and prohibit judicial review. A rider to the congressional budget introduced on January 11, 2017 (S. Amnd. 151), would remove jurisdiction over greater sage grouse habitat lands from the Fish and Wildlife Service and bar listing of that bird for (a rather arbitrary) ten years. The Listing Reform Act (H.R. 717) would require economic analysis before any species listing—which goes specifically against the science-based approach in the original act. The Federal Land Freedom Act (S. 335) would waive ESA requirements for all oil and gas development on federal lands. The State, Tribal, and Local Species Transparency and Recovery Act (H.R. 1274 and S. 735) would require scientific data to be vetted by local governments prior to listing considerations. The National Forest Ecosystem Improvement Act of 2017 (S. 879) would exempt from review under the ESA "forest management practices" (which is pretty broad, considering timber cutting is often considered a forest management practice). Riders to the appropriations acts for Interior, Environment, and several other related agencies would delist the wolf, and also block any funding for wolf and grouse activities.

The most concerning is the Endangered Species Management Self-Determination Act (H.R. 2134 and S. 935). Introduced in the 114th Congress and reintroduced by the 115th on April 25, 2017, this legislation would require the Department of the Interior and (surprisingly) the Department of Commerce to obtain the consent of each state in which a species appears before proposing a listing. It would require Interior to submit a list of species to Congress, which must give a joint resolution of approval (meaning both House and Senate) before a listing can take effect. It proposes to require automatic removal of a species from the endangered species list after five years—unless Interior petitions for it to remain on the list. Citizen petitions would be banned. It gives to states the exclusive power to regulate species that appear only within that state, with no federal oversight whatsoever. And (yes, there's more) it would allow landowners or lessees to apply to Interior to determine whether a proposed use would violate the Endangered Species Act. Non-response by Interior after ninety days would mean the use is compliant by default. And if Interior says the use might violate the act, the owner or lessee is entitled to compensation.

Imagine this scenario: An oil and gas company or a mining interest wants to lease federal land (this happens all the time, by the way) to drill, dig, or extract. Department of Interior staff—already way overworked from managing species on the list, petitioning Congress to relist species at their five-year deadlines, getting states' consents and congressional approval for adding new species that need protection, and defending lawsuits from both sides of the debate (all in the context of reduced overall funding for the department)—fails to respond within ninety days to some of the many hundreds of likely applications. Some of the most controversial projects of the day—frac sand mining in the Mississippi River valley, copper-nickel mining in the Superior National Forest, major logging leases in the north woods—all these could move forward without any endangered species review, even if on federal land. The Self-Determination Act, if passed, would make the Endangered Species Act nonfunctional. It's not officially a repeal, but it might as well be.

All the legislation listed here is currently under consideration. The Self-Determination Act sits in the House Committee on Natural Resources. It asserts that the ESA has been a failure, with less than one percent of listed species recovered. It fails to recognize that possibly a far smaller number of listed species have gone extinct, even in the context of continued habitat loss, climate change, resource extraction, and persecution. It is highly ironic that the same people, including legislators, who repeatedly insist upon the delisting of the wolf because it has recovered are working to gut the act for failing to recover species.

And in terms of successes, even speaking locally to the Midwest, the wolf isn't the only one. Butterflies are being reintroduced to the prairies because of breeding programs and habitat protections encouraged and funded by the ESA. Agencies have come together to work on the study and reintroduction of endangered mussels in the heart of the Twin Cities metro area. The State of Minnesota and the federal government have acquired land to protect the prairie bush clover, the dwarf trout lily, the Leedy's roseroot, the western prairie fringed orchid, and multiple butterflies. Piping plover numbers have dramatically increased in Michigan—and in 2017 plovers nested in Lake of the Woods for the first time in a decade. These species were on the brink of extinction. Some species have only been recognized as endangered for five years or less. Nature takes a long time to recover. It is not time to give up.

My unscientific but educated case for the Endangered Species Act comes down to three ideas: keystones, unknowns, and owning up. The act has protected species that are critical to the overall health of our landscapes. Without keystone species like the wolf, ecosystems can collapse, with economic ramifications. Aldo Leopold saw this in the western mountains as wolves were being exterminated, then spent a lifetime studying this phenomenon. Forests, deserts, prairies, and wetlands cannot exist without certain plants and animals. The act ensures those animals survive to play their essential role.

To crib from Leopold again: "To keep every cog and wheel is the most intelligent form of tinkering." We don't know exactly what Leedy's roseroots, dwarf trout lilies, Topeka shiners, and many others provide in the environment—beyond some contribution to the food chain, that is. Their larger roles are unknown. Maybe they are keystones. Maybe they provide some particular nutrient to the soil. Maybe they could be used for medicine. We don't know, so we better keep them around. Most scientists and plant lovers operate under this principal: study it and protect it because, well, you never know.

Each of those two arguments can be translated, through some creative math, into potential economic benefit. But alongside the calculus there is responsibility. Whether you believe the universe is a fully formed gift from God, an endlessly circulating weave of energy, a mess of chemical reactions, or some combination of these, we can and do control the destiny of other species. What does it say about us if we allow our fellow beings to wink out? How will we tell our children that once there were butterflies? That once there were twelve-inch-long mussels that lived to be a hundred years old? That once there were mammals that flew in the night and tracked mosquitoes with sonar?

We humans need to own our role as the ultimate keystone species. We need to own up to the disaster we're effecting and do something about it. The ESA is one tool—one we should keep and honor because it is working. We have learned more about hundreds of species than we ever would have. We have saved some and in so doing protected and improved entire landscapes.

Landscapes. That's how I came to this topic. I never saw a northern long-eared bat. I never saw a lynx or a wolf in the wild, nor any of the endangered mussels snug in their riverbeds. I was about fifty-fifty at seeing Minnesota's federally listed species in the wild (and the plants drove up my average). But I did love the boreal forest in winter, the nighttime deciduous woods, and the sluggish prairie creeks of southwestern Minnesota. I loved being on the big river blocks from my home and on an ocean lagoon hundreds of miles away. The aspen parklands intrigued me, and the cliffs of the Whitewater River valley surprised and delighted me.

I had never been to many of these places. The wild and rare plants and animals drew me to them. The rare ones did not always show themselves, but their coinhabitants did, unexpectedly at times: an upland sandpiper at Bicentennial Prairie, a tiny painted turtle brought up in a Rock River seine, a broad-winged hawk perched in a dead tree a short bushwhack up from Namakan Lake, American redstarts flushing insects with flashing red tail feathers, a river of bright yellow marsh marigolds alight in the spring-brown forest.

When you go to a wild place—be it days from a trailhead or in your local city park—think a moment about the rare species around you. They may remain unseen, but they live in the landscape in a way that makes the landscape whole. You may never know if a lynx is watching you from behind a copse of black spruce. You may miss the bloom of the dwarf trout lily by just a few days. You will likely never see the mussels and shiners beneath the surface of muddy, turbulent waters. You won't know if those bats above your backyard are northern long-eareds. But their existence is important. Many people are working to ensure they live on.

Your role? Notice the subtle details of our often underappreciated upper midwestern landscape. Help protect the Endangered Species Act. Go outside, learn, and enjoy.

Narrative Bibliography

The vast majority of the information in this book comes from my own interviews with individuals named in the book. In general, their official titles, agencies, and roles appear in the text. These people are considered authorities in their respective subject matters. My interviews and experiences with them took place between 2007 and 2017 and often during fieldwork, in which I joined them as an observer and occasional participant. All the dialogue contained should be considered actual quotes verifiable through recordings I made of these interviews. Furthermore, all scientific information was reverified by these experts prior to the book's publication.

Much of the information about the landscape of Minnesota comes from my own personal experience in the field, either alone or during the above-mentioned field interviews. Many of the facts included in the book that relate to particular landscape features—whether historical or ecological—come from brochures, interpretive plaques, and brief onsite conversations with site managers. This knowledge gained while exploring the state's landscape has been augmented by subsequent review of site managers' and owners' websites, including most notably those of the Minnesota Department of Natural Resources and the National Park Service.

Information about the discovery, listing and management histories of particular species appears throughout the book. In these cases I rely on two primary sources: the US Fish and Wildlife Service's endangered species web pages and fact sheets, and the Federal Register. The former is used for general species information and historical overviews, while the latter (which is the official mouthpiece for the US government's rule-making) is used to construct the listing histories and to communicate the rules, issues, lawsuits, and public comments associated with each species. Much information comes from the recovery plans and five-year species reviews, which can be found on the USFWS web page. In all cases, these narratives have also been reviewed with the species experts.

The native/indigenous history of the region is admittedly still an open discussion. Ever-evolving research is changing, exposing, and expanding the narrative, language, and even facts of the European take-over of America. I have not sought to break new ground with research on this topic in this book and am relying primarily on today's accepted understanding—with the recognition that certain stories may not be entirely true and that other stories remain untold. I will refrain, therefore, from citing specific sources. Primarily I have used onsite interpretive information (especially that at Fort Snelling State Park, including the Dakota Memorial there, Pipestone National Monument, and Jeffers Petroglyphs state historic site) and general Minnesota history volumes.

Some chapters rely on additional specialized sources, documented by chapter below.

Introduction

The number of wolves in Minnesota, approximately twenty-five hundred, comes both from an interview with David Mech and the 2016 wolf survey performed by the Minnesota DNR and available on that agency's website. The history of wolf persecution comes from several sources, including *Of Wolves and Men* by Barry Lopez (New York: Scribner, 1979), *Wolves of Minnesota: Howl in the Heartland* edited by L. David Mech (Minneapolis: Voyageur Press, 2001), and the interpretive exhibit at the International Wolf Center. The picture of children with wolf skins specifically referenced is one of many such photos included in the above sources and available in the Minnesota Historical Society's image library.

Lily

The discussion of the dwarf trout lily's original description and the subsequent searches for more plants is outlined in the species' five-year reviews and was further confirmed by personal communication with Nancy Sather. The information on the Decorah shale was first described to me by Nancy Sather, and it also appears in the federal reports on the species. For backup, I have referred to Richard W. Ojakangas's books *Roadside Geology of Minnesota* (Missoula, MT: Mountain Press Publishing Company, 2009) and *Minnesota's Geology* (Minneapolis: University of Minnesota Press, 1982). The reference to the percentage of lilies flowering in a population at the arboretum was confirmed by David Remucal at the Minnesota Landscape Arboretum. The biographical information on Eloise Butler and the discussion of the founding of the wildflower garden is drawn primarily from *The Wild Gardener: The Life and Selected Writings of Eloise Butler* by Martha E. Hellander (St. Cloud, MN: North Star Press, 1992), from *Minneapolis Star* newspaper articles from the era, and from interpretive information at the garden itself. The contents of Butler's dwarf trout lily index card were provided to me by the garden's current curator, Susan Wilkins.

Mussels

The number of species of mussels in Minnesota comes from the Minnesota DNR and was confirmed by Mike Davis. The description of Twin Cities geology is compiled from the two geology books referenced above, as well as interpretive plaques at various locations around the metro area. The history of upper Mississippi navigation and the US Army Corps of Engineers comes from that agency's website and from interpretive information at Lock and Dam No. 1 and the St. Anthony Falls Visitor Center. Information on zebra mussels comes from the Minnesota DNR's invasive species web page. Background on Hall's Island and the River-First Master Plan can be found on the website of the Minneapolis Park and Recreation Board. The story of the Scioto River in Columbus, Ohio, is based on my own research for an article that appeared in *Landscape Architecture Magazine* in May 2014.

Plover

The presumed life history of the plover Z12 is pieced together from several known sightings of that individual bird provided to me by David Newstead, along with an understanding of general piping plover habits and habitats. This semi-fictitious narrative was reviewed by the plover experts named in the chapter. All information related to the legal cases comes from official federal documentation and official court documents available online. The data on plovers in Minnesota is contained in a pair of 2011 presentations at a national conference by Minnesota DNR staff, which can be found on the DNR's plover website. The Instagram feed segments come courtesy of Plover Lovers, a volunteer organization in Ontario, Canada. The fact that Lake Superior is warming is from a 2016 NASA/National Science Foundation study of 235 lakes on six continents, which found that Lake Superior is warming by about two degrees Fahrenheit per decade, which is one of the fastest warming rates in the world. The Gulf Coast sea level rise information is from the National Oceanic and Atmospheric Administration, which has monitoring stations along the coast.

Roseroot

This plant's history and taxonomy is drawn from the federal documentation associated with this species, with help from Joel Olfelt. The basic geology narrative is drawn from the geology reference books noted in previous chapters, again, with help in comprehension from Joel Olfelt. The Minnesota and Wisconsin DNR websites also feature specific pages about algific talus slopes. Information on the monkshood and the Pleistocene snail was verified through the USFWS endangered species websites and documentation in the Federal Register.

Bush Clover

The description of the survey crew as it moved across the landscape is constructed from several sources used in combination to create the overall narrative. The surveyors' names and roles are contained in the original survey books, available at the Minnesota Historical Society. The process for surveying is mostly contained in *Measuring America: How the United States Was Shaped by the Greatest Land Sale in History* by Andro Linklater (New York: HarperCollins, 2003), a book that cites various primary sources about the surveying process. Linklater's book is also the source for the historical description of American measurement, the Northwest Ordinance, and Jefferson's role in those endeavors. The principal meridians can be viewed on the website of the Bureau of Land Management. Quoted land price sources vary by era. I calculated the per-acre price of the Louisiana Purchase based on its total and area and the historical record of its purchase, drawn from archival federal documentation. The 1864 prices are contained in the early land records for the area that I viewed in New Ulm. The present-day prices are from the US Department of Agriculture's Economic Research Service.

The general history of Jeffers Petroglyphs state historic site appears in the interpretive information at that site. Details about the bush clover itself is from federal documentation and personal conversations with Nancy Sather. The history of Cottonwood River SNA comes entirely from land records held by Brown County in New Ulm. The very general note about coal mining has its basis in the 1916 *History of Redwood County, Minnesota*, by Franklyn Curtiss-Wedge. Redwood County is located directly west of Brown County. Some exploration for a low-grade type of coal was done in the area, but no commercial mines were ever opened. Though the company Redwood Coal is not mentioned in the *History*, it seems likely that this was a failed speculative commercial venture. The final section of the chapter, which envisions the survey crew passing along the present-day property lines, includes ownership information from county records. Of course, land changes hands, so this is a snapshot in time.

Butterflies

The brief history of Bicentennial Prairie appears on an interpretive sign at the site. All pesticide information comes from the Environmental Protection Agency. Basic information on neonicotinoids, including the

history of their development, is currently scattered about in various scientific studies and consumer information papers—some of which take
an activist bent. A worthwhile summary appears on Texas A&M University's "Insects in the City" website. The EPA, in its analyses of this class
of chemical, also provides background information on its function and
chemical makeup. Federal policy documents relating to pollinators are
found on either the current White House website, the archived Obama
White House website, or both. It seems some of this documentation
may be migrating back into easy public access after an initial removal
upon the inauguration of President Trump. Availability of and access to
these documents may remain in flux for some time.

Lynx

The statement that the boreal forest is the largest terrestrial biome is
supported by a variety of credible sources, including, most accessibly,
Arizona State University's "Ask a Biologist" life sciences website. Canadian Shield geology information comes from the geology references cited
in earlier chapters, along with several publications of Natural Resources
Canada, a government agency. As with other chapters, the information
on lawsuits comes from actual court documents and the Federal Register. Trapping records are maintained by the Minnesota DNR. The most
recent are available online, and older ones are documented in Federal
Register reports and other federal documentation. Life histories of lynx
based on scat collection were provided to me by Dan Ryan after analysis.
All climate data references were initially encountered through regular
reporting on Minnesota Public Radio in the spring of 2017 and corrobo-
rated by data from the Intergovernmental Panel on Climate Change. A
Truffula tree, of course, is the fictional species clear-cut nearly to extinction in *The Lorax* by Dr. Seuss.

Orchid

The entire CITES list is available online and is sortable and searchable
by species, family, genus, and more. The number of orchids on the list
comes from my own analysis of the list. The TRAFFIC report is also

available online at that group's website. The fact that orchids are the most abundant and varied plant family is drawn specifically from a 2016 article by Maarten J. M. Christenhusz and James W. Byng called "The Number of Known Plants Species in the World and Its Annual Increase," published in *Phytotaxa* 261 (2016): 201–17 and using data from the Royal Botanic Gardens at Kew. According to the article, orchids just edge out asters in abundance, but species are being described all the time, and asters may eventually catch up. The number of orchids in Minnesota (forty-three) comes from the Minnesota DNR. The 2016 orchid success information is from personal interviews with Nancy Sather.

The details about Pipestone (both the place and the stone) are found in the interpretive information at Pipestone National Monument, which I visited, though that visit does not appear in the book. Louis Agassiz is profiled extensively online, including at several reputable universities, including Harvard and the University of California, Berkeley. In addition, two books offer comprehensive profiles of the man: *Louis Agassiz: Creator of American Science* by Christoph Irmscher (Boston: Houghton Mifflin Harcourt, 2013) and *Louis Agassiz: A Life in Science* by Edward Lurie (Baltimore: Johns Hopkins University Press, 1988). I drew from these sources to create the brief biography included in the chapter. Information about Lake Agassiz is included in the two geological books noted in the dwarf trout lily chapter, as well as the North Dakota Geologic Survey. The books also feature brief biographies of Warren Upham and the history of the naming of Lake Agassiz. This information is further confirmed by Warren Upham (himself) in *Minnesota Place Names: A Geographical Encyclopedia,* 3rd edition (St. Paul: Minnesota Historical Society Press, 2001). Details about the various Lake Agassiz beach ridges come partly from the geological books referenced just above, but also from Nancy Sather's patient and careful explanations, including a map she was able to provide that uses LIDAR data to trace them across Minnesota. This map was prepared by DNR staff but is not generally available to the public. Details about the Svalbard Global Seed Vault and the Center for Plant Conservation come from the websites of those two organizations.

Shiner

The Minnesota buffer law has been widely reported in the *Star Tribune* and on Minnesota Public Radio, along with other news outlets. The full text of the bill can be found on the website of the Minnesota Revisor of Statutes. Information on the floods that wiped out the lower dam at Blue Mounds State Park is drawn from *Star Tribune* and Minnesota Public Radio reporting on the event, while the discussion about whether or not to rebuild (and the eventual decision not to) comes from public information issued by the Minnesota DNR.

Wolf

The listing, delisting, and legal wrangling around the wolf, including legislative actions, is a long and complicated story. I have used a wide variety of sources to reconstruct the timeline: Federal Register documents, public court records, and press releases issued by the US Fish and Wildlife Service, the Center for Biological Diversity, and other parties to petitions and lawsuits. The timeline was reviewed both by David Mech and by Noah Greenwald of the Center for Biological Diversity. Because the nuance of the discussion plays extensively into each side's cases, I have strictly used actual ruling language to discuss the timeline, while drawing from personal interviews, summaries of public meetings, and public comments included in the official Federal Register documents to characterize sentiments. The examples of wolves inhabiting areas very near the Twin Cities come from personal interviews with David Mech. References to delistings or down-listings of other animals come from the official federal documentation of those species. Data on the Minnesota wolf hunt can be found on the website of the Minnesota DNR and has been reported by Minnesota Public Radio.

Bat

All information on white-nose syndrome is drawn from a website called whitenosesyndrome.org, which is a collaborative effort between multiple agencies and conservation groups. Details on current legislation that affects the Endangered Species Act comes from actual bill text and information found on the websites of the US House of Representatives and the US Senate. The Center for Biological Diversity publishes a list of all legislation that organization feels is a threat to the ESA, along with bill numbers and the current status of each. I used this guide to locate bills, then examined each on the respective congressional websites.

Acknowledgments

The greatest thanks goes to Kerri, my wife, for her support and inspiration. This book would not have come to be without her belief in me, without the time she allowed me to travel and write, and without the undercurrent of love I felt all along the way. Ethan and Mason, my sons, also had evenings and weekends with Daddy gone. Their understanding, coupled with their own curiosity and knowledge, drove me forward.

The team at the Minnesota Historical Society Press—Josh Leventhal, Shannon Pennefeather, and especially Ann Regan—were extraordinary to work with. They molded the words of this inexperienced writer into something much more memorable and beautiful. Ann saw the potential in this book from the beginning and then shepherded it carefully, compassionately, and expertly into your hands.

Six people have been important in my writing, across a timeline beginning well before this book was even a spark. They deserve my thanks for sculpting and challenging me as a writer and offering me opportunities to question, research, produce, refine, and publish. Thanks are due Frank Edgerton Martin, J. William Thompson, Douglas Glover, Patrick Madden, Kurt Caswell, and Robert Vivian.

This book would be nothing without the scientists, advocates, and volunteers who study and love these wild and rare species. In particular, Rich Baker and Nancy Sather gave me invaluable background, context, and guidance. Nancy's lifetime of work with Minnesota's rare plants is unfortunately not well known, but we should all be grateful for her tireless passion. Rich has stewarded threatened and endangered species in this state for decades with a combination of smart policy work, good humor, and heart. The list of other specialists who were so generous with their time and knowledge is long: Derek Anderson, Jerry and Karen Ibberson, Susan Wilkins, Mike Davis, Zeb Secrist, Bernard Sietman, Robyn Cobb, David Newstead, Beau Hardegree, Mike Lange, the volunteers at Plover Lovers in Ontario, the folks at Bugsy's on Lake of the Woods who rented me a boat and hand-delivered my passport back to Minneapolis, Joel Olfelt, Brian Teichert, Nelson Gonzalez, Shelley Olson, the patient librarians at the Minnesota Historical Society and the Brown County Courthouse in New Ulm, Erik Runquist, Cale Nordmeier, Dan Ryan, Pat Ceas, Jay Hatch, Margaret Edwards, the shiner survey fisheries students, Morgan Swingen and her merry band of bat-catchers, Noah Greenwald, and David Mech.

Finally, I am sure you have enjoyed the excellent ink drawings throughout the book. They are the work of my good friends Amber Sausen and Daniel Green, with whom I have traveled this great state on many occasions. I am thankful for their illustrations and their friendship.